The Learner-Centered
Classroom and School

The Learner-Centered Classroom and School

Strategies for Increasing Student
Motivation and Achievement

Barbara L. McCombs
Jo Sue Whisler

Jossey-Bass Publishers • San Francisco

Substantial discounts on bulk quantities of Jossey-Bass books are available to corporations, professional associations, and other organizations. For details and discount information, contact the special sales department at Jossey-Bass Inc., Publishers (415) 433–1740; Fax (800) 605–2665.

For sales outside the United States, please contact your local Simon & Schuster International Office.
Jossey-Bass Web address: http://www.josseybass.com

 Manufactured in the United States of America on Lyons Falls Turin Book. This paper is acid-free and 100 percent totally chlorine-free.

Library of Congress Cataloging-in-Publication Data

McCombs, Barbara L.
    The learner-centered classroom and school : strategies for
increasing student motivation and achievement / Barbara L. McCombs,
Jo Sue Whisler.—1st ed.
      p.   cm.—(The Jossey-Bass education series)
    Includes bibliographical references (p.) and index.
    ISBN 0-7879-0836-3 (alk. paper)
    1. Educational innovations—United States. 2. Learning,
Psychology of. 3. Classroom environment—United States.
4. Motivation in education—United States. 5. Academic achievement—
United States. I. Whisler, Jo Sue. II. Title.
III. Series.
LB1027.M224   1997
371.39—dc21   96-52661

FIRST EDITION
HB Printing   10 9 8 7 6 5 4 3 2 1

The Jossey-Bass Education Series

Contents

We dedicate this book to all concerned students, educators, and parents who know what schools can be and who are ready to create classrooms and schools where all learners experience the joy of learning for a lifetime.

Preface

Efforts to reform and transform the U.S. educational system to better educate all students are intensifying. As the current wave of reform and transformation continues, more and more schools and districts are focusing their efforts on standards and ways of assessing what students learn in school. Although this is a necessary focus, a second necessary focus is emerging. It is that the educational system of the future must embrace a learner-centered perspective to maximize high standards of learning, motivation, and achievement for *all* learners—for both students and their teachers (see, for example, Brooks & Brooks, 1993; Comer, 1993; Gardner, 1991, 1995; McCombs, 1993).

In spite of increasing advocacy for a learner-centered perspective, approaches that focus on learners and learning are often based on conflicting assumptions about what is needed for learners to achieve desired learning standards and outcomes. On the one hand, these approaches may look at the learner and learning primarily from the educator's point of view and decide, *from the outside* and *for the learner,* what is required—defining for students the characteristics of standards, instruction, curriculum, assessment, school management, and family and community support needed. On the other hand, these approaches may look *with the learner* at what learning means and how it can be enhanced from *within*—drawing on the learner's unique perspectives, talents, capacities, and experiences as educational standards and frameworks are created and implemented. In the first case, it is assumed that educators need to do things to and for the learner, to engineer conditions outside the learner. In the second case, which reflects a learner-centered perspective, it is assumed that educators need to understand the learner's reality and to support the basic learning needs and capacities existing in the learner.

Our position is that *learner-centered* can be defined as an empirically informed philosophical perspective that begins with a focus on *knowing* and *understanding each learner*. That is, this perspective begins with a full comprehension of how the learner understands his or her world and approaches the process of learning inside and outside the classroom. We argue that knowing and understanding each learner is essential to helping the learner feel connected to, supported by, and respected by his or her teachers and other adults in the educational setting. We also argue that the learner-centered perspective goes beyond a personal understanding of the learner. It focuses on the learner in the context of a deep *understanding of the learning process* itself. Thus, it is a perspective that couples a focus on knowing and respecting individual learners with the best available research and practitioner experience about learning. It is also a perspective that is broader than child- and student-centered approaches because it (1) focuses on all learners throughout their lifetimes, from preschool through old age; (2) broadly addresses not only learners' emotional and social needs but also their intellectual and learning needs; and (3) encourages a systemic redesign of educational processes, structures, and policies to support lifelong learning and the valuing of continuous change and improvement of desired learning outcomes for all learners in the system.

We believe, and our research confirms, that when teachers, schools, and districts function from a learner-centered perspective, students achieve desired educational standards at higher levels and the development of their full potential is enhanced. In fact, we believe that it is only by focusing on both the learner and learning that educators will reach the goal of having their students meet rigorous academic standards. Our confirmation comes from a five-year study, conducted at the Mid-continent Regional Educational Laboratory (McREL), to comprehend and define learner-centered classrooms and schools. We started by analyzing research and theory from psychology and education about personal characteristics that most influence learning. We wanted to understand the implications of this research for a systemic redesign of schools that considers the types of classroom, administrative, and social system supports required. Our basic question was this: Are there fundamental research-based principles that define the learner and learning process and thereby provide a foundation for educational reform and transformation?

In partnership with a special task force established by the American Psychological Association, we synthesized research and theory into twelve *learner-centered psychological principles*. From our consideration of these principles, we have distilled the following premises of a holistic and comprehensive model and perspective for practice that maximally facilitates learning, motivation, and school achievement:

(1) Learners are distinct and unique. Their distinctiveness and uniqueness must be attended to and taken into account if they are to engage in and take responsibility for their own learning.

(2) Learners' unique differences include their emotional states of mind, learning rates, learning styles, stages of development, abilities, talents, feelings of efficacy, and other academic and nonacademic attributes and needs. These differences must be taken into account if all learners are to be provided with the necessary challenges and opportunities for learning and self-development.

(3) Learning is a constructive process that occurs best when what is being learned is relevant and meaningful to the learner and when the learner is actively engaged in creating his or her own knowledge and understanding by connecting what is being learned with prior knowledge and experience.

Learning occurs best in a positive environment—one that contains positive interpersonal relationships and interactions and also comfort and order and in which the learner feels appreciated, acknowledged, respected, and validated.

 Learning is fundamentally a natural process; learners are naturally curious and basically interested in learning about and mastering their world. Although negative thoughts and feelings sometimes interfere with this natural inclination and must be dealt with, the learner is not regarded nor related to as deficient or requiring "fixing."

Thus, empirically validated principles—informed by educators' own knowledge, perspectives, and experiences—form the knowledge base for a learner-centered perspective and model of schooling that focuses attention on what should not be ignored in educational reform. This learner-centered model can be the foundation that undergirds other reforms (in standards, instruction, curriculum, assessment, and other structural aspects of schooling). Conversely, if this learner-centered foundation is ignored, we believe that even the best programs will not be optimally effective and will be less likely to reach *all* students, especially those who are most alienated and see school as irrelevant. When this foundation is in place, however, our research and that of many others shows that educators are more likely to maximize motivation, learning, and achievement for *all* students.

What a learned-centered perspective and model helps educators understand is that individual learners, young and old, students and teachers—like all human beings—bring with them a complex array of unique viewpoints, needs, capacities, and strengths. At the same time, they share certain fundamental qualities. The inherent need to grow, live, and develop in a positive direction, for example, is common to all learners. What best supports these inherent capacities and distinctive characteristics? To find out, we asked students and educators what they thought produced the highest levels of learning in not only academic areas but also personal, social, and vocational realms. We read the research literature in these areas, analyzed and synthesized our results, and developed a set of measures that we believe helps define learner-centered schools and classrooms. We gave these measures to students, teachers, and administrators to further examine characteristics that distinguish effective practice from learners' and teachers' points of view. With these data and data representative of the research on effective practices, we have created a synthesis of what it means to be learner centered.

Overview of the Contents

The Learner-Centered Classroom and School presents results of our work and implications of that work for creating classroom- and school-level practices and strategies that can help educators— teachers, administrators, and professional development staff— enhance the learning, motivation, and achievement of each learner. This book also presents our further work on the types of personal change strategies necessary to transform classroom and school practices in keeping with the learner-centered perspective.

Chapter One begins with a definition of learner centered. As we answer the question *what is learner centered?* we take into account both the existing research and teachers' experience. We explore what it means to be learner centered from student and teacher perspectives and share profiles of teachers considered learner centered and non–learner centered. Research evidence on the major factors that define a learner-centered model rounds out the picture. This chapter also presents and discusses the twelve learner-centered psychological principles.

We then move in Chapter Two to a discussion of what many educators and researchers are realizing—the increasing need for a new model of schooling, a model that focuses on both learners and learning and that supports individual learning needs as integral to successful learning. We also share what students and teachers say about what makes schools places in which optimal learning occurs.

Chapters Three and Four address specific features and characteristics of both learner-centered classrooms and schools. We focus on examples of practices that are consistent not only with our definition of learner centered but also with the experiences of teachers and administrators who use such practices to meet their learners' increasingly diverse needs. Putting together what students, teachers, and other educators say with what is "said" by the research synthesis, we outline what a learner-centered model and perspective adds to new designs of classroom practice and schooling, and we look at implications for curriculum, instruction, assessment, teacher preparation, and school management and policy.

Finally, in Chapters Five and Six, we discuss what it takes to move toward a learner-centered design. We suggest that learner-centered schools and classrooms will not have a single blueprint, that they will be as diverse as the students and communities served in our nation. We further suggest that the process of change toward learner-centered practice is a personal journey—a journey of lifelong learning, transformation in thinking and practice, and continuous improvement. We provide opportunities for teachers and school leaders to assess their own beliefs and practices and identify if and where *they* might become more learner centered. We provide strategies for creating action plans for implementing and assessing personal progress in reaching learner-centered educational goals and standards.

Audience

We invite readers to read and reflect on the ideas and concepts that follow. We are addressing this book to teachers, school administrators, and other educators concerned with enhancing the learning and positive development of each of their students as well as of themselves. We believe the benefits to these audiences will be not only an increased understanding of how to reach each student but also how to maximize each student's learning and achievement. We also hope that readers will be as inspired as we are to join in the learner-centered transformation of our nation's classrooms and schools, maximizing their own motivation and learning, and reconnecting with the passion that brought them to the field—making a difference for each student.

Acknowledgments

The creation of this book and the process of bringing it to fruition rested on the encouragement, support, and effort of many friends and colleagues. We want particularly to thank Raymond Wlodkowski for the personal investment and involvement that included reviewing and editing early drafts of this book. We also thank our colleagues Diane Swartz, Jerome Stiller, and Audrey Peralez, who contributed thoughts and insights about our early conceptualizations of a learner-centered model. For her unwavering patience and support in preparing various drafts of the book, we owe a debt of gratitude to Jan Birmingham. We thank, too, our many colleagues at McREL—particularly Bob Marzano—who have contributed their expertise, support, and friendship in numerous ways and instances, providing us with a supportive context within which to work and write. Finally, we thank our families for their understanding, encouragement, and pride in our accomplishments and their endurance of long nights and weekends when we were writing and less available than we like to be.

Aurora, Colorado   Barbara L. McCombs
January 1997   Jo Sue Whisler

The Authors

Barbara L. McCombs received her Ph.D. degree (1971) in educational psychology from Florida State University. She is senior director for the human development and motivation group at the Mid-continent Regional Educational Laboratory (McREL) in Colorado. She has more than twenty-five years of experience directing research and development efforts in a wide range of basic and applied areas. These include large-scale projects for the U.S. Department of Education on learning and motivational strategies for students and teachers and on social skills training curricula for enhancing job success.

McCombs's particular expertise is in motivational and self-development training programs for empowering youth and adults. She is coauthor of the *McREL Middle School Advisement Program* for enhancing student self-development in critical nonacademic areas. A member of the American Psychological Association's Task Force on Psychology in Education that produced *Learner-Centered Psychological Principles: Guidelines for School Redesign and Reform*, she is also the primary author of that document. Under her direction, the McREL human development and motivation group has recently completed a professional development program for teachers that is based on the principles and entitled *For Our Students, for Ourselves: Putting Learner-Centered Principles into Practice*. In addition, she is directing a project to inspire a new vision of U.S. education and to use telecommunications technologies to bring information and useful strategies related to effective practice to school administrators, teachers, parents, and school boards. Included in these strategies is the use of the All Children's Education Network (ACEnet) on the Internet for the professional development of teachers of students at risk of educational failure. Finally, her work extends to designing and implementing systemic reform strategies including community involvement and empowerment programs for schools with a high percentage of students at risk of school failure.

Jo Sue Whisler received her B.A. degree (1962) in education at the University of California at Los Angeles (UCLA) and her M.A. degree (1964) in psychology at California State University at Northridge. She has completed courses toward her doctorate in educational psychology at the University of Denver. Whisler is a senior associate at McREL and has been involved in K–12 education for more than thirty years. During her career, she has gained experience as a classroom teacher, designer of gifted and talented programs, staff developer, and consultant. She also has experience as an adjunct instructor at the university level. As an international trainer, she works with schools, school districts, state departments of education, intermediate service agencies, and professional organizations as they work to understand learner-centered classrooms and schools and standards-based education.

Whisler is one of the authors and developers of a number of McREL products: *Comprehensive Model of Assessment; Creating a Culture of Transformation Workshop; A+chieving Excellence: An Educational Decision-Making and Management System; Interdisciplinary Curriculum Framework Workshop; Middle School Advisement Program;* and *Dare to Imagine: An Olympian's Technology.* She is also the author of several articles and monographs on middle-level education and the importance of positive teacher-student relationships to student achievement, and part of the author team that works with, trains in, and updates the programs entitled *Dimensions of Learning* and *Performance Assessment,* using the Dimensions of Learning Model.

The Learner-Centered
Classroom and School

1

What Is "Learner Centered"?

> I love my teacher and I love learning in this class. She knows
> me and makes learning fun.
>
> —Middle School Student

> I used to think I was a good teacher, but now I know I'm even
> better. I used to reach one end of an audience before. Now I
> reach both ends of that audience and students leave my class
> knowing that I've made a difference.
>
> —High School Teacher

Many educators and psychologists have been urging us to reexamine our concepts of education, schooling, and whom the system
serves (for example, Lincoln, 1995; Marshall, 1992; Sarason, 1995a).
Consensus is emerging that schools are *living systems*—systems fundamentally in service to students—and that they serve the basic function of learning for the primary recipient (the student) and also for the
other people who support the learning process (including teachers,
administrators, parents, and other community members). Proponents
of this *learner-centered* perspective further add that to support the function of learning for all learners, education and schooling must concern
themselves with how to provide the most supportive learning context
for diverse students—a context that is shaped primarily by the teacher
and where that teacher "comes from" in terms of valuing and understanding the rich array of individual differences and needs that

students present. From this perspective, curriculum and content are important but not exclusive factors in students' desired motivation, learning, and achievement. What is as important as curriculum and content, and fundamental to the learning of curriculum and content, is attention to meeting individual learner needs.

The importance of meeting the basic needs of all learners in a learner-centered educational system is becoming particularly acute as this nation's schools face increasingly diverse student populations. What do we mean by *learner centered*? How do we distinguish this concept from *child* or *student centered*? How, too, do we differentiate it from older more traditional concepts of education and schooling? The purpose of this chapter is to define learner centered from a research and theory base that integrates what is known today about learners and learning.

When learner centered is defined from a research-based perspective including both learning and learners, we believe that definition establishes a foundation for clarifying what is needed to create positive learning contexts at the classroom and school levels, contexts in which the likelihood of more students experiencing success is increased. This goal is critical if this country is to achieve increased motivation, learning, and academic achievement for a much larger number of students, including many who are currently underachieving or dropping out. This research-based foundation that focuses on both learners and learning can also lead to increased clarity about the dispositions and characteristics of those who are in service to learners and learning—including teachers, administrators, parents, other community members, and the students themselves. Finally, a clear definition of learner centered will lead to clear definitions of the practices, programs, and policies that characterize learner-centered classrooms and schools.

The Learner-Centered Psychological Principles

In 1990, the American Psychological Association (APA) appointed a special Presidential Task Force on Psychology in Education whose purpose was twofold: (1) to determine ways in which the psychological knowledge base related to learning, motivation, and individual differences could contribute directly to improvements in the quality of student achievement and (2) to provide guidance for the design of educational systems that would best support individual student learning and achievement. One task force project, directed by Barbara McCombs, was to integrate, from psychology, education, and related disciplines, research and theory concerned with education and the process of schooling. The purpose was to surface general principles that could form a framework for school redesign and reform. The resulting document, *Learner-Centered Psychological Principles: Guidelines for School Redesign and Reform*, specified twelve fundamental principles about learners and learning. Taken as a whole, they provide an integrated perspective on factors influencing learning for *all* learners.* Together, they are intended to be understood as an organized knowledge base that supports a learner-centered model.

No one principle can be considered in isolation if maximum learning is to occur for each student. The principles are categorized into domains of basic factors that cannot be ignored in understanding individual learners and the learning process, as they provide the foundation for sound teaching practices. The domains describe areas identified in the research as having an impact on learning. The factors making up the domains are related to the intellectual aspects of learning (metacognitive and cognitive factors); motivational influences on learning (affective factors); individual differences in intellectual, social, emotional, and physical development areas (developmental factors); influences of the individual's own self-assessments and the assessments of others on learning (personal and

---

*Because our purpose in this book is to lay out implications of the twelve principles for a new model of learner-centered classrooms and schools, we do not review the research that supports each principle here. For readers interested in this research support, several sources are relevant. The specific research and theory reviewed in developing the principles is described by McCombs (1994a).Further research support is described by Alexander and Murphy (in press) and McCombs and Lambert (in press).

social factors); and differences in family backgrounds, cultures, and other experiences that influence learning (individual differences factors). Exhibit 1.1 presents the individual principles and explanations of each. Exhibit 1.2 summarizes definitions of the domains into which the principles are divided.

Looking at the twelve principles, we can see that they apply to all learners—young and old. As complex human beings, we each approach learning situations with fundamental human qualities in common. At the same time, however, we bring to these situations unique ways of learning based on our heredity and prior learning experiences as well as our special characteristics such as interests, talents, and intellectual or physical capabilities. Our common characteristics allow a definition of a general model of schooling; our unique characteristics determine the adaptations that schools and classrooms must make so that they are set up to meet the learning and motivational needs of all learners. The principles remind us that when it comes to meeting learning needs, we are all learners—teachers, administrators, parents, and community members—with learning and motivational needs similar to the students we serve.

The twelve principles form a systemic framework that can guide decisions about content, environment, and opportunities for learning, for the student in the classroom and beyond, and that can help define a dynamic learning context that is continuously improving. Of perhaps even greater importance, the principles both confirm and validate the knowledge and experience of the best teachers by providing research justification for their practices.

Defining Learner Centered

We believe a lot of confusion has existed about what is meant by *learner centered*. Some people equate learner centered with *child* or *student centered*. Generally, child or student centered refers to the use of schooling and learning practices that apply to learners from the ages of two to twenty-one or twenty-five, learners in preschool through secondary or postsecondary school. We think the focus

EXHIBIT 1.1 Learner-Centered Psychological Principles.

METACOGNITIVE AND COGNITIVE FACTORS

Principle 1: The nature of the learning process. Learning is a natural process of pursuing personally meaningful goals, and it is active, volitional, and internally mediated; it is a process of discovering and constructing meaning from information and experience, filtered through the learner's unique perceptions, thoughts, and feelings.

Principle 2: Goals of the learning process. The learner seeks to create meaningful, coherent representations of knowledge regardless of the quantity and quality of data available.

Principle 3: The construction of knowledge. The learner links new information with existing and future-oriented knowledge in uniquely meaningful ways.

Principle 4: Higher-order thinking. Higher-order strategies for "thinking about thinking"—for overseeing and monitoring mental operations—facilitate creative and critical thinking and the development of expertise.

AFFECTIVE FACTORS

Principle 5: Motivational influences on learning. The depth and breadth of information processed, and what and how much is learned and remembered, are influenced by (a) self-awareness and beliefs about personal control, competence, and ability; (b) clarity and saliency of personal values, interests, and goals; (c) personal expectations for success or failure; (d) affect, emotion, and general states of mind; and (e) the resulting motivation to learn.

Principle 6: Intrinsic motivation to learn. Individuals are naturally curious and enjoy learning, but intense negative cognitions and emotions (e.g., feeling insecure, worrying about failure, being self-conscious or shy, and fearing corporal punishment, ridicule, or stigmatizing labels) thwart this enthusiasm.

Principle 7: Characteristics of motivation-enhancing learning tasks. Curiosity, creativity, and higher-order thinking are stimulated by

EXHIBIT 1.1 *(continued)*

relevant, authentic learning tasks of optimal difficulty and novelty for each student.

DEVELOPMENTAL FACTORS

Principle 8: Developmental constraints and opportunities. Individuals progress through stages of physical, intellectual, emotional, and social development that are a function of unique genetic and environmental factors.

PERSONAL AND SOCIAL FACTORS

Principle 9: Social and cultural diversity. Learning is facilitated by social interactions and communication with others in flexible, diverse (in age, culture, family background, etc.), and adaptive instructional settings.

Principle 10: Social acceptance, self-esteem, and learning. Learning and self-esteem are heightened when individuals are in respectful and caring relationships with others who see their potential, genuinely appreciate their unique talents, and accept them as individuals.

INDIVIDUAL DIFFERENCES

Principle 11: Individual differences in learning. Although basic principles of learning, motivation, and effective instruction apply to all learners (regardless of ethnicity, race, gender, physical ability, religion, or socioeconomic status), learners have different capabilities and preferences for learning mode and strategies. These differences are a function of environment (what is learned and communicated in different cultures or other social groups) and heredity (what occurs naturally as a function of genes).

Principle 12: Cognitive filters. Personal beliefs, thoughts, and understandings resulting from prior learning and interpretations become the individual's basis for constructing reality and interpreting life experiences.

Source: Presidential Task Force on Psychology in Education, American Psychological Association, 1993, pp. 7–9. Reprinted with permission of Mid-continent Regional Educational Laboratory.

EXHIBIT 1.2 Domains of Learner-Centered Principles.

METACOGNITIVE AND COGNITIVE

These four principles (1 through 4) describe how a learner thinks and remembers. They describe factors involved in the construction of meaning from information and experiences. They also explain how the mind works to create sensible and organized views of the world and to fit new information into the structure of what is already known. They conclude that thinking and directing one's own learning is a natural and active process and, even when subconscious, occurs all the time and with all people. What is learned, remembered, and thought about, however, is unique to each individual.

AFFECTIVE

These three principles (5 through 7) describe how beliefs, emotions, and motivation influence the way in which people perceive learning situations, how much people learn, and the effort they are willing to invest in learning. Individuals' emotional state of mind, beliefs about personal competence, expectations about success, and personal interests and goals all influence how motivated they are to learn. Although motivation to learn is natural under conditions and about things people perceive to be personally relevant and meaningful, motivation may need to be stimulated in situations that require individuals to learn what seems uninteresting or irrelevant to them.

SECONDARY or SUPPLEMENTARY MOTIVATION

DEVELOPMENTAL

This principle (8) recognizes capacities for learning that are known to develop or emerge over time. It is based on research documenting the changes in human capacities and capabilities over the lifespan. It informs us about the identifiable progressions of physical, intellectual, emotional, and social areas of development that are influenced by unique genetic or environmental factors. These progressions vary both across and within individuals and thus cannot be overgeneralized for any one individual or group of individuals because of the risk of limiting opportunities for learning. The important generalization in this domain is that individuals learn best when material is appropriate to their developmental level and presented in an enjoyable, interesting, and challenging way.

EXHIBIT 1.2 *(continued)*

PERSONAL AND SOCIAL

These two principles (9 and 10) describe the role that others play in the learning process and the way people learn in groups. These principles reflect the research that shows that people learn from each other and can help each other learn through the sharing of their individual perspectives. If learners participate in respectful and caring relationships with others who see their potential, genuinely appreciate their unique talents, and accept them as individuals—both learning and feelings of self-esteem are enhanced. Positive student-teacher relationships define the cornerstone of an effective learning environment—one that promotes both learning and positive self-development.

INDIVIDUAL DIFFERENCES

These two principles (11 and 12) describe how individuals' unique backgrounds and capabilities influence learning. These principles help explain why individuals learn different things, at different times, and in different ways. Although the same basic principles of learning, thinking, feeling, relating to others, and development apply to all individuals— what they learn and how this learning is communicated differs in different environments (for example, cultural or social groups) and as a function of heredity. From their environment and heredity, people create unique thoughts, beliefs, and understandings of themselves and their world. Appreciating these differences and understanding how they may show up in learning situations is essential to creating effective learning environments for all students.

should be broader because it is clear that the twelve principles apply to all individuals, from the very young to the very old, from students in the classroom to teachers, administrators, parents, and others influenced by the process of schooling and by other formal and informal learning experiences.

Some people equate learner centered both with child or student centered and with a focus on the affective side of education—the quality of interpersonal relationships and learning environments. They equate it with creating climates of caring and with focusing on fostering students' self-esteem and sense of well-being. Again, we believe these are important but make up only part of the picture. The domains covered by the principles—the metacognitive and cognitive, affective, personal and social, developmental, and other individual differences factors—emphasize *both* the learner and learning. A central understanding that emerges from an integrated and holistic look at the principles is that for educational systems to serve the needs of *all learners,* it is essential that they have a focus on the individual learner as well as an understanding of the learning process. Thus, we have evolved the following definition of learner centered:

DEFINITION OF "LEARNER CENTERED"

The perspective that couples a focus on individual learners (their heredity, experiences, perspectives, backgrounds, talents, interests, capacities, and needs) with a focus on learning (the best available knowledge about learning and how it occurs and about teaching practices that are most effective in promoting the highest levels of motivation, learning, and achievement for all learners). This dual focus then informs and drives educational decision making. The learner-centered perspective is a reflection of the twelve learner-centered psychological principles in the programs, practices, policies, and people that support learning for all.

This definition in company with the principles themselves leads to five fundamental conclusions about learners and learning.

Because these conclusions offer a distillation of the principles and a holistic and integrative view of key assumptions about the meaning of learner centered, we call them *premises* of a learner-centered model. Later on we will use these premises to organize implications for practice in order to simplify the discussion.

Premises of the Learner-Centered Model

1. Learners are distinct and unique. Their distinctiveness and uniqueness must be attended to and taken into account if learners are to engage in and take responsibility for their own learning.

2. Learners' unique differences include their emotional states of mind, learning rates, learning styles, stages of development, abilities, talents, feelings of efficacy, and other academic and nonacademic attributes and needs. These must be taken into account if all learners are to be provided with the necessary challenges and opportunities for learning and self-development.

3. Learning is a constructive process that occurs best when what is being learned is relevant and meaningful to the learner and when the learner is actively engaged in creating his or her own knowledge and understanding by connecting what is being learned with prior knowledge and experience.

4. Learning occurs best in a positive environment, one that contains positive interpersonal relationships and interactions, that contains comfort and order, and in which the learner feels appreciated, acknowledged, respected, and validated.

5. Learning is a fundamentally natural process; learners are naturally curious and basically interested in learning about and mastering their world. Although negative thoughts and feelings sometimes interfere with this natural inclination and must be dealt with, the learner does not require "fixing."

None of these premises needs to take a particular form or look a particular way. However, they must be reflected in the beliefs, characteristics, dispositions, and practices of teachers. When this occurs, teachers' interactions with learners and the programs and practices they adopt can maximize learning for each student. Generally this means that (1) learners are included in educational decision-making processes, whether those decisions concern what learners focus on in their learning or what rules are established for the classroom; (2) the diverse perspectives of learners are encouraged and respected during learning experiences; (3) the differences among learners' cultures, abilities, styles, developmental stages, and needs are accounted for and respected; and (4) learners are treated as cocreators in the teaching and learning process, as individuals with ideas and issues that deserve attention and consideration. The learner-centered model can be diagramed as an integration of all this knowledge about learners and learning (see Figure 1.1). Applying this knowledge goes further, however. For teachers, it means *functioning in a manner consistent with the foundational knowledge represented in the premises of the model. This knowledge shows up in teachers' beliefs, dispositions, characteristics and practices.*

To make this model more meaningful and further clarify how learner centered differs from child or student centered, consider the following two examples.

ELEMENTARY EXAMPLE

Ms. Jordan teaches second grade. She loves this age level and shows it in her caring attitude toward her students. When a student doesn't feel like putting in a lot of effort and hard work on a project, she finds something else for the student to do and may even excuse him from the assigned schoolwork. Her students love her but know she won't demand much from them. Many of them later report that they wish she had also been a little more demanding of them in their learning and work.

Conversely, Ms. Williams, who also teaches second grade, expects all her students to work hard and develop a sense of responsibility for their own learning. She takes time to know each student personally and knows their strengths and interests.

FIGURE 1.1 Learner-Centered Model: A Holistic Perspective.

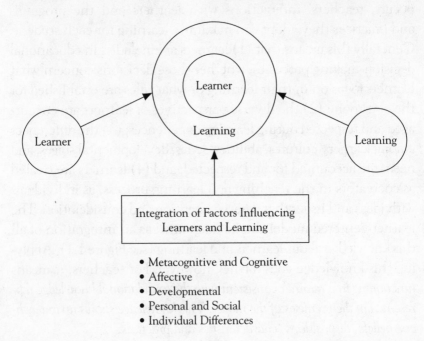

When a student doesn't feel like putting in the effort and hard work she expects, she sits down with the student, and they talk about what issues or problems the student may be having that are interfering with wanting to learn. She assumes that once the student feels listened to and taken seriously, his or her natural motivation to learn will return. She continues to expect and "demand" the student's best effort and good work.

SECONDARY EXAMPLE

Mr. Jacobs teaches algebra to freshmen students. He knows that many of the freshmen are probably not going to use algebra in their other courses or jobs, so he spends most of the class period relating to the students, telling jokes, and making the class fun. The students don't learn a lot of algebra, but they think Mr. Jacobs is a great guy who really cares about them.

Mr. Stevens's freshmen algebra class is very different. He starts the class with exercises that help the students get to know him and each other as they apply simple algebraic concepts such as grouping relationships in equations. In this familiar context in which they are interested and having fun, the students realize that algebra can be a useful subject. The students leave Mr. Stevens's class believing that he knows them and respects them. They also know that they have been helped to learn a valuable subject they may not have thought they could learn or use.

Although these contrasts between child-centered and learner-centered practices may seem extreme, they represent what most individuals have experienced or observed about various educational practices. Many people see child centered practices as "soft," not rigorously attentive to the effective learning of needed knowledge and skills. Even though this characterization may be unfair, it exists, and one reason we have chosen the term learner centered is to move clearly beyond that concept to one that couples a concern with the individual learner with the best available knowledge about how learning occurs and with the use of practices that best promote high levels of learning, motivation, and achievement.

From Content to Learning and Learners

In the past, educators have most often approached the business of schooling with a concentration on the teaching of content—that is, on what and how much must be taught in various traditional academic subjects. Learning and learners are, at best, an implied component. This is particularly true at the high school level and beyond and is supported by the dominant method of teacher preparation: a focus on discipline knowledge often to the exclusion of pedagogical knowledge and skills. With the popularity of the standards movement, which identifies what is important for learners to know and be able to do, this attention to content has moved to in-service teacher education as well. That is, with this shift from what to *teach* to a focus on what must be *learned* by each student, attention moves to the learner's performance or demonstration of the knowledge or skills identified as important by the standards.

This shift in focus from teaching required content to learning valued knowledge and skills goes only half the distance necessary, however, if the goal is to educate *all* students. Why? Because without a corresponding focus on individual learners, educators are in danger of continuing to ignore students' calls for help when these students say they think school is irrelevant, report feeling disconnected from their teachers and peers, or drop out mentally or physically because they just do not want to be in school. It takes more than the identification of the most important knowledge and skills to address these concerns, although student interest in standards and even input into the process of selecting them can contribute to addressing some concerns. Focusing on standards and learning is necessary but is in itself not sufficient.

The learner-centered model focuses equally on the learner and learning. The ultimate goal of schooling is to foster the learning of learners; and learners learn best when *they* are an integral part of the learning equation. This means that the following are recognized and taken into account in students' schooling experiences: the relevance and meaningfulness of what students are being asked to learn, students' distinctiveness and uniqueness, the support available to students from the environment, the relationships within which students' learning occurs, and educators' beliefs about the naturalness of students' learning. And as we stated earlier, it is by focusing on what is known about both learners and the learning process that educators gain a chance at having each student meet high academic standards.

The learner-centered model best serves as a lens through which to view and plan for schooling—from student-adult relationships to curriculum, instruction, and assessment to policies, procedures, and structures in classrooms, buildings, and districts. When educators adopt the learner-centered model, the five premises that emanate from the learner-centered psychological principles become the foundation upon which they function. Although specific actions and programs may be extremely diverse, where people come from as they engage in those actions and programs is common and consistent, as is their understanding of what promotes maximum motivation to learn and successful learning by *all* learners. This commonality and consistency are reflections of the learner-centered model and its five premises.

Deborah Meier, founder and director of Central Park East School in New York City (a school with a more than twenty-five-year history of success), has stated that the educational system needs a wide diversity of schools that support stable personal relationships more than ever (Meier, 1995). We believe that educators also need to acknowledge that equal attention must be given to learners' individual needs and attributes if schools are to maximize the likelihood that all students will achieve identified standards. (And we agree that fundamental knowledge and skills do exist without which it is difficult for anyone to function in life and make the most of whatever gifts he or she has to offer.) We also believe that educators' thinking needs to take advantage of students' rich diversity of individual differences and talents, all of which are needed in today's complex world. We ought to honor multiple intelligences (Gardner 1993, 1995) as well as the goal that Elliott Eisner (1994, pp. 6–7) describes: "Rather than trying to ensure that every student gets to the same place at the same time, schools should strive to raise the mean in performance and increase the variance of students' interests and strengths. Educators ought to be cultivating productive idiosyncrasy, playing to the youngsters' talents . . . because in the long haul it's the cultivation of these positive aptitudes that will feed back into the culture."

How can we who are educators accomplish this goal? When we use a sound set of principles that guide our hearts, thinking, and decision making, we have a foundation for developing significant educational models that help all learners develop their unique capacities and talents and maximize their learning of those things deemed critical by society. When we focus on learners—on our understanding of their needs and how they learn best—as well as learning, more students will be both more successful and more satisfied in school. In addition, many of our current innovations will be more effective in eliciting motivation, learning, and achievement from more of our students.

What needs to happen to shift educators toward this learner-centered approach? As stated earlier, it requires an understanding of the learner-centered psychological principles, the foundational knowledge of the learner-centered model, and functioning with beliefs, characteristics, dispositions, and practices that are aligned with the principles and the model. The remainder of this chapter explores learner-centered beliefs, characteristics, and dispositions.

Shifting Beliefs and Assumptions About Learners, Learning, and Teaching

Throughout history, all major changes have required a transformation in thinking, seeing, or interpreting reality—what is often called a *paradigm shift*. In this current era of educational reform, many shifts in thinking are being proposed. Educators are being asked to adopt thinking that holds that "all students can learn" and to see education as a "shared responsibility" among all constituencies—students, teachers, administrators, parents, and community members. Educators are also being asked to confront old models and beliefs about how individuals learn and how best to promote the learning process. In any time of significant change, people are forced to confront old beliefs and assumptions and to challenge themselves to revise these views based on evidence that a change is needed. For this process to be successful, however, people need to know why such a shift is needed, what the shift entails, and how to make the shift. This certainly is the case when educators are asked to adopt a learner-centered approach.

One current problem is that neither the public nor many educators are convinced that change is needed. Because all people have

been educated, most often by attending schools, they consider themselves experts about schooling and learning. Many people flock to
their children's teachers, principals, and school boards and tell them
what should be taught and how. Often they argue for a return to "how
it used to be, because if it was good enough for me, it is good enough
for my child." We believe this happens largely because people do not
have sufficient knowledge of education beyond their own experience
and fail to examine the knowledge they do have in light of the mon-
umental changes in this society over the past fifty years. For example,
all of us now live with tremendous technological tools such as the
microwave oven, laptop computer, and cellular telephone—all of
which were unknown even thirty years ago to all but the scientists
developing them. Access to tremendous sources of information
through the Internet is an even more recent development that is
changing what and how people learn. At the same time, most people
are unaware of what has been discovered about learning and learners
in recent years and thus cannot take into account the implications of
this new knowledge base.

Contrast the way people interact with educators with the way
they interact with medical practitioners. Few people tell their doc-
tors what to do or recommend treatment that "was good enough for
me thirty years ago." They seem to understand that medical practitioners have at least some level of expertise in their fields and that
new knowledge and conditions dictate new solutions and new ways
of thinking. Yet when it comes to education, people often offer sim-
plistic and familiar solutions and are quick to play expert.

Educators themselves are also often resistant to change. First,
there always seems to be a new bandwagon, one that frequently
"comes in with a bang and goes out with a whimper." Policies, programs, and practices commonly change with changes in school
administrations or legislative mandates. Rather than evaluate the
educational impact of each bandwagon, many educators, somewhat
understandably, hope it will go away as have so many others before
it. Second, educators often feel saddled with all the responsibility
for student success or failure in school and in life. They know that

what they do in school, no matter how positive, can get "undone" outside of school. Such concern is valid, and the teacher's work *is* often undermined outside the classroom, yet one teacher often can make the crucial difference for an otherwise certain-to-fail student (see, for example, Gordon, 1992, and Levine and Nidiffer, 1996, for stories of individuals from poor and disadvantaged situations who have "beaten the odds" because of teacher support).

Even educators who are open to change feel uncertainty about what kind of changes will be most effective and how best to go about making them. They also question whether any changes can be successful given what appears to be a complex and overwhelming set of problems and issues underlying educational systems change. Feelings of fear, frustration, hopelessness, and despair abound, as well as a sense that "we're already doing so much—how can we possibly do more?" In such an atmosphere, it is easy to hold on to old beliefs and assumptions, to stay within the comfort zone of old ways of thinking about and doing education, and to avoid the issue as long as possible. Is there a way to break through this resignation and inertia? What might increase hopefulness about change and thus willingness to change?

Self-Assessing Personal Beliefs

We have been taking these questions seriously as we ourselves examine our own beliefs and thinking about learning, learners, and teaching. We have looked to the research literature to inform us about what needs to change and why. We have challenged ourselves to discover a sound foundation of research-based principles that can guide the change process. In our efforts, we have learned to question even the most pervasive assumptions and ideas being proposed. For example, we have learned from the research that not only *can* all students learn but all students *do* learn. Research from cognitive and developmental psychology clearly supports the view that learning is a natural and ongoing process, that it occurs continuously for all learners, cradle to grave (Alexander & Murphy, in press; McCombs, 1994c). We have examined the differences in educational systems based on the "can learn" versus the "do learn" philosophy and have seen clear evidence of the superiority of those systems that assume all students do learn (McCombs & Stiller, 1995). The "do learn" environments respect and accommodate student diversity by assuming that learning and motivation are natural and that students can be trusted to guide their own learning process; they do not have to be sorted by others into presumed categories of ability. Learning methods, content, and performance demonstrations are variable and determined with student input, not selected for students in ways that may limit student potential. Practices are inclusive and accepting of multiple abilities, and they value the cultivation and demonstration of diverse talents, both academic and nonacademic.

Our examination has led us to a recognition that educational systems are more successful with more learners when they are designed from a research-based set of principles that *focus on learners and learning* and that are translated into a core philosophy and culture. We also have realized that change is more likely to occur when educators and others are assisted in self-assessing and reflecting on their basic beliefs and assumptions, and in engaging in critical inquiry about issues identified in the research on learners and learning. We believe these are essential steps in the change process. We now challenge *you*, our readers, to assess your fundamental beliefs and assumptions about learners, learning, and teaching. Take a few minutes to engage in the self-assessment exercise in Exhibit 1.3. The more truthful you can be in your responses and the more you resist the temptation to give what you believe to be "acceptable" or "right" answers, the more useful the results of this assessment will be to you. To determine how your beliefs "measure up" to those identified as learner centered, turn to Appendix A for self-scoring instructions and score explanations.

Do teachers' learner-centered beliefs have a positive impact on student motivation, learning, and success? Our research (McCombs & Stiller, 1995) looked at the impact of teacher beliefs on teacher perceptions of their classroom practices and at how teacher perceptions

EXHIBIT 1.3 Teacher Beliefs Survey.

Please read each of the following statements. Then decide the extent to which you agree or disagree. Circle the number to the right of the question that best matches your choice. Go with your first judgment and do not spend much time mulling over any one statement. PLEASE ANSWER EVERY QUESTION.

	Strongly Disagree	Somewhat Disagree	Somewhat Agree	Strongly Agree
1. Students have more respect for teachers they see and can relate to as real people, not just as teachers.	1	2	3	4
2. There are some students whose personal lives are so dysfunctional that they simply do not have the capability to learn.	1	2	3	4
3. I can't allow myself to make mistakes with my students.	1	2	3	4
4. Students achieve more in classes in which teachers encourage them to express their personal beliefs and feelings.	1	2	3	4
5. Too many students expect to be coddled in school.	1	2	3	4
6. If students are not doing well, they need to go back to the basics and do more drill and skill development.	1	2	3	4
7. In order to maximize learning, I need to help students feel comfortable in discussing their feelings and beliefs.	1	2	3	4
8. It's impossible to work with students who refuse to learn.	1	2	3	4
9. No matter how bad a teacher feels, he or she has a responsibility not to let students know about those feelings.	1	2	3	4

	Strongly Disagree	Somewhat Disagree	Somewhat Agree	Strongly Agree
10. Addressing students' social, emotional, and physical needs is just as important to learning as meeting their intellectual needs.	1	2	3	4
11. Even with feedback, some students just can't figure out their mistakes.	1	2	3	4
12. My most important job as a teacher is to help students meet well-established standards of what it takes to succeed.	1	2	3	4
13. Taking the time to create caring relationships with my students is the most important element for student achievement.	1	2	3	4
14. I can't help feeling upset and inadequate when dealing with difficult students.	1	2	3	4
15. If I don't prompt and provide direction for student questions, students won't get the right answer.	1	2	3	4
16. Helping students understand how their beliefs about themselves influence learning is as important as working on their academic skills.	1	2	3	4
17. It's just too late to help some students.	1	2	3	4
18. Knowing my subject matter really well is the most important contribution I can make to student learning.	1	2	3	4
19. I can help students who are uninterested in learning get in touch with their natural motivation to learn.	1	2	3	4

EXHIBIT 1.3 (*continued*)

	Strongly Disagree	Somewhat Disagree	Somewhat Agree	Strongly Agree
20. No matter what I do or how hard I try, there are some students who are unreachable.	1	2	3	4
21. Knowledge of the subject area is the most important part of being an effective teacher.	1	2	3	4
22. Students will be more motivated to learn if teachers get to know them at a personal level.	1	2	3	4
23. Innate ability is fairly fixed and some children just can't learn as well as others.	1	2	3	4
24. One of the most important things I can teach students is how to follow rules and to do what is expected of them in the classroom.	1	2	3	4
25. When teachers are relaxed and comfortable with themselves, they have access to a natural wisdom for dealing with even the most difficult classroom situations.	1	2	3	4
26. Teachers shouldn't be expected to work with students who consistently cause problems in class.	1	2	3	4
27. Good teachers always know more than their students.	1	2	3	4
28. Being willing to share who I am as a person with my students facilitates learning more than being an authority figure.	1	2	3	4

	Strongly Disagree	Somewhat Disagree	Somewhat Agree	Strongly Agree
29. I know best what students need to know and what's important; students should take my word that something will be relevant to them.	1	2	3	4
30. My acceptance of myself as a person is more central to my classroom effectiveness than the comprehensiveness of my teaching skills.	1	2	3	4
31. For effective learning to occur, I need to be in control of the direction of learning.	1	2	3	4
32. Accepting students where they are— no matter what their behavior and academic performance—makes them more receptive to learning.	1	2	3	4
33. I am responsible for what students learn and how they learn.	1	2	3	4
34. Seeing things from the students' point of view is the key to their good performance in school.	1	2	3	4
35. I believe that just listening to students in a caring way helps them solve their own problems.	1	2	3	4

Source: Developed by Mid-continent Regional Educational Laboratory (McREL), 1994. Reprinted with permission of McREL.

of practice differ from student perceptions of these same practices. In a large-scale study, we confirmed our hypothesis about the positive impact of beliefs and practices consistent with the research on learners and learning. We also found that teachers who are more learner centered are more successful in engaging more students in an effective learning process and are also more effective learners themselves and happier with their jobs. Furthermore, teachers report that the process of self-assessment and reflection—particularly on discrepancies between their own and their individual students' experiences of classroom practices—helps them identify areas in which they might change their practices to be more effective in reaching more students. This is an important finding that relates to the "how" of transformation. It says that helping teachers and others engage in a process of self-assessment and reflection provides a respectful and nonjudgmental impetus to change. Combining the opportunity for teacher self-assessment of and reflection on beliefs and practices with skills training in how to create learner-centered schools and classrooms can help complete the transformation.

Profiles of Learner-Centered Teachers

To show a clear picture of the differences between a learner-centered and non-learner-centered orientation, we have created two contrasting profiles, each based on the beliefs described in the Teacher Beliefs Survey (Exhibit 1.3). As in any two-category profile, assumptions must, by necessity, fall into one category or the other, and thus the profiles may appear to paint absolute pictures. However, in reality, most teachers do not subscribe to all the beliefs in either profile but have a combination of beliefs, although usually attributes of one profile or the other will be dominant.

PROFILE OF TEACHER WITH
LEARNER-CENTERED ASSUMPTIONS

All students have the potential to learn. In order to maximize learning, I need to help students feel comfortable discussing their feelings and beliefs. Addressing students' social, emotional, and physical needs is important for learning to occur. Helping students understand how their beliefs about themselves affect learning is as important as working on their academic skills. Students have the natural ability to direct their own learning.

When teachers are relaxed and comfortable with themselves, they have access to a natural wisdom for dealing with even the most difficult classroom situations. Being willing to relate to each student as a unique individual facilitates learning more than does being an authority figure. In addition to focusing on what needs to be taught, teachers need to support students in pursuing their own interests in school and in connecting learning to their life situations.

Accepting students where they are—without condoning their behavior—makes them more receptive to learning. I have faith in my ability to make a difference with all students. Seeing things from the students' point of view is a key to their good performance in school. I believe that listening to students in a caring way helps them solve their own problems.

PROFILE OF TEACHER WITH
NON-LEARNER-CENTERED ASSUMPTIONS

If students are not doing well, they need to go back to the basics and do more drill and skill development. My most important job as a teacher is to help students meet established curriculum standards. Left to their own devices, most students can't really be trusted to learn what they need to know. If I don't prompt and provide direction for student questions, students won't get the right answer. Knowing my subject matter really well is the most important contribution I can make to student learning. Good teachers always know more than their students.

There are so many complex reasons why students misbehave that it's not worth my time to figure out what I should do. Besides, I can't affect the things that happen outside of school. If I give too much control to students in my class, they will take advantage of me. For students to respect me as a teacher, it is essential that I maintain my role as an authority figure. One of the most important things I can teach students is how to follow rules and to do what is expected of them in the classroom. Innate ability is fairly fixed and some children just can't learn as well as others. Some students just don't want to learn. Teachers shouldn't be expected to work with students who consistently cause problems in class. I know best what students need to know and what's important; students should take my word that what I'm teaching will be relevant to them sometime in their lives.

Again, most teachers do not fall totally within one profile or the other but share some attributes of each. In general, however, we have found that teachers who lean toward the non-learner-centered profile tend to direct what students learn and how they learn it, assert their authority through dictates and arbitrary rules, try to keep students on their toes (by giving pop quizzes, for example), concentrate solely on building students' intellectual capacity, and focus on getting through the required curriculum.

Those who tend toward the learner-centered profile focus on the student as well as on the student's learning. A focus on the student generally entails better communication and cooperation with the student. These teachers are more likely to take into account what students want to learn, include students in the set-ting of learning goals, and support students as they learn to take increasing responsibility for their own learning, sometimes individually and sometimes in cooperative groups. These teachers are more inclined to draw on students' unique talents, capacities, and strengths to bring about desired learning outcomes—that is, they focus on learning outcomes desired by both teacher and student. Learner-centered teachers also have a propensity to cultivate not just intellectual but also social and emotional growth within and among students.

Teacher Beliefs About What It Means to Be Learner Centered

Conversations with teachers clearly reveal that they have very different beliefs and assumptions about what it means to be learner centered. Teachers, like everyone else, form their beliefs and perceptions from personal experience, education, and values. Teachers' fundamental beliefs about education are important because they consciously and unconsciously shape how teachers see and relate to learners, learning, and teaching. For example, teachers can see learners from a *strength* or a *deficit* perspective (as having everything they need within them to succeed or as missing motivation and capability to learn, which qualities then need to be added or fixed); they can see learning as a natural process or as something students have to be taught to do; and they can see teaching as a process of facilitation and guidance or a process of directing and controlling learning. Thus, what teachers believe and assume about learners, learning, and teaching affects what they do, their behaviors and practices at the school and classroom levels. More importantly, teachers' *awareness* of their specific assumptions and beliefs about learners, learning, and teaching helps prevent *hidden cultures* in classrooms, cultures that are felt by both students and teachers but that cannot be addressed because they are unacknowledged.

It is thus important to define and help teachers become more aware of those beliefs and assumptions about learners, learning, and teaching that are consistent with an instructional orientation toward the *learner's needs, capacities, and perspectives* and toward *learning as a process of personally constructing meaning*. These are the beliefs and assumptions that lead to practices that are respectful, empowering, and facilitative of learning. These beliefs define the learner-centered teacher. Conversely, beliefs and assumptions about learners, learning, and teaching that reflect a deficit perspective about students and an interest in content alone are often but not always consistent with a traditional orientation that can be defined as non–learner centered. One of our goals in our ongoing research and examination became to define these two orientations more specifically; that is, to identify those beliefs that help learners feel valued and respected as individuals and those beliefs that alienate students or lead them to feel devalued as learners.

We found in our research that teachers were not absolutely learner centered or completely non–learner centered. Different learner-centered teachers had different but overlapping beliefs. At the same time, however, because specific *beliefs or teaching practices* could be classified as learner centered or non–learner centered, learner-centered teachers can be simply defined as those that have more learner-centered than non-learner-centered beliefs and practices. Clearly, *believing that all students learn* is quite different from and more learner centered than *believing that some students cannot learn*. Learner-centered teachers see each student as unique and capable of learning, have a perspective that includes the learner (knowing that this promotes learning), understand basic principles defining learners and learning, and honor and accept the learner's point of view (McCombs & Stiller, 1995). As a result, the student's natural inclinations to learn, master the environment, and grow in positive ways are enhanced.

Characteristics and Dispositions of Learner-Centered Teachers

Learner-centered teachers also tend to have some general characteristics and dispositions in common. McKeachie (1990, 1992, 1995) talks about what makes a good teacher great. We believe that those whom he and others call good teachers have characteristics and dispositions we call learner centered. Evidence from the Purdue studies (Remmers) that took place from the 1920s to the 1960s shows that student ratings identify good teachers as those who demonstrate interest in their subject, a sympathetic attitude toward students, fairness in grading, a sense of humor, and a liberal attitude. The Michigan studies of the 1950s (described in Pintrich, Brown, & Weinstein, 1994) show that students believe that good teachers put across material in interesting ways, stimulate intellectual curiosity, give clear explanations, are skillful in observing student reactions, are friendly, and provide clear structure and organization to the materials presented. Good teachers are also found to give quality feedback, are available and helpful, are fair, have a concern for their students, are enthusiastic about their subject matter and teaching, organize materials and information, and give clear explanations.

McKeachie also reports what teachers believe to be characteristics of good teachers; most of these characteristics overlap with those students identify. Good teachers are enthusiastic, seem interested in teaching, use good examples, are concerned about student learning, encourage students to express opinions, and are well organized.

What do good teachers do? Observations of good teachers (Murray & Renaud, 1995) show that good teachers speak expressively, move around, use humor, are enthusiastic, are clear (use concrete examples, signal transitions, repeat difficult material), call students by name, ask questions of students, are respectful of students, and have rapport with them (these teachers are friendly, flexible, available to talk to, and the like). Again, many of these actions are ones we define as learner centered.

Interestingly, many of the characteristics and dispositions that we believe define learner-centered teachers are similar or identical to those that describe *expert teachers* as well. For example, in a study aimed at differentiating between expert and experienced teachers, Henry (1994) cites the following as differentiating an expert teacher: knows the content, works with all students, nurtures, takes risks, respects students, is interested in individual student needs, participates in continuing professional growth, is self-confident and reflective, adjusts the context to learners, is slow to close the learning process, makes multiple concept connections, is enthusiastic, uses teachable moments, uses a variety of strategies, has good classroom management, and acknowledges own lack of knowledge (shares the ownership of knowing).

Findings from Henry's comparison of experienced teachers (six-teen or more years of teaching experience) and expert teachers (an average of twenty years of experience that met the criteria just listed) reveal that expert teachers are more concerned with student enjoyment while learning and with the compatibility of the instruction to their own philosophy and experiences of success. Expert teachers' decision-making process is centered in the self; that is, it is compatible with their values and beliefs about their role as teacher, is directed by personal feelings of competence, and is primarily student centered (concerned with how instructional practice will motivate students and enhance student understanding and enjoyment). Outside influences are significantly less relevant to the expert than to the experienced teacher.

Bernieri (1991) studied the relationship between student achievement and teachers' interpersonal sensitivity in teaching interactions and found a cluster of teacher qualities to be strongly related to learning. Again, many of the qualities found were ones we would call learner centered. Bernieri's cluster includes seeing things from the student's perspective, being genuinely interested in and concerned for the students, being person oriented and involving, displaying responsibility, and valuing order. Similarly, research by Helmke and Schrader (1991) found that classes in which students both learned the most and had the highest positive attitudes toward themselves (their self-concept of ability) and learning had teachers characterized as (1) sensitive to, tolerant of, and patient with student differences in learning ability; (2) adaptive to individual student differences in their instructional approach; (3) task oriented, focused, and presenting content in interesting and involving ways; (4) attentive to affective climate, using praise and humor; and (5) able to present information clearly and make sure students are comprehending what is presented. This study, too, found that it is the teacher—as opposed to the classroom context—that plays the central role in the achievement of multiple goals. (Teachers exhibiting the qualities that produced the most favorable results were in relatively "unfavorable" or "difficult" contexts—classes that had students of lower ability, had more foreign students, and were of moderate size. The positive (favorable) results were clearly a function of the positive teacher qualities and practices because the contexts were not favorable.)

Another characteristic shared by teachers who are both great and learner centered is the willingness and inclination to listen to students. Said another way, these teachers acknowledge student voice. Oldfather (1993, p. 3) describes "the keys" to this recognition of student voice as "a deep responsiveness to students' self-expression—to their ideas, opinions, feelings, needs, interests, hopes, and dreams— and an emphasis on the students' construction of meaning. In short, this learner-centered classroom honored students' voices and emphasized students' making sense of things together." Oldfather's research shows that honoring students' voice fosters motivation, learning, and achievement.

Nolen (1994), too, finds there are good reasons to listen to students. By listening to what students have to say, educators are more able to (1) transform schools to better educate students, (2) understand the sense students are making of the curriculum so as to decide how to change it, (3) understand diverse perspectives that need to be part of the theories of learning and teaching, and (4) demonstrate respect for students that is likely to be returned. Such educators show students that their knowledge and understanding is valuable and pay them ultimate respect by letting their opinions inform both policy and practice. Nolen also points out that *students have a lot to say about what motivates them to learn*. Too often teachers pay attention only to *what they think are the important variables* then often discover these variables do not make a difference to student motivation, learning, and achievement. Nolen argues that teachers need to trust that if they listen to students they not only will discover ways to make their classes more motivational but also will promote deeper learning. In discussing reasons "not to listen," Nolen says (pp. 6–7):

If one admits that students can contribute to decisions about their schooling, that they have something to offer to us, this distance (between students and their teachers and administrators) is eroded. And with distance lies safety, insulation from students' potentially difficult and disturbing lives. Hierarchies are maintained. If we don't listen to our students' critiques, we don't have to learn the shortcomings of our own teaching. We don't have to publicly address the powerlessness we may feel in the face of a difficult teaching situation. We don't have to explore the limits of our knowledge of the subjects we teach, or the places where those subjects intersect with our students' lived experiences. So we maintain the silence, the expectation that the teacher will make educational decisions, and that the students should bow to their superior knowledge of subject matter and curriculum.

A caveat we repeat throughout this book is that learner centered education does not take only one form nor look one particular way. The characteristics and dispositions of learner-centered teachers are not all the same. McKeachie (1995) says it well when speaking of great teachers. As stated earlier, we believe great teachers are great because they are learner centered and fit McKeachie's description (1995, pp. 7–8): "Great teachers come in all sorts of shapes and sizes. What makes one teacher great may be completely missing in others. A teacher who is great for one student may not be great for another. A teacher who is great at one moment may not be great at another moment. There is no teacher who has never made a mistake. Great teachers are not a distinct caste set aside from the rest of us poor untouchables. Rather, to paraphrase, 'We have met the great teachers and they is us.'"

Summary

In answer to the question what is *learner centered?* we emphasized that it is not the same as what some have referred to as child centered or student centered. Rather, we based our definition on an understanding of the twelve learner-centered psychological principles. Learner centered applies to all learners, in and outside of school, young and old. Learner centered describes a certain set of beliefs, characteristics, dispositions, and practices of teachers—practices primarily created by where the teacher is coming from. When teachers function from an understanding of the knowledge base represented by the principles, they (1) include learners in decisions about how and what they learn and how that learning is assessed; (2) take each learner's unique perspectives seriously and consider these perspectives part of the learning process; (3) respect and accommodate individual differences in learners' backgrounds, interests, abilities, and experiences; and (4) treat learners as cocreators in the teaching and learning process.

When school learning experiences are learner centered, learners experience many of the following practices: they are *challenged*, are *given an explanation of what is expected*, have *choice and control*, may *work cooperatively with others*, see activities as *personally interesting and relevant*, believe they have the *personal competence to succeed*, believe they are *respected and that their opinions are valued*, have *individualized attention to personal learning preferences and needs*, are *trusted to be responsible for their own learning*, and have some *input into what standards and methods will be used to evaluate their learning*.

While any single learner-centered experience will not necessarily include every one of these attributes, many, if not most, will be present. What is key is the explicit inclusion of personalized attention to the learner. Each learner is considered an important and central part of the learning equation. Attention is paid to the learner's personal needs, preferences, interests, and competencies. As a consequence, learners have the sense of being known, respected, challenged, and supported while learning. This personalized support does more than just make the learner feel good; it greatly enhances the likelihood that he or she will learn important knowledge and skills.

An understanding of the learner-centered psychological princi-ples leads to five premises about learners' uniqueness, the ways their differences are expressed, their personal construction of information to make meaning and connect new information to prior knowledge and experience, the types of positive climates for learning that are needed to facilitate learning and motivation, and the importance of seeing both learning and motivation to learn as natural processes in supportive contexts. Of critical importance are teachers' beliefs and basic assumptions about learners, learning, and teaching—and particularly the match of these beliefs and assumptions with what is known about learning and about the influence of individual dif-ferences among learners on the learning process. Whether they are explicit or implicit, a teacher's basic beliefs and assumptions trans-late into a core philosophy and culture. That is to say, if teachers and other educators within a school do not make their beliefs and assumptions known, these beliefs and assumptions will still operate as a hidden culture that is felt by students and teachers. Thus, it is important for teachers to become more aware of their personal beliefs, to know how their beliefs relate to their practices, to know how their practices are perceived by individual students, and to learn what changes would produce beliefs and practices facilitative of learning and motivation for all students. Allowing time for teacher self-assessment and reflection is essential to the change process and to the development of the learner-centered cultures at the school and classroom level that you will read about in Chapters Three and Four.

In this chapter, we emphasized that learner centered *is not defined by one kind of teacher or one set of practices*. It is defined by *a perspective that couples a focus on individual learners and their needs as central to decisions about teaching and learning at both the school and classroom levels and an understanding of the research on the learning process, as it interacts with, informs, and is informed by teachers' under-standing and experience of the process, how the process occurs, and how the learning process can be enhanced for all learners.* The learner-centered model thus reflects the necessity of a focus on both learners and learning. Unless all of us take into consideration learner needs and teacher dispositions and beliefs that support the natural learning and motivation of all students, our understanding of the learning process will continue to provide incomplete information for engaging all learners in school learning.

2

Why Learner Centered?

This place hurts my spirit!
—High School Student quoted in Poplin and Weeres, 1992

You're on constant management and police patrol. If you let up your guard for a second, you don't know what's going to happen in the room. I try to maintain high standards in my room and I will not allow anything to go on that will infringe on a child's safety, but I go home drained because you can never rest or relax.
—Middle School Teacher quoted in Poplin and Weeres, 1992

We now think it is fair to ask the question why learner centered? You, too, might be wondering why you should consider such a model. We are proposing that to better meet the needs of more students—that is, to have more of them stay in school, learn, and exit school with the knowledge and skills needed to become productive and satisfied citizens and with the desire to continue learning after formal schooling has ended—educators and students should use the learner-centered model as a framework for the design and planning of educational systems and classrooms.

But before we address what this model might look like in classrooms and schools, we would like *you* to consider whether or not our current educational system is working for most students. If it is, invoking a new model might not be necessary. An old saying states, "If the wheel ain't broke, don't fix it."

However, we—along with a number of researchers, educators, and students—assert that the "education wheel" is not working for many students and teachers and that definite signs support this assertion. As we have worked with educators from across the country on implementing learner-centered practices, they typically and consistently report the following signs that the educational system is not working as it should:

High dropout rates

Low achievement by too many poor and minority students

Low attendance by students who are at risk of failing

Low graduation rate of these at-risk students

Low student motivation to learn or devaluation of learning

Student complaints that school is "boring"

Student disrespect for adults and authority figures

High incidence of teenage pregnancy

High youth suicide rate

Violence in schools

Apathy and disinterest on the part of many students

Frustration among educators at not being able to make a difference with many students with very diverse needs

We have also asked students themselves what signs they see that the educational system is not working for them. Interestingly, their answers are quite different. Their comments suggest that they:

Believe the curriculum is not relevant to the real world

Feel alienated from teachers and peers

Believe they are not given the supports they need to
  succeed

Feel as if they do not belong

Feel misunderstood and not cared about as human beings

The two lists include some interesting differences. Educators, for the most part, tend to focus on the results that indicate that the system may be "breaking" (student performance and behavior) while the students focus on their feelings and needs that are not being met.

Thus, there are a host of signs—from both teachers and students—that the system is not working. On the one hand, teachers and other educators are concerned because students emotionally or physically leave school; do not attend regularly or achieve academic, personal, or social success; are unmotivated, disinterested, and apathetic; seem bored with school; don't seem to value learning; or have increasing disregard for what adults can teach them. On the other hand, increasing numbers of students tell us they do not experience school as relevant to their personal interests or to life, do not believe most teachers care about them or what they think, and are frustrated by a system in which teachers or other adults seem burned out or are "going through the motions." Educators think students do not care, while the students tell us they do care about learning but are not getting what they need. Furthermore, educators are frustrated because they do not know how to deal with the increasing diversity of students in today's schools, do not understand how best to meet the many and different needs of individual students, and do not believe their administrations and communities are supporting them by sharing responsibility for rigorous accountability standards.

Given signs that the educational system is not reaching all learners, policymakers and citizens are placing pressure on educators to reform or redesign schools in ways such that more students achieve academic success on rigorous academic standards. In this high-pressure context, we believe that teachers, in particular, need to be empowered, validated, and encouraged to gain a deep understanding of the knowledge base and practices that enhance motivation, learning, and achievement for more students, including those hardest to reach. Specifically, we propose that policymakers and the public should come to understand that the educational system that works for more of its constituents is the one grounded in research on learners and learning, that is, the learner-centered model.

Although we recognize that even in the most dismal situations some students have some positive learning experiences and excel in school, we also believe that the learner-centered model—with its combined focus on *learning* and *learners*—provides a framework for increasing the likelihood of positive student experiences, resulting in increased student motivation, learning, and achievement as well as teacher satisfaction and excitement about reaching more students. We believe, in fact, that if the issues and concerns addressed by the learner-centered model are ignored, efforts to raise the educational achievement levels of all students will be undermined, the sustainability of needed changes in the educational system will be impeded, and increased frustration and burnout of educators and students alike will result. A brief review of the characteristics of learner-centered and positive learning experiences helps to show how we have come to this conclusion.

In general, when people are asked to remember their most positive learning experiences in school settings, although they may remember *what* they learned, what stands out most is how they *felt* and what it was like while they were learning. Usually they felt good about themselves as learners, were motivated to learn, and did learn important and interesting content. What most people remember as contributing to the positive feelings within the experience are the teacher's personal concern and support, enthusiasm, high expectations, trust, and respect—all of which are central to positive student motivation, learning, and achievement. They contribute to the establishment of a positive climate for learning. In fact, when we have asked teachers to list attributes of their most positive learning experiences, including the qualities and characteristics of their best teachers, the lists of all groups are basically the same. Teachers identify these qualities and characteristics as primarily motivational, personal, and interpersonal; they say they felt cared about, challenged, accepted, and respected.

Beyond the affective and feeling level, when asked what they remember about positive learning experiences in school, most people also recall being able to pursue things they were interested in and being given reasons for why they were being asked to learn something or trusted to make other learning choices. These are attributes that help students meet personal needs for control and responsibility over their own learning. Achieving this outcome requires teachers to attend to what and how students learn and how to assess that learning. People further note that these successful learning experiences challenged them to learn things they might have been afraid to tackle or gave them an opportunity to demonstrate particular skills and talents. These are attributes that meet personal needs to succeed and to demonstrate competence. To sum up, *from the learner's perspective* there are three areas of personal needs to be met: the needs to belong and feel supported, to have personal control and responsibility, and to demonstrate personal competence through challenging educational experiences (see, for example, Deci & Ryan, 1991; Karsenti & Thibert, 1995; McCombs, 1993, 1994c; Thorkildsen, Nolen, & Fournier, 1994).Thus, one of the big benefits of the learner-centered model is that it addresses these needs of students, which, in turn, contributes to reducing students' feelings of alienation and boredom and their sense that what they are learning is irrelevant to personal and real-life issues.

The question why learner centered? necessarily concerns the issues that are of current concern to students, educators, parents, and other community members as they look at what is needed once students leave school and become contributors to society. In fact, it is in what people generally agree to be the mission of schools that we can see another set of reasons for being learner centered.

The Mission of Schools

One of the problems with any discussion about our educational system is that the varying factions may be talking apples and oranges. That is, conversations often do not get anywhere because the basic assumptions underlying what is being discussed are not articulated. Thus, we start here by explicitly stating our view of the mission of schools. (You may or may not agree with our view, but you will at least understand why and how we have come to our conclusions.) Our belief is that the mission of schools is twofold: (1) to ensure that students learn and are able to use important (as defined by society) knowledge and skills so as to become members of an educated, productive, and satisfied citizenry; and (2) to promote the valuing of learning as a lifelong pursuit. If this is the schools' mission, how does adopting a learner-centered model better ensure this result? We would like to share our journey in thinking about why learning centered? and the supporting research in the remainder of this chapter.

Where our thinking about the need for learner-centered practices began was with an analysis of how learning in school settings and learning in life settings other than school differ in ways that can influence motivation to learn and how much is learned. The critical learning outcomes of motivation and achievement also look different in life and school settings. To see how these differences are related to basic principles of learning, we first looked at what differs in the conditions of learning. In life, much of what is learned is decided on by the learner on the basis of whether it is perceived to be needed, important, or personally relevant. For example, learning to talk, drive, cook, or play a sport usually happens because these activities are perceived as important in and of themselves or are connected to some personal need or goal. In school settings, however, the content of learning is prescribed by others—teachers, parents, school boards, or educational leaders—based on what these adults value. Choice and control as well as perceived meaningfulness and relevance may be missing in the view of individual students.

Not only do schools, by necessity, have to teach content that learners may not *want to learn* and may not perceive as relevant, but schools also have prescribed times within which learning must occur and methods of learning that may or may not be optimal for all learners. As a result, students may not always be motivated to learn, may not believe they can be successful, and may not perceive that they have the personal and physical resources they need to become responsible for and successful in their own learning.

The most important differences between life and school learning that we saw lie in the *content and context of learning*. On the one hand, life learning experiences usually offer

- An opportunity to follow natural curiosity and personal interests.
- Lots of natural choices and decisions to make
- Time to excel and natural feedback on how well the learner is doing
- Family and friends to encourage and support learning

On the other hand, school learning experiences often

- Ask students to learn something that may not be of personal interest
- Give students little or no control and choice
- Do not engender students' confidence about their personal ability to succeed
- Lack external support and resources needed for student success

To understand why these differences are important, we then considered what we knew about learners and learning that could enhance or offset these potentially negative influences of schooling on motivation, learning, and achievement. Our premise for doing this was that this knowledge could be used to design schools that are places where students want to be, excel in their academic pursuits, come to value lifelong learning, and adopt the discipline of self-directed learning in areas they need for success in life (see Chapters Three and Four for more specific examples).

What Has Been Missing?

We next explored recent educational reform efforts and noted that increasingly they are based on the research on learning (see, for example, Brown, 1994; Darling-Hammond, 1996; Lewis, Schaps, & Watson, 1995; Lieberman, 1995; Marshall, 1992; McCombs, 1993, 1995a; McCombs & Lambert, in press; Resnick, 1987). We noted that this reliance on the research on learning has resulted in a growing emphasis on high standards, thematic and integrated curricula, instructional practices that help students take a more active and responsible role in directing their own learning, and assessment methods that focus not only on what students know but what they can do to demonstrate and apply that knowledge in real life or lifelike settings. We saw changes in school organization, management structures, and policies that acknowledge the important social and organizational factors that contribute to effective schooling. These factors include physical space and facilities for organizing teachers and students in teams, reorganizations to increase the time spent on learning activities, and changes in policies that govern grading practices and graduation requirements so that all students are held accountable for reaching high academic standards.

These technical changes (that is, changes in the domains of educational systems design that are concerned with standards, curriculum, instruction, and assessment) and organizational changes (changes in management structures and policies) have occurred in response to what we now know about how learning occurs best. However, although part of the focus may be on learning and on developing teaching methods that generally are engaging for learners and necessary for achieving higher levels of learning, the focus has not included addressing the diverse needs of individual learners and helping learners feel connected to their teachers and to the learning process. Educators have given little attention to the impact of technical changes in standards, curriculum, and assessment as they relate to measures other than student achievement in content areas. Measures of student involvement and success in school such as high attendance, no or low discipline problems, and school leadership are largely ignored. And, we noticed, students are rarely asked what they want in and from school.

We came to believe, and found that the research demonstrates (see, for example, Fullan, 1996; Joyce & Calhoun, 1995; Maehr, 1992), that technical and organizational changes do not sufficiently address these measures of student involvement because they often downplay the role of the learner and the learning environment. Similarly, they rarely focus on or provide effective strategies for offsetting the problems of student alienation, fear of failure, or disinterest in school.

To address motivation, learning, and achievement and such related variables as attendance and staying in school, we concluded that in addition to a focus on *learning*, it is critical that there be an equal focus on the *learner*. The knowledge base about both *learners* and *learning* must be considered if new designs for schools are going to have maximum impact on increasing motivation, learning, and achievement for more of our learners. This implies that there must be increased attention to the *personal* domain of educational systems design (that is, the domain concerned with support for personal, motivational, learning, and interpersonal needs) in addition to the more commonly addressed technical and organizational domains of school design.

We found, to our delight, that in fact more and more educators, researchers, and parents are arguing that to be most effective schools should treat the student as a "whole person" (for example, Bosworth, 1995; Brown & Campione, in press; Burke, 1996; Chaskin & Rauner, 1995; Comer, 1993; Eisner, 1991; Hanson, 1995;

Lipsitz, 1995; McCombs, 1995a, 1995b; Meier, 1995; O'Neil, 1995; Wang, 1992; Wlodkowski & Jaynes, 1990). Treating students as whole persons means building on their personal histories and experiences and their cognitive and social competencies; paying attention not only to their academic but also to their personal, social, emotional, and physical needs; and giving all students the same chance to blossom in learning and in life. Many educators also are concerned with making schools more equitable, making schools more just, and respecting the integrity and experiences of every child. This, again, requires a greater sensitivity not only to the needs all children share but also to the needs of each individual child.

In spite of growing agreement that schools must focus on learner needs as well as learning outcomes, it often appears that such human issues matter little because they are infrequently discussed in policy reports authored by panels of business executives, academicians, politicians, and leaders of professional organizations. These experts focus on educational problems such as low student achievement, the need for clear standards, the deficiency of time in the classroom given what needs to be learned, the lack of choice in schools to attend, and the poorly structured teaching profession. Missing from most of these discussions is an equal focus on individual student learning needs. As Poplin and Weeres (1992) argue, such problems are no more than consequences of a much bigger one: too many administrators, teachers, students, and parents feel disrespected, feel disconnected and alienated from each other, and/or believe school is irrelevant to pressing individual and social needs. This bigger problem expressed by key "customers" of the educational system is often not understood by well-meaning "experts" who have great influence on educational policies and programs. Thus, our exploration journey in thinking about why learner centered? led us to the realization that the answer lies in the ability of the learner-centered model to address a major missing piece: the personal domain.

The Learner-Centered Model Addresses What Is Missing: The Personal Domain

Why and how does the learner-centered model address the personal domain? We needed to first look at some specific examples to answer this question. We then explored several ways in which learner-centered approaches in education address the personal domain; why they contribute to student motivation, learning, and achievement. We considered, too, the specific research that supports each area or practice we will recommend at the classroom and school levels in Chapters Three and Four.

Examples abound of schools that are implementing practices consistent with research on learning (for example, Ancess & Darling-Hammond, 1995; Boyer, 1996; Glasser, 1990; Kindel, 1995). In some cases, these schools are showing high success rates in enhancing student motivation, learning, and achievement. In others, they are not. What accounts for this difference? When we analyzed successful schools, we found the critical difference to be in *how* the practices are implemented and in whether there is explicit and shared attention given to the individual learner and the learner's unique needs. In other words, the critical difference is in whether or not the practices are learner centered, whether or not they focus on the personal domain.

In order to illustrate concretely what we are suggesting, we present two hypothetical schools. Both are focused on student learning, but one is learner centered and the other is not. In the first case, teachers and other adults in the school are explicitly supported by their administration and community in continual learning and given time to explore, inquire about, and understand the knowledge base that addresses individual differences in cognitive and metacognitive abilities important to learning, the role of affective and motivational variables in influencing these cognitive and metacognitive differences, the ways different personal and social needs can influence learning, the ways individuals differ in their development across physical and emotional as well as intellectual domains, and the ways various cultural and family backgrounds and experiences may enhance or impede school learning. Based on an understanding of this knowledge base, there is a shared commitment to know and respect each learner and to provide the personal context that best meets each learner's needs. Time and attention are devoted to the personal domain.

In the second case, the knowledge about and commitment to individual learners is only implicitly recognized, is often given lip service, and is attended to by only some of the staff. The focus is on learning outcomes and accountability, and there is an atmosphere of stress and pressure that often alienates students and staff. Although standardized test scores are among the highest in the district, many students are just going through the motions and are developing negative attitudes about school and learning. Other indicators of student dissatisfaction are beginning to rise, such as low attendance, fewer students going on to higher education, and greater discipline problems. In this school, there is little if any attention given to the personal domain; the focus is on the supposed "business of education."

The result in the first school is that all students know they have the respect and support they need; in the second, some students believe they have the respect and support they need but others do not. Attendance, dropout rate, and achievement levels are more positive in the first school than the second in spite of the fact that they share many of the same practices—practices that have been shown to increase learning. Furthermore, measures of learning and achievement are higher in the first school because motivation to learn is higher. Perhaps the most important difference is that more students in the first school choose to stay in school, thereby increasing their potential for lifelong learning and leading productive lives.

Following our examination and analysis of examples such as this, we then looked at specific practices that are learner centered and thus address the personal domain. The accompanying research elucidates why learner-centered practices are needed. That is, it describes practices that address the personal domain and result in increased student motivation, learning, and achievement.

Sharing Power and Control with Students

Sharing power and control with students certainly addresses the personal domain. It is a learner-centered practice that results in increased motivation, learning, and achievement. Many teachers have discovered that "some amazing things happen" when they allow students to have a voice and make choices about their own learning (Vatterott, 1995). For example, students often choose tougher and more challenging learning tasks or more stringent classroom rules than teachers would have established. Because students are empowered and feel ownership over their own learning by virtue of having a voice and choice, they *are more willing to learn and be involved in their own learning.* Learning occurs *constructively,* in accordance with the research-based theory of constructivism, which explains that learning occurs through active interactions with the environment during which personal constructions of meaning are made by the individual learner as he or she connects new concepts to existing knowledge (DeVries & Kohlberg, 1987; Piaget, 1954). When teachers' practices are consistent with this research-based learning theory, the learning process is "honored" with opportunities for students' choice in meeting their needs and making personal connections with prior and new knowledge. Motivation thus is enhanced (Brooks & Brooks, 1993; Glasser, 1984), which ultimately contributes to greater student achievement.

Further evidence of the rewards of a more positive and supportive student-teacher relationship is reported by Voelkl (1994). In a study of more than 13,000 eighth graders, student perceptions of school warmth (defined as a supportive environment in which students feel understood and connected to their teachers and to learning) were positively related to their active participation in classroom activities, which in turn was highly predictive of student achievement. For example, when students perceived that their teachers valued and respected them, they were more actively involved in their own learning, and as a result, their achievement was higher than that of similar students who did not perceive that their teachers were supportive. The important lesson from this research is that when students feel accepted and comfortable in school, they are more likely to be involved, and this involvement leads to high levels of achievement. There is a powerful interplay between achievement and practices such as giving students more control, encouraging active learning, and supporting individual student learning needs.

More and more, distinguished educators concerned with equity are calling for democratic schooling and instructional methods that build on each student's background, experience of reality, and perspective (for example, Bartolome, 1994), methods that address the personal domain. For practices such as these to become realities, however, teachers need to become more aware of "their relationship with students as knowers and active participants in their own learning" (p. 173). When power is shared by students and teachers, teaching methods become a means to an end rather than an end in themselves. Bartolome (1994, p. 190) contends that the "critical issue is the degree to which we hold the moral conviction that we must humanize the educational experience of students from subordinated populations by eliminating the hostility that often confronts these students. This process would require that we cease to be overly dependent on methods as technical instruments and adopt a pedagogy that seeks to forge a cultural democracy where all students are treated with respect and dignity." That view addresses nicely the greater goal of learner-centered practices at the school and classroom levels—and the question why learner centered?

In a further understanding of the benefits of teachers' sharing power with students, Vatterott (1995) points out that although teachers are held responsible for student learning, it is the student who makes the decision to learn. Teachers *cannot make learning happen*; they can encourage and persuade with a variety of incentives. But teachers know only too well that many incentives (grades and fear of discipline, for instance) work only for some students. Further, when teachers try to overly control the learning process or to get students to take responsibility within the teacher's parameters and by the teacher's rules, they may get obedience but they will not get responsibility. In this scenario, students know who has the power, and being responsible has no payoff unless the students see the task as being intrinsically rewarding (that is, interesting, relevant, or of some personal value). When the task is not perceived as intrinsically rewarding, students are likely to choose not to do it or not to do it well, just going through the motions to get it done. What Vatterott (1995) suggests is that teachers set up a system that gives students more independence as learners and more control over their learning, without giving up control of the classroom. The control that is given up is "the standardized task with one standardized way of doing the task" (p. 28). In its place is "student-focused instruction," in which students have some control and choice; not all students necessarily are doing the same thing at the same time.

By the time students reach middle school, they are fast on their way to adolescence. From this point on in their development, they need and want more control over their own learning (Vatterott, 1995). They want to have their ideas and opinions heard; they want to have some voice and input over classroom decisions. As Ridley, McCombs, and Taylor (1994) have argued, student responsibility—or anyone's responsibility for that matter—begins with making choices. Without the opportunity to choose, to make decisions for oneself, and to face the consequences of those decisions, there is no sense of ownership. A sense of ownership, resulting from choices, is empowering. The wise teacher thus knows that having some choice is motivating for students and brings a level of excitement to the classroom. Learning is more fun and exciting for both students and teachers, and "students themselves become co-operators who share in the pleasures and responsibilities of control" (Ridley, McCombs, & Taylor, 1994, p. 54). Self-directed and self-regulated learning requires at least some learner input, choice, and autonomy. In the for-

How can you have choices without options?

mal school setting, teachers and students share the responsibility and the power for learning—a key feature of learner-centered practices and one that addresses the personal domain.

Zimmerman's research (1994) goes even further. It demonstrates that intrinsic motivation and self-regulation are, by definition, only possible in contexts that provide for choice and control. If students do not have options to choose among or if they are not allowed some control in critical dimensions of their learning (such as what topics to pursue, how and when to study, and the results they want to achieve), regulation of thinking and learning processes by the self is not fully possible. Externally imposed conditions then regulate the content, structure, and process of learning. Zimmerman goes on to argue that if students are not allowed some choice and control, they are not likely to learn strategies for regulating their own learning and, as a result, will not attach value to self-regulation strategy training or *willingly* self-initiate and control the use of various strategies. Training in such self-regulation strategies as monitoring one's comprehension while learning, setting learning and performance goals, and controlling negative emotions and cognitions has been shown to enhance school learning and performance (Zimmerman, 1994). But if the major conditions required for self-regulation (choice and control) are not present, schools will actually work against helping learners *want to learn and self-regulate their learning*.

Many teachers are understandably skeptical and even fearful about what will happen to classroom order and discipline if students are given some choice and control over their own learning. Remarkably, when teachers take this risk, they are often surprised to see that there are *fewer not more* classroom management and discipline problems. This is not an accidental occurrence; it is easily predictable from the research base as summarized by motivational researchers Deci and Ryan (1991; Ryan, 1995): "First, the research is clear that motivation to learn and to take responsibility for one's own learning is enhanced when the basic needs for autonomy and control over the learning process are met. Second, once ownership over the learning process occurs, learning becomes intrinsically motivating because one is in charge of making decisions that are fueled by personal interests and goals" (Ryan, 1995, p. 401).

Simply put, it is in the nature of human beings to strive for control and autonomy, to believe they are masters of their own destinies. When opportunities are provided to meet this innate need, when this element of the personal domain is addressed, the student's natural response is to feel empowered—personally motivated and excited about learning. Thus, we see that the results of sharing power and control with students, help answer the question why learner centered?

A related practice is involving students in the learning process. It, too, in addressing the personal domain, helps answer the question why learner centered?

Involving Students in the Learning Process

A recent national survey of what motivates students to stay in school also offers valuable information about students' perspectives regarding what makes schools into places where they want to be and want to learn (Strong, Silver, & Robinson, 1995). High school students from around the country were consistent in naming four student opportunities that create a positive motivational context in a school: (1) the opportunity to *demonstrate competence and success*, (2) the opportunity to *become curious about and develop a desire for a deep understanding of new subject matter*, (3) the opportunity to *exhibit self-expression and originality in learning activities*, and (4) the opportunity to *feel connected to and involved in relationships with others in the school environment*. What is particularly notable in this study is that the major components of schooling that students say increase their motivation to learn and to stay in school are also the conditions that major researchers say foster intrinsic motivation: meeting the needs for mastery, understanding, self-expression, and involvement with others (see, for example, Deci & Ryan, 1991; McCombs, 1995a). The research helped us understand that students need and want opportunities to understand their own needs and to define criteria for success. Students also need and want work that stimulates their natural curiosity and desire to know and master their environment; need and want activities that permit them to make choices, express their autonomy and originality, and enable them to discover themselves and their personal goals; and finally, need and want opportunities to form relationships, connect with those around them, and become interpersonally involved with teachers and peers. All these needs and desires relate to the personal domain; they are addressed in a learner-centered context.

Ornstein (1993) argues that teaching and teachers that emphasize the personal and social development of learners are key in fostering motivation and engagement in learning. He cites a variety of research indicating that people perform best when they feel respected and valued, when they can develop their own unique strengths, and when they are helped to take control of their learning and their lives. Furthermore, Oldfather (1991) contends that students' continuing impulse to learn is propelled and focused by conditions that are learner centered as defined from the perspectives of students. Her research indicates that higher levels of intrinsic motivation are evoked in contexts that honor students' self-expression—contexts in which their voices are heard, taken seriously, and acted upon.

Developing student potential is underscored in the research of Renzulli, Reis, Hebert, and Diaz (1995) who discuss "the plight of high-ability students in urban schools." The bottom line of this research is that all urban youths, and high-ability students in particular, benefit from an educational system that values and supports their gifts and diversity—that addresses the personal domain. Renzulli's schoolwide enrichment model, which lets students pursue curricula matched to their interests, has demonstrated that schools need to broaden their limited stereotype of human potential (defined by achievement and intelligence test scores). When students are allowed to govern their own learning process by following their interests and goals (rather than being sorted into enrichment clusters based on assessments of their abilities or other categories that carry negative limits to potential), they benefit from both a motivation and achievement perspective. They see their environments as rich, challenging, personally relevant, accepting, and supportive. The key is to relate to every student as being gifted in some way and to design learning experiences and environments that enhance the individual potential of all students.

One of the most successful urban schools in this country—as evidenced by a twenty-five-year history of consistently educating high-risk students—is Central Park East in New York City. In talking about what makes this a school where students want to be, founder and director Deborah Meier discusses what she believes are major ways in which schools can be crafted to provide better alternatives to traditional schooling for students considered at risk of school failure (Scherer, 1994). At the core of these alternatives is the personal domain—the opportunity for each student to be involved in and have a say in her or his own learning process—what she or he wants to learn and how she or he wants to learn. Parents are also encouraged to be involved in watching their children make important learning decisions such as the kinds of projects they choose for demonstrating achievement, thereby gaining confidence and becoming comfortable with school. Furthermore, the school is kept small enough to create a sense of community among peers and adults. Meier maintains that "all members of the community should have at least an initial choice about being at that school, and they should know the rules for getting out if they should want to leave" (Scherer, 1994, p. 6). The curriculum differs from student to student because there are multiple paths for accomplishing negotiated outcomes, so the curriculum is perceived as interesting and stimulates students' curiosity and thinking abilities. Standards but not standardization are in place, along with ongoing conversations between and among teachers and students about what it means to be an educated person. There is flexibility and respect for multiple conclusions. As Meier sums it up, "Schools have to be communities that nourish our common values and our differences" (Scherer, 1994, p. 8).

Shifting Teacher and Student Roles

Shared ownership and responsibility for learning that occurs be-tween teachers and students strongly addresses the personal domain and thus is a cornerstone of learner-centered practices and produces outcomes that answer the question why learner centered? A criti-cal defining characteristic of this shared responsibility is the nature of the teacher and student roles and relationships it requires. Cur-rent practices often necessitate a shift from traditional roles. According to Vatterott (1995), teachers no longer deliver the cur-riculum but mediate it in three ways. (1) Teachers design active learning tasks in which students learn by doing; there are opportu-nities for choice, autonomy, integration of content from more than one subject, application of content knowledge, and demonstrations of creativity and personal expression in student projects and prod-ucts. (2) Teachers design assessments, ideally in partnership with students, as exhibitions or performances that encourage students to produce knowledge, create products, or engage in personal reflec-tions. (3) Teachers direct time and energy away from content pre-sentation or paper grading and toward the development of activities that focus students on their learning and how they will articulate or demonstrate that learning. Teachers also develop options for struc-turing and individualizing learning that are based on learning styles or multiple intelligences. Students' roles become more active— they construct their own knowledge, make their own meaning, and participate in the evaluation of their own learning—leading, of course, to enhanced motivation and academic achievement.

Perhaps of most importance, however, is a change in the teacher-student relationship. This relationship becomes more collaborative, students have more voice, and there is an underlying trust and respect often absent in traditional teacher-centered models of learning. Stu-dents are given opportunities and encouraged to take responsibility for asking questions and guiding their own learning. The result, again, is higher student motivation (interest and engagement in learning activities) and achievement (on both traditional paper and pencil and newer performance-based measures of learning outcomes and standards).

Benefits of Learner-Centered Schools

The result of our journey in thinking and research led us to the conclusion that learner-centered schools benefit both students and educators. In this section, we articulate and pull together some of those benefits.

In our study of successful schools—as judged by high levels of student engagement, motivation, learning, and achievement for all students—our analysis revealed a powerful and persuasive set of attributes among school staff: high energy, positive attitudes, feelings of hopefulness, and commitment to making a difference for all students (see, for example, McCombs, Swartz, Wlodkowski, Whisler, & Stiller, 1994). Many teachers expressed that teaching in these schools had rejuvenated them and helped them reconnect with their initial teaching goals. Because students were learning and were motivated to learn, teachers and administrators felt reinforced, and parents were enthusiastic and willing to be involved in their children's education. The students themselves were "turned on" to school and to learning, and a positive reciprocal cycle was in place for *all learners* in the system.

In contrast, in less successful schools—even those with a learning focus—many of these attributes were noticeably absent. (Exceptions occurred in isolated classrooms in which teachers intuitively implemented learner-centered approaches and in schools in which administrators intuitively implemented learner-centered approaches with their staffs. These educators had learned from personal experience or, often, had validated their intuition by personally pursuing the emerging research on learning and individual differences, research that concludes that attention to individual student needs is central to student motivation and achievement.) We thus learned that an understanding—or at least an intuitive sense—of basic psychological principles of learning, human development, motivation, and individual differences was common to those successful schools. A learner-centered approach was critical to the creation of optimal learning climates at all levels of the system and for all participants. Successful schools operated as learning communities and learning was explicitly valued. The *systemic* implementation of learner-centered principles had the effect of enhancing the well-being and learning of all.

Specifically, as we noted earlier in this chapter, research shows that teaching guided by a learner-centered perspective can enhance students' motivation to learn and, more importantly, their actual learning and performance (see, for example, Deci & Ryan, 1991; McCombs, 1993, 1994c; Zimmerman, 1994). When students, guided and supported by teachers, can be involved in directing their own learning and making important decisions about classroom procedures, instruction, and curriculum; when students believe that teachers listen and try to get to know them; when students think that what they are learning is somehow connected to the real world and their personal interests—then their natural curiosity will guide their learning. They become more effective, more independent, and more interested learners. They develop skills, such as learning to question, analyze, think about their thinking, and make decisions. They also develop social skills; a deeper respect for their teachers, classmates, and other individuals; and realize how much they can learn from each other.

Work by Damico and Roth (1994) bears out that compared to students who drop out, students who want to learn and stay in school characterize their schools as having a facilitative orientation toward students and as having adults who treat students in positive ways, communicate high expectations, and also advocate joint responsibility for learning among staff and students. For this study, tenth- and eleventh-grade student samples from six high schools, matched in ethnic mix and socioeconomic status but differing in graduation rates (three high, three low), were selected. Students in schools with high graduation rates reported that their schools had strong support systems, fair and consistent discipline policies, and gave students a strong and active role and voice in school practices. Conversely, schools with low graduation rates were described by students as being punitive and authoritarian, being unfair and inconsistent, having demoralized faculties, and paying little attention to individual student learning needs and the learning environment. Students were very clear about what needs to change. Damico and Roth concluded that for schools to change in positive ways—ways that will make a difference in whether students stay in school and graduate—students need to be included in regular assessments of specific school policies and practices, particularly those that contribute to a positive learning environment. Beyond this, students need to be involved on the front end in defining these policies and practices. The more voice and control learners have in their own learning process, the more commitment and ownership are established, resulting in increased motivation, learning, and academic achievement and success.

In addition to the benefits in enhanced motivation to learn, the research shows a number of other benefits from interventions that are learner centered and focus on providing learner choice and control. Students display more active planning and monitoring of their learning, demonstrate higher levels of awareness of their own learning progress and outcomes, exhibit more resourcefulness and efficiency in using learning resources, and display higher levels of sensitivity to the social learning context (Zimmerman, 1994). Further benefits include broader educational outcomes such as staying in school, higher academic performance, self-regulation of learning (doing schoolwork, for example), feelings of competence and self-esteem, enjoyment of academic work, and satisfaction with school (Deci, Vallerand, Pelletier, & Ryan, 1991).

From our work with learner-centered models of education (McCombs, in press; McCombs, Swartz, Wlodkowski, Whisler, & Stiller, 1994)that build on the learner-centered psychological principles (Presidential Task Force on Psychology in Education, 1993), it is clear to us that redesigning school and classroom practices and structures in keeping with what is known about learners and learning can also lead to such extended outcomes as enhanced student valuing of schooling and learning and a reduction in students' feelings of alienation, boredom, and frustration. In turn, when schools function from a learner-centered model and perspective—including strategies that provide for critical dimensions of choice, relevancy, control, responsibility, and connection with others—other outcomes are possible, such as reduced dropout rates and a reduction in such associated problems as drug use, gang involvement, and other negative behaviors.

Teachers also often report that being learner centered in their relationships with students, other teachers, and administrators is crucial if they are to feel good about their teaching. In fact, a common reason teachers report being in education is to connect with students. Teachers we have talked with about what matters most say such things as these:

> "For this reform agenda to work, it's got to be about making connections with kids. I know I'm being successful when I connect. That's when I know all kids have the capacity to learn."

> "Teaching is hard, particularly with all the issues kids bring into the classroom today. But I have support from my kids and that gives me everything I need."

> "Centering on the kids and what they needed was, quite frankly, a career saver. I moved away from delivering the same old curriculum in the same way year after year to a new and different approach of dealing with human beings, the kids in my classroom."

Learner-centered practices can also make an educator's life more satisfying. Far less energy is needed to devise new ways to keep students involved in class or to make learning interesting to them. With a learner-centered approach, teachers report that there is less student disruption and fewer discipline problems (McCombs &

Stiller, 1995). And there is more time to spend with individual students. The point is, when educators put learners squarely in the center of the learning process, they do what works best for each student as an individual learner. The result is increased motivation, learning, and achievement.

Generally speaking, then, the benefits of a learner-centered perspective and corresponding learner-centered practices are attributable to coupling what is known about individual differences in will to learn, intrinsic motivation, and self-regulated learning (in other words, what is known about the learner) with what is understood about the learning process. That is, the learner-centered model focuses both on an understanding of basic learner needs, interests, and learning capacities *and* on an understanding of the personally and socially constructed nature of the learning process. Findings from psychological research in such areas as human development, learning, cognition, and motivation are being integrated in ways that can contribute directly to practices responsive to the individual learner and to the personal domain.

In order to better understand how to implement the learner-centered model, however, it is necessary to clearly articulate foundational principles derived from the knowledge base on learning and learners and to describe the implications of these principles for practices at all levels of the educational system. With such an articulation, it is possible for educators to validate and defend what needs to be designed and why. As we mentioned earlier, many excellent teachers have arrived at these principles intuitively and experientially, but until they can defend their methods as implementation of research-based, learner-centered practices, there is little likelihood of systemic application at community, district, school, and classroom levels. We further realize that the learner-centered principles also define a change process that is in keeping with this knowledge base and that addresses personal as well as technical and organizational dimensions of systemic educational change. Learning is change, and change involves learning. Both processes are continual and ongoing; they are complementary and reciprocal. We thus have yet more evidence that answers the question why learner centered?

Summary

There is little argument that traditional modes of schooling are no longer adequate. Students—and, for that matter, all individuals in the educational system—operate as whole persons, with intellectual, emotional, social, and physical needs. In addition, students' behavior is based on their perceptions and evaluations of situations from their own perspective—a perspective that considers meaning and value relevant to personal and cultural contexts. Because conventional education often ignores current understandings of learners and learning, it does not incorporate student perspectives, needs, and talents. The result is the increased devaluing of schooling and learning by too many of our students.

Many of these students are frustrated by the lack of caring they experience in their schools as well as the absence of a sense of relevancy about what they are being asked to learn and do. This is true for many urban, suburban, and rural students of all ability levels but is particularly true for minority students, for whom race and culture can be sources of alienation. More students of color are entering schools and are finding the dominant school culture to be in conflict with their home culture. Many teachers have difficulty working with ethnic minority students. Understanding and accommodating different frames of reference can be an enormous and overwhelming challenge.

Not only are students left wanting something different but teachers also feel frustrated. They report that relationships with students have suffered as they feel pressured to cover curriculum and prepare students for tests. They also report a lack of administrative support, and relationships with administrators that are mostly centered around rules, regulations, and results. Teachers complain about not being trusted or respected by legislators, parents, and even colleagues. Policymakers may generate mandates without understanding what really goes on in classrooms or what it takes and how long it takes to bring about personal and systemic change. Teachers thus feel confused and put upon by these mandates because the mandates often do not take into account the realities of schooling and what is involved in bringing about change.

Administrators also feel pressure to meet policy-driven demands and are frustrated because they have little time to devote to the fundamental issues of teaching and learning or to meeting with teachers about their work in the classroom. Administrators are often the ones who are called on to negotiate problems between teachers and parents, having to walk a fine line between the two. In short, such forms and degrees of alienation among such key participants make it hard for schools to do their best. The time has come to reevaluate the foundational principles that underlie this country's educational system, a task we have addressed in the first chapter.

The answer to the question why learner centered? can be summarized as follows:

- The research evidence is abundant and accumulating that motivation, learning, and achievement are enhanced where learner-centered principles and practices are in place— practices that address the personal domain, which is often ignored.

- The benefits of learner-centered practice extend to students, teachers, administrators, parents, and all other participants in the educational system.

- The changes in our society necessitate a change in the role and function of schools so that they better meet the needs of the learner as a whole person, whether that person is a student, teacher, administrator, or parent.

- Change itself requires a transformation in thinking (and thus a process of learning); this transformation can be facilitated by an understanding of basic principles about learning and learners.

3

The Learner-Centered Classroom

As a teacher, I must first slow down in order to acknowledge the
voices of my students—to take these moments to give value to
what is being said no matter how loud or soft, gentle or angry,
relevant or irrelevant it may seem.

—Elementary School Teacher

JO SUE WHISLER'S FIFTH-GRADE TEACHER

Miss Slike, my fifth grade teacher, was not only my favorite
teacher but inspired me to become a teacher myself. I loved
her and worked harder in her class than I ever had before. Yet
when I look back on my experience of fifth grade, some of
what Miss Slike did, on the surface, does not appear to be or at
least was not always learner centered. She gave us some but
not a lot of choice about what we wanted to learn. She often
proffered the "right" answer in lieu of inquiry. We more often
worked independently than in groups. She was what we called
"strict," being somewhat directive as she provided structure.
However, in many ways, and certainly in my experience, Miss
Slike was very learner centered.

When I look at the results she produced and examine
her ways of being and other practices, the point that
learner centered does not look any one particular way is
driven home.

First, she did give us choice, encouraged inquiry, and arranged for group work some of the time. And her directiveness engendered a sense of safety and comfort in that we knew what was expected of us! Furthermore, our class was heterogeneous: there were smart kids and not-so-smart kids. Yet Miss Slike had high expectations of and challenged everyone. And all of us rose to the occasion and did better than we had done in earlier grades and classes. She did design tasks and provide learning activities that were interesting, challenging, and enjoyable, and she herself was enthused about what she was teaching. She presented information and asked questions that stimulated our thinking and facilitated participation of all students. She demonstrated affection, caring, respect, and interest in each and every student. And we loved and did our best for her.

There are many Miss Slikes in the world of teaching. All teachers have their own styles and ways of being with students. Given this, it is fortunate that learner-centered education does not have to look a certain way or necessarily include all attributes or practices from a checklist such as Characteristics of Learner-Centered Classrooms (Exhibit 3.1) or a survey such as Teacher Classroom Practices (Exhibit 3.2) or any other such checklist or survey, although such lists are useful as guidelines and for self-assessment. Learner-centered practice has a lot to do with a way of being, a disposition, a place to come from that honors students, is responsive to their individuality and uniqueness, and respects and appreciates them as human beings. Teachers could adopt most or even all of the practices and strategies from the checklist or survey yet just go through the motions of being learner centered, doing things considered learner centered but without the heart, mind-set, and beliefs that should match the actions.

Consider this analogous example: a teacher assigns a project to her class and accompanies the assignment with a checklist. Many students complete the assignment and provide or accomplish everything on the checklist. Do all these students receive A's or whatever

EXHIBIT 3.1   Characteristics of Learner-Centered Classrooms.

In learner-centered classrooms, the **students**
- [ ] Choose their own projects
- [ ] Work at their own individual pace
- [ ] Show excitement about learning new things
- [ ] Work with students of different ages, cultures, and abilities
- [ ] Demonstrate their knowledge in unique ways
- [ ] Are actively engaged and participating in individual and group learning activities
- [ ] Go beyond minimal assignments

In learner-centered classrooms, the **teacher**
- [ ] Makes it clear that he/she has high expectations for all students
- [ ] Listens to and respects each student's point of view
- [ ] Encourages and facilitates students' participation and shared decision making
- [ ] Provides structure without being overly directive
- [ ] Encourages students to think for themselves
- [ ] Emphasizes student enjoyment of activities
- [ ] Helps students refine their strategies for constructing meaning and organizing content

In learner-centered classrooms, the **instructional strategies and methods**
- [ ] Use time in variable and flexible ways to match student needs
- [ ] Include learning activities that are personally relevant to students
- [ ] Give students increasing responsibility for the learning process
- [ ] Provide questions and tasks that stimulate students' thinking beyond rote memorizing
- [ ] Help students refine their understanding by using critical thinking skills
- [ ] Support students in developing and using effective learning strategies
- [ ] Include peer learning and peer teaching as part of the instructional method

EXHIBIT 3.1 (*continued*)

In learner-centered classrooms, the **curriculum**
- [ ] Features tasks that stimulate students' varied interests
- [ ] Organizes content and activities around themes that are meaningful to students
- [ ] Has explicit built-in opportunities for all students to engage their higher-order thinking and self-regulated learning skills
- [ ] Includes activities that help students understand and develop their own perspectives
- [ ] Allows learning activities that are global, interdisciplinary, and integrated
- [ ] Encourages challenging learning activities, even if students have difficulty
- [ ] Features activities that encourage students to work collaboratively with other students

In learner-centered classrooms, the **assessment system**
- [ ] Assesses different students differently
- [ ] Includes student input in design and revision
- [ ] Monitors progress continually in order to provide feedback on individual growth and progress
- [ ] Provides appropriate opportunities for student choice of types of products for demonstrating achievement of educational standards
- [ ] Promotes students' reflection on their growth as learners through opportunities for self-assessment
- [ ] Allows diversity of competencies to be demonstrated in a variety of ways

Source: Developed by Mid-continent Regional Educational Laboratory (McREL), 1994. Reprinted with permission of McREL.

EXHIBIT 3.2 Teacher Classroom Practices.

Please read each of the following statements. Then decide how often **in this class** you do what is described in each of the statements. Circle the number to the right of the question that best matches your choice. Go with your first judgment and do not spend much time mulling over any one statement. PLEASE ANSWER EVERY QUESTION.

	Almost Never	Sometimes	Often	Almost Always
1. I demonstrate to each student that I appreciate him or her as an individual.	1	2	3	4
2. I allow students to express their own unique thoughts and beliefs.	1	2	3	4
3. I teach a variety of strategies for organizing content.	1	2	3	4
4. I change learning assignments only when students appear to be failing.	1	2	3	4
5. I provide positive emotional support and encouragement to students who are insecure about performing well.	1	2	3	4
6. I provide opportunities for students to learn perspective taking.	1	2	3	4
7. I help students clarify their own interests and goals.	1	2	3	4
8. I group students from different grades together.	1	2	3	4
9. I demonstrate to students that I care about them.	1	2	3	4
10. I encourage students to challenge themselves while learning.	1	2	3	4
11. I help students understand how to link prior knowledge and new information in ways that are meaningful to them.	1	2	3	4
12. I encourage students to express their preferences for different ways of learning.	1	2	3	4

EXHIBIT 3.2 *(continued)*

	Almost Never	Sometimes	Often	Almost Always
13. I appreciate my students for who they are beyond whatever their accomplishments might be.	1	2	3	4
14. I help students understand different points of view.	1	2	3	4
15. I plan activities that help students understand how they can reflect on their thinking and learning processes.	1	2	3	4
16. I teach students how to deal with stress that affects their learning.	1	2	3	4
17. I help students value their abilities.	1	2	3	4
18. I encourage students to think for themselves while learning.	1	2	3	4
19. I encourage students to monitor and regulate their own thinking and learning processes.	1	2	3	4
20. I get to know each student's unique background.	1	2	3	4
21. I help students feel like they belong in the class.	1	2	3	4
22. I ask students to listen to and think about their classmates' opinions, even when they don't agree with them.	1	2	3	4
23. I am able to change my teaching when students are having difficulty.	1	2	3	4
24. I treat students with respect.	1	2	3	4
25. I provide activities that are personally challenging to each student.	1	2	3	4

Source: Developed by Mid-continent Regional Educational Laboratory (McREL), 1994. Reprinted with permission of McREL.

the top grade is? Most teachers will answer no. There is usually, if not always, more involved in getting an A (or doing exemplary work) than doing what is on the checklist. The same is true for teachers using checklists of learner-centered practices. Checklists can act as guidelines but in and of themselves are not enough.

Given this caveat, we next explore the learner-centered classroom, first looking at specific ways in which each learner-centered psychological principle might manifest in the classroom.

Learner-Centered Psychological Principles in the Classroom

In this section, we look at how the twelve principles get played out in learner-centered classrooms. Later in this chapter we look at the learner-centered classroom through the three broad areas of teacher-student relationships and classroom climate; curriculum, instruction, and assessment; and classroom management. In all of this, we consider the impact on student motivation, learning, and achievement.

Metacognitive and Cognitive Factors

Principle 1, the nature of the learning process, affirms that learning is a natural process of pursuing personally meaningful goals, and it is active, volitional, and internally mediated. Further, it is a process of discovering and constructing meaning from information and experience, filtered through the learner's unique perceptions, thoughts, and feelings. How might this principle manifest in the classroom?

One way, particularly in this day of instant gratification, fast-paced media presentations, and student skepticism about the relevancy of what they are being asked to learn, is that teachers might share their own enthusiasm about the topics they are teaching or, if they themselves were not initially enthused, share how they made the topics personally meaningful. Teachers might spend time helping students connect what they are being asked to learn with goals of their own or, at least, helping them to see how what they are learning might be relevant to their current life or to the future. They might encourage students to set personally meaningful goals connected to what they are learning. For example, a student might not be particularly interested in learning about the Civil War (yet must because it is part of the curriculum). The teacher might encourage the student to generate some reasons why this topic is considered important enough to be included in the curriculum, ask and listen to what students have to say about what they already know and might like to know about the Civil War (Donna Ogle's KWL process, 1986), and suggest that students create some questions or a project about the Civil War that would be personally interesting and meaningful. Teachers also might consciously elicit and value students' differing perspectives about what they are learning.

Principle 2, goals of the learning process, states that learners seek to create meaningful, coherent representations of knowledge regardless of the quantity and quality of data available. The implication here is that learners will make sense of what they are learning, whether or not their interpretation is valid from an objective perspective. With time and encouragement from a teacher who is aware that this is natural in the learning process, students will refine and revise their concepts, fill in gaps, and resolve inconsistencies. Thus, a teacher would not test too soon material that is complex and open to varied interpretation, but allow time for students to construct their meaning, while gently validating their process of refinement and revision.

Facilitating this process can be tricky. It is important that a teacher check for understanding as students are constructing meaning, yet just as important for that teacher not to create a situation wherein the student feels invalidated or "stupid" for construing something inaccurately. Just knowing and being sensitive to this possibility alerts the teacher to proceed with caution and sensitivity. This practice might look like identifying common misconceptions where these are well known to the teacher, articulating them, and acknowledging how easy it is to come up with such misconceptions. Asking students to sum up their learning periodically is a good way to check for understanding, taking the precaution to create a safe context for that checking.

Principle 3, the construction of knowledge, tells us that the learner links new information with existing and future-oriented knowledge in uniquely meaningful ways. It is important for teachers to know that not everyone constructs meaning or organizes information in the same way. This knowing might result in students sharing their differing understandings as they are acquiring and integrating knowledge. For example, as students view a film or read new material, the teacher might stop the activity after ten or fifteen minutes and use the three-minute-pause strategy (pairs of students share what each has just learned). Teachers might teach students different ways of organizing information; the formal outline is just one method (although the only one we, and probably many of you, learned when in school). Some other methods are webbing, using pictographs, and applying various formal organizational patterns (for example, concept patterns, sequence patterns, cause-effect patterns, and so forth), possibly through graphic representations (see Figure 3.1). Thus, students would have many organizing tools available to them and could, in any particular learning situation, select the one that best helps them make sense of and organize the information they are learning. Similarly, teachers might equip students with different strategies to help them remember important or interesting information (for example, memory frameworks or mnemonic devices that help students associate new information with something they already know, such as connecting a date in history with a friend's or relative's birthday). Again, knowledge of a variety of tools allows students to select the ones that work best for them or best suits the information. When teaching processes or skills, teachers might provide a variety of ways for students to learn the steps, not just demonstrate them. And teachers would allow students time to practice and thus internalize important processes and skills.

Principle 4, higher order thinking, reminds us that higher-order strategies for "thinking about thinking"—for overseeing and monitoring

FIGURE 3.1 Six Graphic Organizers.

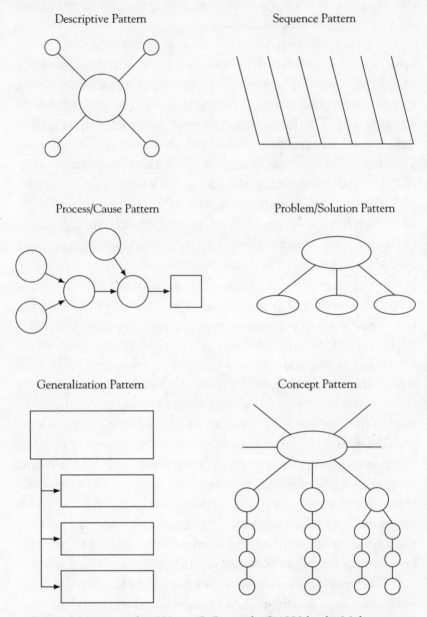

Descriptive Pattern

Sequence Pattern

Process/Cause Pattern

Problem/Solution Pattern

Generalization Pattern

Concept Pattern

Source: Marzano et al., 1992, p. 45. Copyright © 1992 by the Mid-continent Regional Educational Laboratory. Reprinted with permission.

mental operations—facilitate creative and critical thinking and the development of expertise. Thinking about our own thinking, or *metacognition*, develops during early to middle childhood. Teachers who know the role of metacognition in learning are not only aware of it but consciously and explicitly teach, model, and provide opportunities for students to become aware of themselves and their thinking in a variety of ways (asking themselves, for example, "What am I thinking when the teacher asks me to do something I don't want to do?"). They might be shown how to engage in self-inquiry (asking, for example, "What do I do when I can't easily find the answer or solve a problem?") and how to monitor and regulate themselves (asking, for example, "How am I doing on my project? Will I finish it on time?"). Teachers might teach strategies to help students in this domain and provide opportunities that would allow for the development of such thinking. For example, teachers might set up projects that require work over an extended period of time; ask students to create goals and a time line for the project and assess themselves as they go along; and upon completion, reflect on the process and articulate what worked, what did not work, and what they learned from going through the process.

Engaging students in the use of specific complex reasoning processes, from the more simple, such as comparison and classification, to the more cognitively complex, such as decision making and invention, encourages divergent and original thinking—the production of new knowledge—rather than the simple reproduction or recalling of knowledge. In addition to engendering higher-order thinking, the use of these kinds of processes with content knowledge is intrinsically more interesting, engaging, and challenging for students and deepens and extends their understanding of content as well.

Affective Factors

Principle 5, motivational influences on learning, states that the depth and breadth of information processed, and what and how much is learned and remembered, are influenced by (1) self-awareness and beliefs about personal control, competence, and ability; (2) clarity and saliency of personal values, interests, and goals; (3) personal expectations for success or failure; (4) affect, emotion, and general states of mind; and (5) the resulting motivation to learn. Sometimes regarded, especially by upper-level content teachers, as "that fuzzy stuff," these five motivational influences all are foundational to motivation, learning, and achievement. To the degree to which they are positive, learning is enhanced; to the degree to which they are negative, learning is hindered.

Teachers who know and appreciate the role of motivation in learning will spend time and energy creating a climate in which positive beliefs, attitudes, perceptions, and feelings are developed and nurtured. For example, these learner-centered teachers might be conscious of giving *all* students, whether male or female, high or low achievers, equal attention and opportunity to respond. GESA (Gender Expectations and Student Achievement, Grayson & Martin, 1977) and TESA (Teacher Expectations and Student Achievement, Kermon, Kimball, & Martin, 1980) are two staff development programs that address the issue of giving all students equal opportunity in the classroom. Teachers might be sensitive to students' moods and, upon noticing one or some students in a low mood, might explicitly acknowledge it, give the students a chance to talk about what is going on, and do something appropriate that might elevate their moods. Teachers might teach students strategies that could help them change their own motivational influences, strategies such as using positive self-talk (thinking, "I can learn to do this math," rather than, "I'm terrible at math and will never learn this") or bracketing (a method for setting aside troublesome thoughts and feelings). A kindergarten teacher, for example, the week before the Christmas holidays, taught her students to bracket their thoughts and feelings about the upcoming vacation. She had them "take their thoughts and excited feelings, make them into a tiny imaginary ball, put them into an imaginary box and put the box into their pocket or desk." She assured them that they could retrieve their thoughts and excitement at the end of the day. The teacher reported that she had a very productive week rather than the usual "lost" week at that time of year. Teachers might be sure, in other words, that the motivational influences were positive so that the foundation for learning was in place.

Principle 6, intrinsic motivation to learn, points out that individuals are naturally curious and enjoy learning but that intense negative cognitions and emotions (for example, feeling insecure, worrying about failure, being self-conscious or shy, and fearing corporal punishment, ridicule, or negative labels) may thwart this enthusiasm. Teachers cognizant of this principle might not be in the business of "fixing" students but instead would be with students in such a way and with such activities as to elicit their natural love of learning and desire to learn. These teachers would encourage, support, and be interested in their students as people. They would see beyond students' external presentations and facades.

For example, when we visited a class in an alternative high school, the most consistent comment from the students about why they liked the school and believed they did better there was that the teachers related to them as human beings and saw beyond their external appearances and what those appearances might suggest (for example, the teachers did not think that girls who dressed in sexy outfits were interested only in boys, not in learning). One girl said of the alternative school staff: "Just because I dress in a way the teachers might think is dopey, the teachers here don't treat me like I'm a dope. I just want to learn and do a good job here. Here I'm OK even though I'm different. At my other school they just thought I was weird and wrote me off." Students at this alternative school also were treated with respect and trusted, even though some of their past behaviors might have suggested they be treated otherwise. The teachers were rewarded with positive results: returned respect, trustworthy behavior, motivation, and improved student achievement.

Principle 7, characteristics of motivation-enhancing learning tasks, reminds us that curiosity, creativity, and higher-order thinking are stimulated by relevant, authentic learning tasks of optimal difficulty and novelty for each student. The trend toward more authentic learning and assessment reflects an acknowledgment that when learning is of the real world and students perceive the relevance of what they are being asked to learn, they are motivated and learning is enhanced.

Learner-centered teachers, where possible and appropriate, will seize real-world opportunities for learning. For example, a middle school math teacher who was teaching a unit that had as its goal the students' understanding of the concepts of perimeter and area and the ability to compute them, knew that the schoolyard needed resurfacing and that there was no money for having it done. She used the situation as an opportunity for the authentic use of math knowledge and skills. Accordingly, she shared the schoolyard information with her students, suggesting that this might be a real-life situation in which they could use their new knowledge and skills. Together they decided to measure the yard to see how much area there was to resurface. Then they came up with an idea for financing the project: The school could "sell" various sized rectangles of playground to parents and community members to finance the resurfacing. The students could then create a model of the yard to be displayed in the front-hall case, complete with rectangles marked with the names of their "owners," or sponsors. The students then determined the sizes of rectangles and costs per size that would be both reasonable enough to sell and profitable enough to pay for the resurfacing. Further, they decided to write a proposal to "sell" their idea to the school administration. The proposal included their ideas, their calculations and plans, an explanation of why it would work and be beneficial, and a request for the administration's support for the plan. Students were excited about this meaningful task they had created and, what's more, learned and used valuable math knowledge and skills. Rather than just memorizing the formulas for area and perimeter and working some problems in a book, the students applied their understanding of the concepts and ability to do the appropriate calculations to a real setting.

At another middle school, located in the upper Midwest, a group of students wanted the school to buy a new stereo system for school dances. They also generated an idea for raising the money: students would make winter car survival kits to sell to the public. This project became multidisciplinary. In science, students researched the history of winters in the state, the impact of long cold spells and unusually long and destructive blizzards, and the kinds of foods that have both a long shelf life and provide the human body with sustainable fuel and energy. They conducted experiments to discover how to keep materials like matches usable even in damp weather. In math, they determined a pricing schedule that would cover the price of the materials for the kits and create a profit, and they eventually created budgets for a small business. Students in language arts studied persuasive talks and written materials and eventually wrote the brochures and marketing materials for the kits. In home arts, with the help of a volunteer tailor from the community, students designed and sewed the bags that would hold the various pieces of the winter survival kit. The business class visited the bank and learned about small business loans. They ultimately applied for and received a loan for their small business. And finally, the technology class designed and produced the brochures, ads, and labels for the kit. Students in all classes took part in the planning, designing, production, financing, and selling of the kits. Attendance during the six weeks of the project hit an all time high; no student wanted to miss being involved. When the students not only raised more than enough money for the stereo but also saw that they had created the seeds of a small business that their rural community had committed to supporting, they expressed enthusiasm and pride—not only at having raised the money and created the business but also at how much they had learned in all the subject areas.

Again, of course, there is a caveat: just because a group of students creates a seemingly meaningful task or teachers create one that the majority of students seem to be excited about, teachers cannot assume that the task is relevant and meaningful to *all* students. A learner-centered teacher will check out students' true feelings and, if he finds students for whom the task is meaningless or irrelevant, will use his knowledge of those students to help them find connections and meaning. There will be times, too, when he might find it appropriate and useful to allow such students to come up with their own projects or tasks that use the targeted information and skills in ways that are meaningful to them.

Developmental Factors

Principle 8, developmental constraints and opportunities, states that individuals progress through stages of physical, intellectual, emotional, and social development that are a function of unique genetic and environmental factors. Knowing this and *taking it into account* when planning lessons, selecting materials, and interacting with students is a learner-centered approach that facilitates learning. During the primary and early adolescent years, when children vary so much in their developmental levels—both from child to child and within each child (for example, a child might be able to think abstractly in one area and not in another), it is particularly important for teachers to understand this principle. Learner-centered teachers, thus, might keep lessons for very young children brief, acknowledging that their attention span is short. Similarly, middle school teachers might provide opportunities for students to explore many and varied subjects and interests to capitalize on youngsters' curiosity at this stage. Always, learner-centered teachers will keep in mind a balance between being developmentally appropriate and providing a challenge. They will see the potential danger of underestimating a child's readiness in the interest of being developmentally appropriate. Also, given the increasing acceptance of the inclusion model, teachers will be aware of and account for the developmental differences of children with special needs, so as to maximize their learning by providing appropriate experiences and materials. These learners, too, need to be approached with a balance of developmental appropriateness and challenge.

Taking developmental factors into account can be complex and challenging. Learner-centered teachers will be familiar with the developmental characteristics of children and know how to consider them in enhancing student motivation, learning, and academic achievement. They also will be aware of specific strategies for developmentally appropriate practice. And again, they will balance the need to be developmentally appropriate against the potential pitfall of underestimating a child's interests or abilities. This will be easier for them than for non-learner-centered teachers because they will know all their students well.

Personal and Social Factors

Principle 9, social and cultural diversity, incorporates the idea that learning is facilitated by social interactions and communication with others in flexible, diverse (in age, culture, family background, and so on), and adaptive instructional settings. Teachers today have a real opportunity to facilitate and maximize motivation, learning, and achievement given the growing diversity of student populations in U.S. schools. Although teachers do need support and knowledge to gain an understanding of the important aspects of their students' differing cultures, they also have a natural setting within which they can help students understand and accept others with differing customs, values, and points of view, and develop flexibility and ability to communicate and interact with people who are different from them. As a result of perspective taking—that is, understanding what is important or meaningful to another and why it is so—students may have insights and breakthroughs to new knowledge that would not otherwise have occurred.

Learner-centered teachers will bring their knowledge and understandings of their students' cultures to their interactions and instruction planning. For example, one teacher was unable to get her Native American students to write letters to the editor of the local paper. Being sensitive to her students, she did some checking and discovered that in the local tribe the accepted behavior was to refrain from expressing an opinion in public. Once she knew this, the teacher quickly changed the assignment for these students; they wrote a personal essay in which they expressed their opinions "privately" and did not violate their cultural norms. Another teacher, understanding the Native American reverence for nature and cultural value of operating in harmony with nature, encouraged his Native American students to bring their culture's perspective, understandings, and insights about nature to a unit on the environment.

Wlodkowski and Ginsberg (1995, p. xi) assert that with the growing diversity of the student population, "Multiculturalism has shifted from a trendy buzzword to a wave of indelible influence on education." They point out that a growing body of literature provides educational practices that both prevent discrimination and affirm diverse student groups, as well as alter routines and practices that unwittingly manifest bias. Their book cites much of this research, provides practical suggestions for working effectively with culturally diverse learners, and offers evidence for the importance of teachers gaining such knowledge and skills.

Principle 10, social acceptance, self-esteem, and learning, points out that learning and self-esteem are heightened when individuals are in respectful and caring relationships with others who see their potential, genuinely appreciate their unique talents, and accept them as individuals. Many students have had a Miss Slike in their life—a teacher who genuinely cared and showed it and who believed in their potential regardless of their history. For some students, that teacher or significant adult made *the* difference—turning a life headed for disaster into one of success and satisfaction. One of the authors of this book attended a seminar several years ago in which the leader shared her view of students in these words: "Each student is unique and has a gift. All are wrapped in different packages. Some of the wrappings are beautiful and some look as if they've been dropped in the mud and stomped upon." Learner-centered teachers find a way to unwrap each and every package so as to reveal the gift inside. They find ways to establish and nurture relationships with their students so that their students feel personally cared about, accepted, and appreciated. These teachers also know that self-esteem and learning have a chicken-

and-egg relationship and are mutually reinforcing—you cannot have one without the other.

Individual Differences Factors

Principle 11, individual differences in learning, reminds us that although basic principles of learning, motivation, and effective instruction apply to all learners (regardless of ethnicity, race, gender, physical ability, religion, or socioeconomic status), learners have different capabilities and preferences for learning mode and strategies. Furthermore, these differences are a function of environment (what is learned and communicated in different cultures or other social groups) and heredity (what occurs naturally as a function of genes). A learner-centered teacher, therefore, will be informed not only about general information about learning, cultures, developmental stages, and the like, but will also become familiar with each student so as to be aware of his or her uniqueness.

Sizer, too, in *Horace's School* (1992), makes the point that students differ in the way they learn and the rate at which they learn. He notes that there is among individual students a variety of learning styles, a variety of sources of abstract reasoning, and a variety of sensing powers as well as the possibility of different intelligences. He argues that schools and teachers must accommodate these differences; although standards for accomplishment can be the same, the means to the ends must vary according to each student's particular differences. Sizer reminds us that people do not learn in the same way. Therefore, it is actually discriminatory to have only one curriculum, one way of teaching, or one type of assessment.

Learner-centered teachers, thus, will know everyone in the classroom well—each student's strengths, weaknesses, worries, and hopes will be known, understood, and accommodated. Additionally, learner-centered teachers will use strategies and practices that address students' uniqueness and their differences. For example, these teachers will know how to teach to different learning styles, will understand the multiple intelligence literature, and will provide for projects that allow students to capitalize on their own strengths and uniqueness while also giving them opportunities to get better in areas where they are less developed.

Principle 12, cognitive filters, refers to personal beliefs, thoughts, and understandings resulting from prior learning and interpretations, that become the individual's basis for constructing reality and interpreting life experiences. Through understanding this phenomenon, a learner-centered teacher will know that each and every student comes to the classroom with his or her own filter or lens through which he or she views and experiences the world. A learner-centered teacher will stand in students' shoes, walk in students' moccasins, to better understand and relate to her students as individuals and understand and honor what is so for them. This knowledge might also help the teacher not to take so personally students' negative comments and actions when they occur; she would be more able to see that even an unpleasant student action or reaction makes sense from the student's point of view.

What this means practically is that a learner-centered teacher will monitor his perceptions, refrain from operating as if he knows for certain what students are thinking or feeling. He will check out his perceptions and ask for information from students that will help him understand what they are thinking and feeling so that he will be more able to appreciate the world from their point of view. Operating from the knowledge that we all have our own realities makes a learner-centered teacher less likely to misunderstand others and behave inappropriately with them. It also increases the teacher's ability to empathize and affords students the experience of feeling understood and known.

The Learner-Centered Classroom: Critical Features

Let us now take another cut on what a learner-centered classroom might be like. (Again, recall the necessary caveat that learner centered does not look any one particular way or include only some programs and not others. Learner centered is as much a *way of being* as it is *doing* one thing or another. As discussed in Chapter One, it has much to do with beliefs, characteristics, and dispositions of teachers.)

As a result of having learner-centered beliefs, characteristics, and dispositions, learner-centered teachers naturally and often intuitively engage in practices that honor the five premises of the learner-centered model delineated in Chapter One. Broadly speaking, learner-centered teachers

- *Acknowledge and attend to students' uniqueness* by taking into account and accommodating practices to students' states of mind, learning rates and styles, developmental stages, abilities, talents, sense of self, and academic and nonacademic needs (premises 1 and 2)

- *Know that learning is a constructive process* and thus try to ensure that what students are asked to learn is relevant and meaningful, and also try to provide learning experiences in which students are actively engaged in creating their own knowledge and connecting it to what they already know and have experienced (premise 3)

- *Create a positive climate* by taking the time to talk with their students on a personal basis, getting to know them well, creating a comfortable and stimulating environment for them, and providing them with support, appreciation, acknowledgment, and respect (premise 4)

- *Come from an assumption that all their students, at their core, want to learn* and want to do well, and have an intrinsic interest in mastering their world and relate to each student's core rather than trying to "fix" or ameliorate a deficiency (premise 5).

Learner-centered teachers almost certainly engage in different practices and use different strategies even though the strategies and practices they do use have the same intent and likely outcome: the enhancement of student motivation, learning, and achievement. Let's look at what research says regarding critical features of learner-centered classrooms.

Generally speaking, as is shown by both Goldenberg (1991) and Resnick (1987), although students themselves tend to focus on affective factors as being most important in teaching and learning, other factors (in this case, particular strategies and practices) can lead to supportive learning environments and, ultimately, to student motivation, learning, and achievement. Goldenberg's and Resnick's research shows that effective teachers provide an optimal amount of structure that is neither laissez-faire nor authoritarian, invite students to participate in classroom decision making, maintain high expectations for all students, instruct in developmentally appropriate ways that challenge all students, help instill a sense of purpose in what students are doing, and encourage students to take responsibility for their own learning, That is, effective teachers have strategies and practices that focus on both the learner and learning. Conversely, research by Wang (1992) indicates that ineffective teachers maintain differential expectations for some students, provide easier work to help "slower" children succeed; provide either too much or too little structure; and take responsibility for entertaining and engaging students, thereby robbing students of the opportunity to take responsibility for their own learning.

Fiske and Clinchy (1992), similarly, describe what could be considered a learner-centered classroom: students work in teams where each person helps everyone else in the group; an agenda is created that allows students to go through materials and discover information by themselves; students are encouraged to share their discoveries by teaching others; drama, songs, satires, essay writing, and other forms of communication are used rather than only books and discussion; oral presentations are given and videotaped so students can learn from their work; and guidance, feedback, and expertise are provided by the teacher when needed. Fiske contrasts this classroom with the "factory-model" school classroom that he asserts has failed: teaching rather than learning is the central activity, students are passive, diversity of learning styles among students is not accounted for, and what goes on in the classroom is incompatible with the current demand for higher-order thinking and problem-solving skills.

In the same vein, Glasser (1994), outlines six conditions that must be in place in the classroom for students to do "quality schoolwork." These conditions could be considered learner centered.

1. *There must be a warm, supportive classroom environment.* In this environment teachers allow students to get to know them and, it is to be hoped, like them. Glasser points out that we work harder for someone we know and like.

2. *Students are asked to do only useful work.* And teachers must explain the usefulness of what they are asking students to do. Information is taught if it is directly related to a life skill, students express a desire to learn it, teachers believe it is especially useful, or it is required for college.

3. *Students are always asked to do the best they can do.* The conditions of quality work include students' knowing the teacher and appreciating that he or she has provided a caring place to work, believing the work assigned is always useful, being willing to put a great deal of effort into their work, and knowing how to evaluate and improve upon their work.

4. *Students are asked to evaluate their own work.* As self-evaluation is a prerequisite to quality work, all students should be taught to evaluate their own work, to improve it based on that evaluation, and to repeat this process until quality has been achieved.

5. *Quality work always feels good.* Students feel good when they produce quality work and so do parents and teachers as they observe this process. Glasser believes that it is this feeling good that is the incentive to pursue quality.

6. *Quality work is never destructive.* Quality is never achieved through doing something destructive such as doing drugs (even though that may produce good feelings) or harming people, property, the environment, and the like.

Finally, the research showing what *students themselves* think about what makes school a place where they want to learn (Poplin & Weeres, 1992) also aligns with what the research says about effective classrooms and teachers, which is, in turn, consistent with the literature on learners and learning. Students want (1) "rigor and joy" in their schoolwork, (2) a balance of complexity and clarity, (3) opportunities to discuss meaning and values, (4) learning activities that are relevant and fun, and (5) learning experiences that offer some choice and require action.

So there are some strategies and practices that capture the spirit of learner-centered teaching more than others. With this in mind, let's look at the learner-centered classroom through the lens of three areas of major importance in creating that classroom, that place where the principles and premises are most obviously played out. The three areas are teacher-student relationships and classroom climate; curriculum, instruction, and assessment; and classroom management.

Teacher-Student Relationships and Classroom Climate

Schooling is more than good programming and pedagogy. The best curriculum or lesson in the world will have no effect in the hands of teachers who do not believe in, respect, and relate to their students. The very foundation of any learning experience resides in the nature of teacher-student relationship and the quality of the classroom climate.

Although all teachers acknowledge the importance of quality teacher-student relationships and positive classroom climate, some give only lip service to these ideas. That is, in the heat of battle—the day-to-day race to get through the curriculum—they unwittingly surrender to covering the content instead of spending time on the relationships and climate that might make more students more successful at the academic pursuits. In September, most teachers make an effort to call each student by name and ask about students' family members or outside interests; by April or May, as burnout sets in, the most well-meaning teachers may forget the positive effect of saying a simple hello to each of their students.

The dimensions of learning model (Marzano & Pickering, 1991) highlights the importance of positive teacher-student and peer-student relationships. In that model, these relationships are part of dimension 1, which deals with positive attitudes and perceptions. An interesting and powerful twist provided by the model is that attitudes and perceptions are seen as a kind of thinking, thus allowing them to be influenced and taught (teachers can both influence students' attitudes and perceptions and teach students how to influence and change their attitudes and perceptions themselves). The model also suggests that teachers *overtly plan* actions and activities that promote positive attitudes and perceptions (or quality relationships and a positive climate) to ensure that they occur. Greeting students, interacting with them about things other than classroom business, doing things for them that signal caring (remembering a birthday, bringing in a book that a student has mentioned wanting to read, acknowledging a holiday or an important event, and the like), treating them not only as students but as human beings, are the kinds of things that learner-centered teachers do and that students say distinguish teachers whom they believe care about them. Consider this observation from a high school student: "Teachers that help you learn talk about life not just school! They share their experiences and views. I find I learn most with teachers who at least try to understand us."

Learner-centered teachers also monitor their own attitudes about their students, especially the more challenging ones, even interacting with these students as if they are the opposite of what they seem to be (for example, a teacher might treat a student as if he is interested in learning even when the teacher is convinced he couldn't care less about school).These teachers know that students tend to live up to what is expected of them (see, for example, Ames, 1992; Covington, 1992; Dweck, 1991) and that teachers should have high expectations of *all* students. Although all teachers know this, learner-centered teachers use the knowledge to inform their practice: they monitor their expectations, make more use of heterogeneous grouping, and are less likely to pigeonhole students based on prior information or performance. Thus, their students are less often relegated to low "tracks" where they feel less capable, less is expected of them, and they learn less.

The learner-centered teacher attempts to connect with each student and, consequently, is better able to respond to students' unique capabilities and needs. Recent work by Gardner (1991) and Gardner and Boix-Mansilla (1994) affirms that all learners possess unique "intelligences," or ways of processing, understanding, and contributing to the world; the learner-centered teacher, often intuitively, discovers and honors these unique and diverse gifts in students. Such teachers are sensitive to cultural issues as well as to student differences in learning styles, values, perspectives, roles, customs, and so forth, and use the information to *better understand yet not stereotype* their students. They are keenly aware, as is pointed out by Wlodkowski and Ginsberg (1995), that they cannot simply assume that all of their students, particularly in classrooms with students from a variety of cultural backgrounds, share the presuppositions held by the dominant cultural group or the same background experience, values, or meanings. To best meet the diverse and unique needs of their many students and avoid the risk of alienating students from cultures other than their own, learner-centered teachers get to know their students and their backgrounds and incorporate a variety of ways for students to learn and to demonstrate or express that learning.

Research by Poplin and Weeres (1992) succinctly sums up the issue: when students feel alienated and disconnected from the process of learning and from the social context of learning, levels of achievement are lowered.

Curriculum, Instruction, and Assessment

The third premise of the learner-centered model states that learning is a constructive process that occurs best when what is being learned is relevant and meaningful to the learner. It is interesting that one of the most common complaints of students is that what they are asked to learn in school is irrelevant to "real life" and is not useful for their future. Dropouts, in fact, give this as one of their major reasons for leaving school (U.S. Department of Education, 1991; Haas, 1990). Student engagement in their education has been shown to be a primary element in programs that do work (U.S. Department of Education, 1991), and Natriello, Pallas, McDill, McPartland, and Royster (1988) name three elements that support such engagement:

- Relevance of school. Classes must make the connection between education and employment.
- Academic success. Classes must be relevant to students' interests, promote higher-order thinking, and provide good preparation for further study and employment.
- Students' positive experience of the school environment. Students must feel safe and secure in order to learn effectively.

Deci and Ryan (1991) also studied students at risk of school failure and dropping out and similarly found that interventions that make a difference with these students in terms of motivation, learning, and achievement are those that help the students (1) see the link between what they are learning and what is important to them; (2) make choices of activities and actions, thereby learning to regulate their learning activities; and (3) experience the pleasure and satisfaction of engaging in learning for its own sake. It behooves all of us, therefore, to do whatever we can do to help students see connections between the curriculum and life, to help them see its relevance or find a way themselves to make it relevant, and to relate what we are doing to their interests. This happens in learner-centered classrooms.

One way teachers might establish connections between curriculum and life is by organizing the information to be learned around generalizations, or "big ideas"—statements at a high enough level of generality that they can apply beyond a specific unit of study. For example, instead of just teaching a second-grade unit on bears, a learner-centered teacher might ask herself, "What do I want my students to walk away from this bear unit knowing, even if they forget the little specifics?" A plausible response might be, "Animals adapt to their environment in different ways." This generalization, while applicable to bears, also applies to all other animals, including animals that the students might have at home, encounter on trips, or see at the zoo. In fact, on any given day of the week in most towns, there probably is at least one article in the newspaper that could be connected to this generalization. While identifying such a generalization or two for units of study is not always easy (it requires that teachers determine what is important about that which they are teaching), learner-centered teachers believe that it is worth the time spent, both because it focuses and refines what gets taught and because it helps them make natural and important connections for students between what they are learning and life (McCombs & Pope, 1994).

Another way learner-centered teachers may help curriculum be more meaningful and relevant to students is to give them choice whenever and wherever possible. Even though there are often constraints in the curriculum, that is, certain content must be taught, learner-centered teachers know that there is always a way to give students some choice—perhaps choosing an aspect of the content they would like to focus on or the product or project through which they will communicate their learning. In addition to giving students a sense of ownership and control of their learning, student choice allows students to make their own connections between learning and life and to select learning topics, experiences, and means of expression that are meaningful for them. Oldfather's research (1993, p. 12) shows that "motivating power was attributed to self-expression, choice, and a responsive teacher who was able to . . . share power and responsibility and provide a continually evolving balance between choice and structure. [Such teachers] . . . negotiate with students when appropriate; they provide ground rules; and they make clear what the 'givens' are and what students' options are within those givens. Students may feel that being able to make even small decisions (e.g., when to use the restroom or sharpen a pencil) are important indicators of their self-determination in the classroom."

In the learner-centered classroom, students are actively involved in their learning. Although students are sometimes found sitting at their tables reading quietly, they may also be found working in cooperative groups, chatting and animated as they find information, make connections, and make discoveries. Similarly, some students might be working in one classroom, others in the media center, and still others outside, and a fourth group might be working with a community member in his or her office. Groups of learners are usually heterogeneous, with students of differing abilities finding ways in which they can contribute their expertise and talents. Learners are frequently active in some way, engaged in acquiring knowledge and in expanding that knowledge and applying it in meaningful situations. At the same time, there is a place for both student-directed and teacher-directed instruction because either can facilitate active learning, thus reaffirming the point that learner-centered teaching does not necessarily look any one particular way or totally reject any particular practice (Weinert & Helmke, 1995).

Learning in learner-centered classrooms, even though mostly centered in the classroom, often extends beyond its walls—to other locations in the building or to locales in the community. And the community is often an important component within the walls of the classroom. Community members may serve as classroom aides, mentors, or resources, lending their expertise and experience to the learning setting. They may appear as guest speakers or work informally with students, individually or in small groups. Many classrooms include opportunities for intergenerational learning experiences, pulling together young students and senior members of the community. Young and old alike report on the richness and rewards of such learning experiences. Finally, there are a host of service learning programs and projects that give students the opportunity to provide service in a selected area in the community (often students get to choose the project they will work on). Service learning includes projects such as spending a day a week reading to the elderly in a nursing home, serving as a candy striper in a local hospital, working in a local animal shelter, and the like.

Students in learner-centered classrooms learn important and interesting content as well as skills needed in the world of work and in daily life. Thus, in addition to reading, writing, math, history, science, literature, geography, and other important academic content areas, complex reasoning, information processing, communication, collaboration, and productive habits of mind such as those outlined in dimension 5 of the dimensions of learning model (see Exhibit 3.3) have an important presence in the classroom. These are habits or dispositions that learners can be taught to bring to the learning situation—and to life in general—in order to think critically and creatively and to regulate their own thinking and behavior. The presence or absence of these habits or dispositions, when and where warranted and appropriate, either fosters or hinders learning. Oldfather (1994), in fact, finds that situations in which students become more motivated are those in which they are encouraged to engage in productive thinking (defined as choosing a positive attitude, choosing open-mindedness, searching for what is worthwhile in learning activities, self-regulating attention, and learning from boredom), to engage in actions that include observing classmates' interests and "plunging" into activities, and to develop an intrinsic purpose for learning.

Assignments in a learner-centered classroom are challenging and require students to use their minds; rather than just reproduce, recall, or restate knowledge, students are asked to engage in

EXHIBIT 3.3 Productive Habits of Mind.

Self-regulation

- Being aware of your own thinking
- Planning
- Being aware of necessary resources
- Being sensitive to feedback
- Evaluating the effectiveness of your actions

Critical thinking

- Being accurate and seeking accuracy
- Being clear and seeking clarity
- Being open-minded
- Restraining impulsivity
- Taking and defending a position
- Being sensitive to others

Creative thinking

- Engaging intensely in tasks even when answers or solutions are not immediately apparent
- Pushing the limits of your knowledge and ability
- Generating, trusting, and maintaining your own standards of evaluation
- Generating new ways of viewing situations outside the boundaries of standard conventions

Source: Marzano et al., 1992, pp. 211–212. Copyright © 1992 by the Mid-continent Regional Educational Laboratory. Reprinted with permission.

reasoning processes—doing comparisons, analyzing errors, inducing or deducing conclusions, making decisions, and solving problems—processes that encourage them to produce new knowledge (Marzano & Pickering, 1991).

Students in learner-centered classrooms are often involved in the selection and planning of lessons, assignments, and even units of study. Similarly, they are given responsibility—to plan, direct, and carry out their assignments. This entails some long-term assignments, assignments that require and promote students' ability to plan, to regulate their own behavior, and to operate autonomously. It also entails helping students select and set goals, monitor their progress toward achieving those goals, and evaluate the process they used to achieve those goals.

As stated earlier, learner-centered teachers take into account the unique and diverse needs and styles of their students. One way teachers might do this is by making sure that at least some lessons are taught so that they fit more than one learning style and so that all students are comfortable because their dominant style is being used some of the time. This practice helps all students learn to develop their less dominant learning styles as well. Bernice McCarthy's 4MAT System (McCarthy, 1980; McCarthy & Leflar, 1983; McCarthy, Samples, & Hammond, 1985) is one model that addresses learning styles. It distinguishes among *innovative learners* (they need to be involved, ask "Why?"); *analytic learners* (they think through ideas, ask "What?"); *commonsense learners* (they seek utility and how things work, ask "How does it work?"); and *dynamic learners* (they seek hidden possibilities and learn by trial and error, ask "What can this become?"). The important point is to be aware that different learners have different preferred styles, just as they have other differences; to be sensitive to this fact; and to take it into account when teaching and interacting with learners.

Assessment in the learner-centered classroom is varied. Conventional tests are used when appropriate but are not the only form of assessment. Performance tasks, portfolios, student self-assessment surveys and probes, peer assessments, journals, logs, products, projects, and other performance-based activities may be a part of the classroom. Sizer (1992) describes "exhibitions" as ways that students can convince themselves and others that they can use the knowledge they have learned. An exhibition is not simply about "covering the content," being informed, or displaying skills but is a demonstration of the employment of skills toward important and legitimate ends.

All assessments are made as "authentic" as possible (as Sizer would contend the exhibition is). Authentic assessments relate in some way to the real world—students demonstrate an understanding of some information or an ability to use a skill that is important in real life, or they demonstrate some understanding or skill in a real-life context or simulation. Most importantly, assessment is conducted in the true sense of the root meaning of the word—"to sit beside." Teachers and students work together to determine what is being learned, how well it is being learned, and what both the teacher and the student might do to facilitate learning.

One assessment element that might be found in learner-centered classrooms is the *rubric*, a set of criteria that defines performance at various levels. Students are given rubrics up front, before they are assessed. Often, they are even involved in developing the rubrics. Thus, in addition to feeling some ownership of the criteria and some buy-in, they know what they need to do to achieve at an acceptable level and what achievement below or above an acceptable level looks like. An example of a rubric is shown in Exhibit 3.4. The three-point level of this four-point rubric designates the targeted level of performance, or the *performance standard*; it is the level teachers want and work to have all students achieve. It is beyond minimum competency; it describes *solid* performance. The four-point level in the rubric describes exemplary performance, the two-point level is developing toward solid performance, and the one-point level describes performance that has serious misconceptions or errors.

Rubrics have a great potential to alter education for our students in that students given rubrics finally know what they need to

EXHIBIT 3.4 Rubric Example from an
Elementary Class Learning Geometry.

4   Demonstrates a thorough understanding of how basic geometric shapes are used in the planning of well-organized communities and provides new insights into some of their use.

3   Displays a complete and accurate understanding of how geometric shapes are used in the planning of well-organized communities.

2   Displays an incomplete understanding of how basic geometric shapes are used in the planning of well-organized communities and has some notable misconceptions about their use.

1   Was unable to offer a rationale for using basic geometric shapes in the planning of well-organized communities.

---

do to succeed. This is not giving them the answers but spelling out the criteria for success. It is not unlike what happens in the Olympics: the competitors know exactly what they need to do to get a 10 on any given event. Although teachers have always had rubrics of sorts in their heads, in learner-centered classrooms these rubrics are now in the hands of the students, where they belong. Ask yourself how much time you spent during your school years trying to figure out what exactly your teachers wanted, and you will get an idea of how much more time you might have had for learning!

Grant Wiggins, during a conference in 1992, once used the following analogy in talking about the value of rubrics: rubrics are for students what road signs are for drivers. Imagine all highway and road signs being eliminated. Now imagine getting from where you live to some distant locale. You probably know enough to get on a highway and get some distance out of town. At some point, however, you will have to stop, knock at a door, and ask someone when you should turn east or north (or wherever) and whether there's a tree or a barn at the intersection so that you'll know it when you come to it. Rubrics are like road signs: they allow students to know where they are with respect to where they need to be and how to get there. They allow students to self-assess, self-correct, and be more self-reliant. Because of their ability to inform students and assist them in excelling, rubrics are usually found in learner-centered classrooms, along with at least some of the numerous other forms of assessment mentioned earlier, where they contribute to increased student motivation, learning, and achievement.

Classroom Management

While the learner-centered psychological principles reflect research that supports the idea that learning is a natural phenomenon and that learners are intrinsically curious and want to learn and master their world, learner-centered practitioners were not born yesterday. They know that not all students behave consistently with this assumption. That is, some students, more than we would like to count, are unmotivated, reject what is being taught, and are downright nuisances in the classroom, actually impeding the learning process. What are some of the ways that learner-centered teachers deal with such students?

One practice learner-centered teachers use, which relates back to ideas in the section on teacher-student relationships and classroom climate, is to place a premium on maintaining positive perceptions about all students, even those that continually cause concern and exhibit negative actions. They remind themselves who these students really are at their core and give them innumerable other chances. In fact, they try to forget the past and start each day as a new beginning. And they find, as with any other expectation, this expectation sometimes pays off—that is, sometimes even the most recalcitrant student comes through with exemplary behavior and work.

Years ago, one of the authors attended a workshop during which the leader (Constance Dembrowsky) told the following true story that reflects this book's perspective on who most human beings are at their core. In the summer of 1986, Dembrowsky donated her time to work with at-risk students (some of them dropouts) in a school district in California. While recruiting participants for a program on developing personal power, she interviewed an eighteen-year-old dropout. When she asked him what he wanted to do with his life, he answered that he aspired to be the biggest drug kingpin in Southern California. Dembrowsky, committed to listening to these students and not judging them, then asked him to tell her more about this goal and what his life might be like if he achieved it. After going on for about ten minutes, extolling the advantages of having the power, money, and women such a position would afford him, he suddenly stopped and said, "But you know what I'd really like to do if I could do anything? I'd like to be the guy who discovers the cure for AIDS. I don't think anyone knows how bad it's gonna get. I'd really love to be the one that figures out how to cure it."

Admittedly teachers might have to dig fairly deep to get to this core in some students, but we do believe that for most students it is there, often buried under layers and layers of anger, hurt, hopelessness, neglect, poor parenting, and the like. And sometimes teachers can access that core by just knowing and remembering that it is there, relating to *it* rather than to the student's immediate behavior, and by giving the student the opportunity to express it.

But what about actually dealing with problems and problem students in the classroom? Fortunately for learner-centered teachers, there are several learner-centered discipline programs. They have in common, first, the belief that misbehavior may be avoided when students' basic needs are met and, second, the goal of teaching students responsibility and respect, rather than trying to teach them to blindly obey authority (Ancess & Darling-Hammond, 1995). Here are some examples of such programs:

- *Discipline with Dignity* focuses on problem solving and prevention. Students are involved in the discipline process, allowing them to internalize the values that underlie desired and acceptable behaviors. The program's authors believe that it is important to enhance the dignity of students no matter what their behavior.

- *Cooperative Discipline* also involves students in the process, as well as colleagues and parents. This program includes identifying the goals of a particular misbehavior and intervening when it occurs. The underlying belief is that students must be affirmed and given the opportunity to share in the responsibility for their own behavior.

- *Positive Classroom Discipline* operates on the belief that classroom management procedures should be gentle and positive, building on cooperation rather than coercion. The program focuses on managing group behavior so as to reduce disruptions, limit-setting, using incentive systems, and giving responsibility training.

- *kids are worth it!* focuses on showing students what they have done wrong, giving them ownership of the problem, and helping them to solve the problem. Its author believes that students can develop self-discipline if they are treated with respect, given responsibilities and choices, and allowed to experience the natural consequences of those choices.

- *Stress-Free Discipline*'s main focus is working with at-risk and special needs students, preventing violence, and controlling gang activity. The author believes that teachers can achieve successful classroom management and discipline with minimal stress while achieving the goal of self-discipline for students.

Many learner-centered teachers use no formal discipline program at all. Because of their basic beliefs about students and the teacher's role in the classroom, they often intuitively respond in ways that reflect many of the goals and underlying beliefs of the programs just described. Their basic respect and caring for students forms the basis for whatever actions they take. Once again, there is no particular way learner-centered classroom management looks.

Some learner-centered teachers have lots of rules and require quiet and strict behavior; others have looser, less formal guidelines. Some are serious; others are funny. Some are more authoritarian (tempered with caring and respect); others are more laissez-faire. Again, being learner-centered is as much a matter of personal disposition—where teachers come from in their interactions—as it is the specific actions teachers take in managing the classroom.

Summary

There is no question that many classrooms in this country produce students who are motivated to learn, learn, and achieve academic success. We have proposed that the classrooms in which this occurs are what we would call learner centered and that many of the teachers in these classrooms are the way they are and do what they do naturally and somewhat intuitively. We also have maintained that being learner centered does not look any one particular way. Not all learner-centered teachers believe or think in exactly the same way or engage in the same practices. We have said repeatedly that learner-centered teaching is as much a way of being, a disposition, as it is doing one thing or another.

At the same time, we have also asserted that there are some important commonalities in beliefs, qualities and characteristics, and practices of teachers whom we would call learner centered. Basically they operate in accordance with the premises that emerge from the learner-centered psychological principles. That is, they *acknowledge and attend to students' uniqueness*, by first getting to know their students well and by then using this information to accommodate students' unique qualities and needs; they know that *learning is a constructive process* and thus they do whatever they can to ensure that what is being taught is meaningful and relevant to students and they provide opportunities for students to be actively involved in the learning; they *create a positive climate* by caring for and respecting their students as human beings with nonacademic as well as academic needs and by providing an environment that is safe, supportive, and comfortable; and they assume *that all of their students want to learn,* and thus they come from that assumption in their interactions.

These premises, as described in Chapter Two, emerge from the learner-centered psychological principles, which reflect the research on both learners and learning. While we acknowledge that many teachers are learner centered somewhat naturally and intuitively, we also believe that these teachers, as well as those who are not particularly learner centered, can benefit from knowing and understanding the principles and thus the research base these principles reflect. For teachers in the former group, learning about the principles might validate their experience, provide them with a rationale for what they are doing, foster more purposefulness in doing what they are doing, reinforce what they are doing well, and perhaps give them a few ideas. For teachers in the latter group, we hope that learning about the principles is an eye-opener, that it gives them a reason to reassess what they are doing and motivates them to recreate their relationship to their students and what they do in the classroom.

Deming (quoted in Glasser, 1990, p. 26) makes an interesting point in creating a case for the importance of understanding theory: "Knowledge is prediction, and knowledge comes from theory. Experience teaches nothing without theory. Do not try to copy someone else's success. Unless you understand the theory behind it, trying to copy it can lead to complete chaos."

While we might not agree entirely with this position, we do believe that there is power in understanding the theory behind why one thing works well and produces the result one is after and another thing does not. Francis Bacon said, "Knowledge is power." We agree. Therefore, we encourage teachers to become knowledgeable about the learner-centered psychological principles that reflect the research about learners and learning from which ways of being, strategies, and practices may be identified that can be used to maximize motivation, learning, and achievement for *all* students.

4

The Learner-Centered School System

> We realized that our school must be more learner centered. We were driven by looking for more equality for all kids and giving all kids the same opportunity to learn.
> —John Davis, Principal, Mundelein High School, Illinois

BARBARA MCCOMBS'S VISIT TO MUNDELEIN HIGH SCHOOL, ILLINOIS

You knew it was a learner-centered school before you walked into the building. The parking lot had many welcoming signs, inviting visitors to park in an ample array of parking spots conveniently located near the school entrance. The grounds were well-kept, and student artwork in the form of sculptures decorated an area off to the front of building, with metal placards honoring the artists and their graduating classes. Once inside the door, you first saw a welcome banner, and conveniently placed signs telling you where to find various administrative offices and school centers. The school's mission—"service to all learners"—was predominantly displayed along with a list of achievement goals and learning standards for all students. Students' special achievements in each area were displayed, leaving you with a clear picture of the diversity of the talents that were recognized and developed. Pictures of students, teachers, administrators, school staff, school board members, and even parents adorned the walls, along with school awards for community service. Halls and offices were attractive, orderly, and neat. You could feel staff and student pride and ownership. Groups of staff and students could be seen walking together in a spirit of camaraderie and mutual respect. There was a sense of positive energy, with smiling faces and genuine regard. It was a friendly place, an inviting place.

Learner-centered schools are recognized by a feeling or spirit of vitality and caring as well as by actual welcoming and inviting physical features or layouts. And as we saw in the research presented earlier on factors that enhance student motivation, learning, and achievement, learner-centered schools can be characterized as attending to individual learning needs through personalized and caring programs, practices, and policies. For example, Anson and Fox (1995) point out that a dominant trend is for the system to become more *personalized*. This means giving greater attention to individual differences, decisions, and creativity and to people supports. Teachers are also learners and are supported by their administration in their efforts to engage in active research on learning. One result is higher student achievement and lower dropout rates. As shown by Damico and Roth (1994), schools with comparatively high graduation rates have learning environments that convey how much the learner and learning are valued. These environments also convey respect and responsibility for the school building. Other benefits of such personalization are student pride and ownership and teacher excitement and renewal.

Designing schools in keeping with the knowledge base on learning, motivation, and individual differences produces many different models. All these models, however, will have certain basic features in common. We will explore these features by first looking at how each of the twelve learner-centered psychological principles might be manifested in schools.

Learner-Centered Psychological Principles in the Schools

In learner-centered schools, we can expect to see many features that clearly reflect the twelve learner-centered psychological principles. We examine critical features of the learner-centered school as they are revealed in the school culture and school practices, structures, and policies, to see how they contribute to learners' motivation, learning, and achievement.

Metacognitive and Cognitive Factors

Principle 1, the nature of the learning process, when applied at the school level, is concerned with opportunities students *and* staff have to express their unique talents and pursue personally meaningful learning goals. This principle shows up in the selection of course requirements, standards (particularly their breadth, for tapping multiple talents), assessment systems, and flexibility in accommodating diverse interests and goals—both for students and staff (professional development opportunities are staff members' "course requirements").

The multiple intelligences theory of Howard Gardner (1995) captures the essence of this principle and that theory is implicitly acted on in school practices such as having a variety of curriculum approaches and perspectives, using assessment strategies that help students display their new understandings in a variety of ways, and personalizing approaches to education in ways such that each child has the maximum opportunity to master the materials. Similarly, one of the authors (McCombs, 1995a) has argued that we need school models that see all children as "gifted" and that use students' interests and goals as the means of sorting students into enrichment clusters—not abilities, grade levels, or other categories that often negatively affect potential.

Principle 2, goals of the learning process, raises the level of generality available for students' *sense making.* That is, opportunities for students to participate in schoolwide projects, debates, and school-community learning experiences may be used to help students test their understanding on the larger moral, social, economic, or political issues that do or will affect their lives.

The promotion of certain traits or characteristics in students supports larger, school-level goals of the learning process. Recent studies of resiliency traits, traits linked to success in school and in life, are particularly relevant as these mirror traits that other research shows makes a school learner centered. A key researcher of resiliency, Bonnie Benard (Berliner & Benard, 1995), outlines resiliency traits that we believe need to be fostered in schools:

- *Social competence*. The ability to establish and sustain positive, caring relationships, to maintain a sense of humor, and to communicate compassion and empathy.

- *Resourcefulness*. The ability to critically, creatively, and reflectively make decisions, to seek help from others, and to recognize alternative ways to solve problems and resolve conflict.

- *Autonomy*. The ability to act independently and exert some control over one's environment, to have a sense of one's identity, and to detach from others engaged in risky or dysfunctional behaviors.

- *Sense of purpose*. The ability to foresee a bright future for oneself, to be optimistic, and to aspire toward educational and personal achievement.

All these traits are consistent with outcomes associated with learner-centered practices at both the school and classroom levels. It is at the school level, however, that the commitment to and valuing of these outcomes creates a climate that can support the work of individual classroom teachers and provide the consistency in message necessary for both students and staff to know this is their school, they belong, and they will be supported. Part of that support comes from educators working with parents or community members to see that students' hopes and aspirations can be realized.

Principle 3, the construction of knowledge, suggests that in addition to trying to make sense of the world, learners also try to relate what they are learning to information they already have or perceive will be important to have in the future. At the school level, this process may be facilitated by helping students make choices about content areas to integrate, putting together their own college prep or vocational courses of study, for example. Obviously, these choices must be supported by adults, but the point is that schools are learner centered with respect to this principle when they include students' ways of making meaning and constructing knowledge as an important component of the decision process.

The value of choice and control in helping learners construct personal meaning is born out in school-level practices that address teachers' needs for collaboration and time for personal inquiry. For example, Clark and Clark (1996) describe reform efforts that provide for collaborative environments, with small groups of staff involved in decision making around school policy and procedures. Benefits are higher teacher motivation and involvement, benefits parallel to those gained when this principle is applied at the classroom level for students.

Principle 4, higher-order thinking, suggests that learning is facilitated when students engage in self-inquiry and other strategies for "thinking about thinking." At the school level, practices and policies consistent with this principle include opportunities for students to reflect on school scheduling, curriculum, assessment, or other policies, and opportunities to examine their own thinking and problem-solving strategies relative to those of other students and adults in the building. It also means that such inquiry happens in all classrooms, not just those in which an individual teacher values it.

This principle also extends to school practices that support teachers' learning and inquiry about the effectiveness of their practices. As suggested by Merenbloom (1996), school organization needs to address flexible scheduling that provides teachers with opportunities to talk with their colleagues about successful strategies and about individual student needs. This time for communication, extended dialogue, and reflection allows for higher-order thinking as a way of doing business at the school level that becomes a model for students.

A major point is that schools need to become contexts within which all learners have an opportunity to be productive thinkers. For example, Sarason (1995b) argues that in attempts to transform schools into institutions dedicated to learning and learners, change starts with the attitudes and conceptions of educators, and that may mean addressing power relationships and how they need to be altered to support learning for students and teachers alike. Giving more voice to students in setting school rules and defining programs to meet students' needs is one way to alter power relationships. If educators want productive thinking, it is also necessary to design productive contexts for learning that can challenge and speak to all learners.

Affective Factors

Principle 5, motivational influences on learning, points to the importance of learner beliefs, values, interests, goals, expectations for success, and emotional states of mind in producing either positive or negative motivation to learn. At the school level, these motivational influences extend not just to motivation to learn but also to motivation to be in school. When this motivation is low, so is attendance; conversely, the dropout rate is high. Practices, policies, and structures that support a positive school environment and culture are those that value and appreciate diversity and also provide opportunities for students to be involved in decision making, setting rules, and having voice in what they consider fair policies. As shown in research by Damico and Roth (1994), schools that seriously attend to student motivational needs have higher graduation rates than schools that enforce non-learner-centered policies and practice.

Sylwester (1994) builds on Dewey's notions about education for the *whole child* and argues that emotion research may be the catalyst for providing this kind of education, education that is learner centered. Emotion research, says Sylwester (1994, p. 65) shows that

- Schools should focus more on metacognitive activities that encourage students to talk about their emotions, listen to their classmates' feelings, and think about the motivations of people who enter their curricular world.

- Activities that emphasize social interaction and that engage the entire body tend to provide the most emotional support.

- School activities that draw out emotions—simulations, role playing, and cooperative projects, for example—may provide important contextual memory prompts that will help students recall the information during closely related events in the real world.

- Emotionally stressful school environments are counterproductive because they can reduce students' ability to learn. Self-esteem and a sense of control over one's environment are important in managing stress. Highly evaluative and authoritarian schools may promote institutional economy, efficiency, and accountability, but also heighten nonproductive stress in students and staff.

Additional examples of school-level practices consistent with this principle include attending to emotional needs of students by providing mental health and counseling services along with academic services. The fifth principle also relates to the use of systems that track or sort students based on ability or other characteristics and that might result in students' feeling ridiculed or insecure about their abilities as learners. Research on the effects of tracking on student motivation and achievement is now fairly clear: such practices are neither equitable nor effective (see, for example, Oakes, 1992; Wells & Serna, 1995). And as always, motivational factors are just as important for staff and their own ongoing learning.

Principle 6, intrinsic motivation to learn, reminds us that students are naturally motivated to learn when conditions of support are present. Supportive conditions include educators and staff who believe in students, refrain from seeing students as unmotivated or not caring about learning, and work with students to elicit this natural motivation when they have difficultly relating to the purpose and meaning of school. For example, Deborah Meier, of Central Park East High School, found that students who were engaged in discussions of the value and meaning of schooling felt more a part of their education and more willing to invest in the "have to's" of schooling (Meier, 1995).

As we saw in Chapter Two, when educators understand the differences between learning in life and learning in school settings, they are better able to see how natural motivation to learn can be positively influenced. Although schools may have little choice about the content that students have to learn (defined as it is by state or local standards), they do have options for how that content is structured, scheduled, and assessed and about the breadth and depth of learning required for each learner. By implementing practices and policies that (1) give students choice and control; (2) support them in meeting learning requirements; (3) help them believe they can succeed; and (4) respect and value the diversity they represent in talents, experiences, and backgrounds, schools enhance intrinsic motivation to value education and lifelong learning. Remembering that adults, too, are naturally motivated to learn when conditions of support are present brings this discussion about intrinsic motivation full circle.

Principle 7, characteristics of motivation-enhancing learning tasks, appears on the surface to be applicable only at the classroom level because it deals with providing authentic learning and assessment practices that are perceived to be relevant by students and of optimal difficulty and novelty. At the school level, however, this principle translates into schoolwide projects and activities that might, for example, involve students in community service projects that meet graduation requirements. It translates, too, into grading policies, assessment strategies, and graduation requirements. All those practices that arouse students' curiosity about how their developing knowledge and skills can be used to create productive lives for themselves and others, and that allow students to engage in creative expressions of their learning and understanding and engage them in higher-order thinking, are in keeping with this principle. Examples of such practices include creating opportunities for students to demonstrate their knowledge and skills to parents and community members in special ceremonies or having students make presentations to local colleges about what they have experienced in their schooling that they would like to carry forward in their postsecondary experiences.

In our own work, we have also stressed the need for models of schooling that meet the needs of all students holistically. One of us (McCombs, 1995a, p. 91) has stated, for example: "Research supports that all learners need and can benefit from learning goals and environments they perceive as rich, challenging, personally relevant, accepting, and supportive. In such contexts, all students have the potential to be highly motivated learners." That such models also apply to teachers' professional development must also be kept in mind.

Developmental Factors

Principle 8, developmental constraints and opportunities, addresses the multiple areas and stages of development that apply to all learners, staff and students alike. At the school level, this principle is reflected in both flexible curricula and schedules for students and flexible roles and responsibilities for teachers and other staff. In learner-centered schools, this principle also plays out in the concept and practice of *inclusion,* wherein learners of a wide range of backgrounds, capabilities, and special needs have opportunities to learn together.

As an example, Katsiyannis, Conderman, and Franks (1996) see the concept of "inclusionary programming" translating into school-level practices that avoid labeling or segregating students. The research is beginning to demonstrate that students with disabilities who are placed in inclusive programs make small to moderate increases in both academic and social outcomes. This validates the positive effects of such programs for students who typically have been assumed to lack required capabilities for inclusion in general or even gifted programs. Katsiyannis, Conderman, and Franks argue that inclusive practices need to be carefully planned to include the necessary supports for students and teachers. They also must be accompanied by ongoing research. In learner-centered schools, such research includes students and teachers, particularly those students who would have been excluded from the mainstream in traditional school models.

Personal and Social Factors

Principle 9, social and cultural diversity, promotes the idea at the school level that the contexts and physical structures of schooling need to support social interactions and communications among diverse learners, young and old. In keeping with this principle, effective school practices are programs such as special academic and social clubs that provide opportunities for students with diverse backgrounds to share common interests. Mentorship programs can also bring adults and youths into communication and enhance the value of positive adult models for student development. Furthermore, structuring large schools into teams or *schools within a school* can create what Wynne and Walberg (1995) say is the critical "intimacy" that fosters more intense and enduring relationships among and between adults and students; these relationships, they suggest, may be the academic and emotional salvation of both groups.

Multiyear teaching is another structural strategy that Hanson (1995) argues can reap both academic and emotional benefits for teachers and students. In this approach, students have the same teacher for two or more years. Students and teachers have a chance to get to know each other, teachers become familiar with students'

personal and academic needs, and both have opportunities to appreciate each other's perspectives—benefits for teachers and students alike.

Principle 10, social acceptance, self-esteem, and learning, builds upon the prior principle and expands educators' understanding of the value of caring and respectful relationships in promoting learning, a sense of self-esteem and competence, and motivation to learn and persist, even in the face of seemingly overwhelming obstacles. Everyone remembers a story about a student who would never have succeeded in school—or stayed in school for that matter—without the special attention, respect, and caring of a particular teacher. When this principle is applied at the school level, it implies that schools need to be structured so that time for one-on-one relating with teachers is encouraged. Programs and policies also need to support the building of adult-student relationships. Again, mentorship programs that include all staff in the school building and perhaps concerned members of the community also are good examples of learner-centered practices consistent with this principle.

Other practices consistent with this principle are described by Williamson (1996) and include changing the use of time and space so that both students and teachers increase their feelings of membership and belonging in the schools. Practices such as multiyear teaming, less departmentalization, mentorship programs, advisor-advisee programs, and more heterogeneous grouping all contribute to teachers' abilities to form more meaningful relationships with students—relationships that pay off in students' increased motivation, learning, and academic achievement.

Individual Differences Factors

Principle 11, individual differences in learning, points educators to the importance of treating all members of the school team—students, teachers, administrators, and other staff—as unique individuals with special needs, talents, backgrounds, and experiences. This principle applied at the school level takes the form of structures, programs, and policies that value diversity, that set up opportunities for all people in the system to get to know each other, and that generate respect and caring such that a focus on strengths and resilience is fostered. Learner-centered schools have the distinction of being communities and cultures of caring and learning that use time and other resources to support personal and technical needs related to learning, motivation, and achievement for all.

The importance of a caring culture, of creating schools as caring communities, is addressed a little later in this chapter. In general, however, at the school level, this principle appears in the establishment of opportunities for collaboration and for creating personal relationships within organizational structures, programs, and policies. As emphasized in the work of a number of important educators (for example, Eisner, 1991; Fullan, 1995; Glasser, 1990), learner-centered practices promote personalized environments in which everyone experiences feelings of belonging and support.

Principle 12, cognitive filters, deals with how each individual constructs reality and how different constructions can lead to different views. Of particular relevance at the school level are the differing beliefs and philosophies among educators, parents, and community members that may underlie reform efforts. Just as students bring to school their own filters or lenses through which they view and experience the world, so do all stakeholders concerned with education. To be learner centered means to try to understand and respect these differing perspectives while moving toward school designs that are more learner centered in their cultures, practices, structures, and policies.

Work by Fullan (1993, 1995) on systemic change is relevant here and exemplifies an understanding of this principle. Fullan talks about the importance of creating cultures in which people are free to share basic beliefs and values and to struggle with bringing them into agreement in a mission and vision for the school. Weinstein (in press) further argues that to accomplish school-level changes, it is necessary to help both teachers and students "change their minds," or modify current thinking. One example of such change in thinking is exemplified by teachers' learning to value student perceptions of practice and using negotiation strategies in which they work together collaboratively with their students to define changes in practice and expectations. When beliefs change, practices and climate change, and student outcomes shift to more positive expectations, higher motivation, increased learning, and higher achievement.

As a summary of this section and a pulling together of the principles and their implications for the design of learner-centered schools, the work of Berliner and Benard (1995) is relevant. Their research contrasts characteristics of two kinds of schools, those with a risk focus and those with a resiliency focus. We suggest that the same characteristics describe the foci of non-learner-centered and learner-centered schools (see Table 4.1).

The Learner-Centered School: Critical Features

Just as we examined critical features of learner-centered classrooms and teachers in Chapter Three against the premises of the learner-centered model outlined in Chapter One, it will be helpful for consistency and understanding to examine the critical features of learner-centered schools vis à vis these same premises. In general, then, staff, practices, structures and policies in learner-centered schools

- *Acknowledge and attend to students' uniqueness* by taking into account and honoring the full range of talents and capabilities students bring with them into the school context in the selection of school mission, learning goals, and performance recognition systems (premises 1 and 2).

- *Know that learning is a constructive process* in which students need to feel ownership by having voice in school decisions and by making choices about programs, practices, and structures in order to develop personal responsibility and respect for the school building and people in it (premise 3).

Table 4.1 Comparison of Conventional and
Learner-Centered School Level Characteristics.

Non-Learner-Centered (Conventional) Focus	Learner-Centered Focus
Relationships are hierarchical, blaming, controlling.	**Relationships** are caring and promote positive expectations and participation.
Curriculum is fragmented, nonexperiential, limited, and exclusive of multiple perspectives.	**Curriculum** is thematic, experiential, challenging, comprehensive, and inclusive of multiple perspectives.
Instruction focuses on a narrow range of learning styles, builds from perceptions of student deficits, and is authoritarian.	**Instruction** focuses on a broad range of learning styles; builds from perceptions of student strengths, interests, and experiences; and is participatory and facilitative.
Grouping is tracked by perceptions of ability; promotes individual competition and a sense of alienation.	**Grouping** is not tracked by perceptions of ability; promotes cooperation, shared responsibility, and a sense of belonging.
Evaluation focuses on a limited range of intelligences, utilizes only standardized tests, and assumes only one correct answer.	**Evaluation** focuses on multiple intelligences, utilizes authentic assessments, and fosters self-reflection.

Source: Adapted from Berliner and Benard, 1995, p. 6.

- *Create a positive climate* in which students, staff, and parents feel welcomed and supported and in which personal and interpersonal concerns have precedence over technical and organizational issues, a climate that at the same time provides diversity and flexibility in technical and organizational features to meet diverse learner needs (premise 4).

- *Come from an assumption that all students, at their core, want to learn* and that any outside interferences with this natural inclination (for example, family or other social pressures or personal health problems) and any inflexible or nonresponsive school-based practices and policies (for example, calendars and schedules that do not accommodate student needs to work or to watch younger siblings, or lack of health and mental health services) may interfere with this natural process and must therefore be dealt with (premise 5).

The learner-centered school extends these premises to include all learners in the school—students, staff, parents, and community members alike.

In line with these premises and as depicted by the recent film *Why Do These Kids Love School?* (produced by Dorothy Fadiman in 1990 and described by Raywid, 1992), schools where students love to be are characterized as being learner centered. That is, they

- Provide the opportunity for individual responsibility by learners

- Have an emphasis on motivation

- Provide a personalized and supportive environment

- Encourage active engagement of students with the material to be learned

- Emphasize the centrality of the human community

- Interweave the affective, cognitive, and social aspects of development throughout the school years

When actual schools begin to transform their practices based on the research on learners and learning, learning looks different and applies to all people in the system. We asked teachers in three high schools that we have studied, as they made their journey to learner-centered practices, what learning looks like in a learner-centered school (McCombs, Burrello, & Dudzinski, 1996).They described the following elements:

- Teams that stay together
- Diverse learning opportunities
- Exhibitions of student learning (integrated and inquiry based)
- High expectations for all students
- Student confidence and caring for each other
- Active learning
- Content related to life and self-knowledge and self-development
- Success with disadvantaged and at-risk students
- Learning challenges for all students
- Collaborative learning opportunities
- Socratic, inquiry-based learning that puts responsibility on students
- Open classrooms in which teachers are not afraid to have visitors

The next section takes a look at what the research says about characteristics of successful schools, schools that we consider to be learner centered.

Research on the Characteristics of Learner-Centered Schools

Think about the kind of school that might result from an application of the twelve learner-centered principles, the premises, and our definition of learner centered. What might you see? What would you probably not see? Based on your understanding of the learner-centered model and principles, reflect on the following studies of what others have defined as successful classrooms and schools and see if you are able to identify practices, structures, and policies that make them not only successful but learner centered. We believe, in fact, that they are successful *because of* their learner-centered features. Each specific research example that follows, discusses issues or elements of education that we believe are integral to what we are defining as learner centered.

Eisner (1991) outlines what he believes are six aims that count in schools: (1) helping children learn that learning and the exploration of ideas can be difficult but can also be exciting and fun, so that they are more likely to pursue studies outside of formal educational institutions; (2) helping children learn problem-solving tactics and strategies so that they are increasingly able to solve their own problems as they get older; (3) helping children learn multiple forms of literacy, thus securing meaning in a wide range of forms that match those in the larger culture, and developing a larger conception of what it means to know through a variety of sources of understanding such as poetry, music, astronomy, science, and the like; (4) helping children learn the importance of "wonder" by providing tasks that stimulate imagination and fantasy; (5) helping children see that they are part of a "caring community" by creating schools that allow personal needs to come into and be met in the classroom; and (6) helping children learn that they have unique and important "personal signatures" that provide inner meaning and purpose, thus discouraging them from relying solely on external knowledge and content, and extending our concept of giftedness to include the development of unique interests and talents, thus expanding rather than diminishing individual differences as a function of schooling.

One critical context for learning is a sense of community. Rossi and Stringfield (1995) recently searched for schools that are successful for students at risk of educational failure and found them to support "community" (having a shared frame of reference and supporting mutual expectations that provide a foundation for positive change) and "consistency" (providing for a high-reliability organization that supports positive change). Ten elements that are present in such schools are shared vision, shared sense of purpose, shared values, incorporation of diversity, communication, participation, caring, trust, teamwork, and respect and recognition. In addition, central goals are clear and widely shared, staff members share a belief that success is critical and failure to achieve core tasks is absolutely disastrous, intensive recruitment and ongoing training are present, staff members are interdependent, standard operating procedures are in place, and flexibility and monitoring of progress are valued parts of the larger organization or district.

Baum, Renzulli, and Hebert (1994) also have studied the issue of students at risk of failure, specifically underachievers. They say the first step toward addressing these students' needs is to understand underachievement from the perspective of the learners themselves. When students are asked why they fail to achieve, the reasons they give are not that they do not study, do not do their homework, do not get good grades, or do not try to please their teachers. All of these reasons may seem true from the perspective of an outside observer, but *from the students' perspectives*, the reasons are associated with such emotional issues as trying to gain positive attention from a caring adult, dealing with peer group pressure to underachieve as a way to gain popularity, or lacking a curriculum that they perceive as interesting and in keeping with how they like to learn. Reversing the underachievement pattern requires that teachers (1) take the time to know each student; (2) use their time with students to facilitate learning rather than to counsel about underachievement; (3) understand students' needs to make choices and share their expertise and competence; (4) recognize the need for observation, reflection, and ongoing experimentation with strategies for helping students overcome their learning and motivational problems; and (5) consistently demonstrate patience and belief in each student's ability to succeed. A *transformation* occurs in thinking and practice as teachers and schools move from a deficit to an enrichment model that encourages students to pursue an area of interest in their preferred learning style. The enrichment model provides students with general exploratory experiences to stimulate new areas of interest, training in research and learning-to-learn skills necessary for pursuing an interest in greater depth, and guidance in pursuing both individual and small-group investigations of meaningful real problems that are designed to have an impact on a real audience. With this model, the underachievement cycle was reversed for nearly 90 percent of students classified as underachievers and the improvements were sustained following the intervention for more than two years (Baum, Renzulli, & Hebert, 1994).

A broader four-year study looked at high schools that were successful for all students. Miles and Louis (1990) found these schools to have five key features: (1) knowledge is clearly communicated; (2) knowledge is relevant to normal life and concerns; (3) action images that help students visualize what they need to do to accomplish academic goals are used; (4) will and motivation to do something with the knowledge learned is present; and (5) skills to engage in the actions required are developed. When there is successful improvement, passionate and shared images of what the school should become are present. When people believe they can make a difference, will is established.

The *quality school* is an example of a school designed in keeping with the research on learning and motivation. Glasser (1990), creator of this model, uses the analogy of schools as serving the job of learning and of students as "workers." He discusses the concept of "lead-management," a form of leadership in which the leader (1) engages workers (students) in a discussion of what they believe should be the quality of work to be done and the time needed, while also fitting the job to worker skills and needs; (2) models the job and its expectations, while seeking constant input from workers; (3) asks workers to evaluate their own work for quality, while providing an attitude of respect and acceptance of workers' ideas; and (4) facilitates conduct of the job, while providing a noncoercive, nonadversarial atmosphere in which to do the job. Glasser describes the essence of good managing as caring and hard work. He also talks about the value of negotiation when teachers and students disagree about quality standards. Based on research on motivation, Glasser holds that people engage in quality work because it feels good. Because coercion is not used, students engage in tasks more willingly; they also have more ownership because they have choice and input.

The concept of the *basic school* is described by Boyer (1996) as a new model for elementary schools. This model conceives of the school as a community that has curriculum with coherence, a positive climate for learning, and a commitment to character development. As communities, effective schools are purposeful, communicative, just, disciplined, caring, and celebrative. Teachers are instructional leaders with knowledge about children, pedagogy, and content; they empower students, are open and authentic, and form partnerships with parents. The curriculum focuses on literacy, very broadly defined. Students learn the language of vital content areas in thematic frameworks with eight core commonalities that spiral upward across grade levels: the life cycle; the use of symbols; membership in groups; a sense of time and space; response to the aesthetic; connections to nature, producing, and consuming; and living with purpose. The climate for learning begins by making sure teachers have what they need to do their jobs successfully, for example, reduced class size, flexibility in grouping students in homeroom and in the classroom depending on instructional purpose, and the like. Support services for students are available to meet health and counseling needs. Commitment to character is concerned with the social, ethical, and moral dimensions of children's lives and strives to develop the "seven virtues" of honesty, respect, responsibility, compassion, self-discipline, perseverance, and giving. These attributes are infused across the whole curriculum, so that the basic school prepares students not only for careers, but also for lives of dignity and purpose.

Specific examples of learner-centered schools abound. One example is Summerbridge in San Francisco, which began in 1972 and has now expanded to seven other major U.S. cities (Kindel, 1995). The school serves inner-city middle school students with a unique educational experience. A key feature of the school is very small classes taught by high school and college students. The curriculum is designed to challenge all students, build self-esteem by teaching students to take control of their education, and provide special tutorial classes to prepare students for top academic high school programs. Student voice and input to decision making are key to defining the program and reaching student learning goals. More than 92 percent of program graduates get into top academic high schools, 100 percent go on to college, and more than 60 percent of the program's young teaching staff go on to pursue careers in education.

Another example is provided by Ancess and Darling-Hammond (1995). International High School in New York City is based on "an instructional commitment to student diversity as a generative focus for learning" (p. 6). Alternative assessment strategies are derived from this learner-centered instructional model; the model and resulting assessment strategies provide a broad context for student learning and deal with the student as a whole person. A physics teacher at the school, David Hirschy explains: "Heterogeneity is not a problem to be solved. In fact when embraced, it is a positive force. . . . Students come to us at different stages of development and levels of preparation, and education increases those differences. In the long run, if a student is good at something, we try to encourage the student to pursue the interest, to excel, which results in inequality, differences, heterogeneity. It happens naturally. It is unreasonable to expect that, as a result of our efforts, students should become less heterogeneous" (Ancess and Darling-Hammond, 1995, pp. 6–7).

The learner-centered instructional model at International High School is also based on collaboration between students and faculty such that they learn from each other's different experiences and knowledge as well as from the synergy of the collaborative process. Diversity is capitalized on and celebrated. This model has the following seven key characteristics (Ancess and Darling-Hammond, 1995, p. 8):

- Heterogeneous and inter-age grouping.
- Creation of a learning community.
- Collaboration (teachers plan together and students work extensively in small groups with teachers alternately coaching, assessing, questioning, and prodding them; students in groups work on individual as well as group tasks).
- Emphasis on critical-thinking skills and in-depth study.
- Active learning (students work extensively on problem-solving projects).
- Whole language learning in context (language skills are taught within the context of subject areas).
- Authentic assessment using multiple perspectives.

Each of these characteristics focuses on human needs—students' and staff's alike.

We began this section by asking you to think about our definition of learner centered as it might be reflected in the studies of successful schools that followed. We asserted that the schools in these studies are successful because they are learner centered. Having read the research and, hopefully, reflecting on the learner-centered model, what do you think?

The next section examines some specific and important components of schools, components that have a major impact on learners' motivation, learning, and achievement: school culture, practices, structures, and policies.

School Culture

As noted in the introduction to this chapter, learner-centered schools are recognized by a feeling or spirit of vitality and caring as well as by their physical features. This feeling or spirit is a product of the school culture. The culture that distinguishes learner-centered schools is one of caring and one that is committed to learning and change and to collaboration. Each of these attributes of the culture contributes positively to student motivation, learning, and achievement.

The Importance of Schools as Caring Communities. A recent issue of *Phi Delta Kappan* was devoted entirely to the concept of the *caring school* and its benefits. In introducing this issue, Smith (1995) argues that a part of caring is helping students care about learning. This happens when students have a caring relationship with teachers and with the subject matter, so that they develop the commitment to a subject required for competent learning. Teachers need to be models of committed learners who care passionately about a subject and are willing to share that passion with their students.

Lipsitz (1995) points out that the development of a caring culture in schools requires a change in attitude—not just a restructuring of policies, curricula, and systems. In essence, schools must be learner centered and consider students' personal needs and development within the larger context of their families and communities. Caring is what Lipsitz argues is necessary for establishing an effective culture for learning. It does not replace the need to have high standards and expectations for learning, but it represents a core set of beliefs about how educators should be with other people.

In describing benefits of caring school cultures, Chaskin and Rauner (1995) focus on an effect of the teacher-student relationship that is often overlooked: its ability to offset students' feelings of frustration with or alienation from school. In research funded by the Lily Endowment's Research Program on Youth and Caring, caring was found to be what differentiated successful from unsuccessful programs. A *caring environment* is defined by Chaskin and Rauner (1995) as one in which (1) an atmosphere is created that helps young people feel welcome, respected, and comfortable; (2) experiences are structured to provide opportunities for students to develop caring relationships with both adults and peers; (3) information is provided to students about what it means to care for themselves and others; and (4) opportunities and training are provided to encourage students to engage in projects that contribute to the "greater good," such as service, advocacy, and active problem solving of critical human issues. Caring involves protecting and investing in students' development and helping students learn to protect the rights and interests of others. Caring works because it responds to basic psychosocial needs, particularly needs for independence and connection, belonging and membership, safety and support, and individual and social competency. It also creates a "context of possibilities" in which genuine education occurs through relationships, settings, and practices that encourage youths to value caring as a way to approach self and others, including the larger community and society. Research has shown that when young people have opportunities to care for others they have an increased sense of social responsibility, higher self-esteem, better school attendance, and decreases in depression. To accomplish lasting effects and true trusting relationships, strategies for promoting cultures of caring in schools need to be implemented gradually and incrementally by committed individuals. We emphasize that there is no single best way, that caring has to be promoted by example, and that to be successful, the particular caring culture that evolves needs to be relevant to particular interpersonal and academic needs of its clients, students and teachers alike.

According to Noddings (1995), the technical and structural changes necessary to create cultures of caring in schools are relatively simple and inexpensive to bring about. The bigger problem she sees is to achieve a fundamental shift in people's attitude, so that in addition to responding to pressure to produce high test scores, they respond to the idea that it is legitimate and even necessary to focus on the development of caring and competent people and to spend time developing trusting relationships, talk with students about central personal problems, and guide students to be more sensitive and competent across all domains of caring.

Bosworth (1995) calls attention to the fact that although adults often think young people do not care, these same adults do not consider what the young people themselves have to say. When asked, adolescents are very articulate about what caring means. Common themes involve relationships and include helping; having feelings of love and friendship, kindness, respect, and faithfulness; and engaging in activities that allow for both giving and receiving. Unfortunately, most schools are structured to provide very few opportunities for either teachers or students to demonstrate caring. Teacher behaviors associated with caring are consistent with learner-centered behaviors. These include helping with school-work, valuing individuality, showing respect, being tolerant, explaining work, checking for understanding, encouraging, and planning interesting and enjoyable activities. Students see these behaviors as characteristics of caring teachers in classrooms. Things teachers do outside the classroom to demonstrate caring include helping with personal problems, providing guidance, going the extra mile, being nice and being polite, being available to help students, being success oriented, and being involved.

We would point out in addition that caring is a style of teaching that puts the needs of individual learners at the center of decision making; that is, caring is learner centered.

The Value of Cultures of Learning and Change and Collaboration. Another contributor to the spirit of vitality of learner-centered schools is that aspect of the culture committed to learning, change, and collaboration. Research shows that for teachers, a culture that supports student motivation, learning, and achievement must be based on principles that also support teachers' needs to be learners. The culture that is formed among teachers committed to high achievement for all learners is one committed to learning and change. Fullan (1993) suggests that the following teacher characteristics construct such a culture: (1) being committed to being agents of educational and social improvement; (2) being committed to continuous improvement through program innovation and evaluation; (3) valuing and practicing exemplary teaching; (4) engaging in constant inquiry; (5) modeling and developing lifelong learning among staff and students; (6) modeling and developing collaboration among staff and students; (7) being respected and engaged as a vital part of the whole system; (8) forming partnerships with relevant groups and agencies; (9) being visible and valued in the local and global community; and (10) working collaboratively to build regional, national, and international networks.

Fullan (1992–1993, p. 14) proposes seven "propositions for success"—positions that define a culture of learning and change. These propositions include the following: "(a) change is learning, loaded with uncertainty, (b) change is a journey, not a blueprint, (c) problems are our friends, (d) change is resource hungry, (e) change requires the power to manage it, (f) change is systemic, and (g) all large scale change is implemented locally."

Areas in which teachers need support to develop a culture of learning and change are outlined by Fullan (1993). Specifically, teachers need the organizational and personal support to become knowledgeable about, committed to, and skilled in

- Working with *all* students in a caring, equitable, and effective manner, respecting diversity and individual student needs
- Being ongoingly active learners and reflective practitioners
- Developing and applying the research knowledge needed to implement and monitor effective and evolving programs and practices for all learners
- Initiating, valuing, and practicing collaboration and partnerships
- Appreciating and practicing the principles, ethics, and legal responsibilities of teaching as a profession
- Developing a personal philosophy of teaching

Many educators and psychologists argue that *motivation to learn* is central not only to academic success but to sustained commitment to learning across the life span, that is, to a culture committed to learning and change. For example, Weinstein (in press) points out that expectations about learning capability play a critical role in motivation. She also notes that efforts to promote *positive expectancy climates* are particularly needed in this time of increasing diversity of learners. The learner-centered psychological principles are seen as helping to define the conditions for creating such climates. Weinstein presents an integrative model that defines effective expectancy practices in terms of curriculum, grouping, evaluation, motivation, responsibility for learning, class relations, parent-class relations, and school-class relations. These practices include strategies that reduce ability comparisons among students, foster beliefs that a range of abilities are valued, promote student choice and agency, increase warmth and trust, broaden communication opportunities, and increase leadership and chances for success at both school and classroom levels.

Three further points are critical in the development of a culture of learning and change. First, the culture must build on the *concept of inclusion*, the true valuing and respect for multiple perspectives, including the perspectives of those who might be seen as resistors. When there is room for everyone's ideas and there is no single "right way" to do things, agreement on a common vision is more likely and negative conflict may often be avoided. Thus, although the process of creating cultures of learning and change may benefit from conflicts that promote interaction and discussion about a vision and although staff can benefit from training in conflict resolution and other team-building skills, a new, more inclusive vision, as advocated by Boyd and Hord (1994), may avoid the negative conflict and need for resistance that has occurred in past reform efforts. When diversity is celebrated by all who serve and are served by the system, a new culture may be created with minimum conflict, as reported by Roesener (1995) after a two-year study of urban reform.

Second, the change literature (particularly that which looks at personal change) supports the role of *hope* and *creative tension* in facilitating willingness to change and the role of *inspiration* or *excite-*

ment in fostering an openness to new options and ways of thinking and acting (see, for example, McCombs, 1995c). One of the by-products that may occur as a result of a shift to understanding change as learning and to the development of a new culture devoted to learning and continuous improvement is the generation of excitement, experimentation, and hope. Directly facilitating an attitude of hopefulness must be a deliberate part of culture-building activities. This may mean developing what Bennett and O'Brien (1994) call a "creative tension" between current reality and the desired future. Strategies such as encouraging a look at discrepancies between ideal and actual practices from varying perspectives, sharing success stories generated by real schools and the people in them, observing a diverse set of successful models and options for reaching a shared vision, and creating positive support teams and networks that go beyond the school walls are all ways that have been successful in generating and sustaining hope (McCombs, 1995c). Models such as (1) *accelerated schools* that are based on a philosophy of providing the best possible education for each child (Keller, 1995); (2) Sizer's *coalition of essential schools* that demonstrates a principle-driven approach to empowering local schools and communities to prepare all students for a twenty-first-century world (O'Neil, 1995); and (3) Comer's model that emphasizes students' social, emotional, and academic development (Ramirez-Smith, 1995) all provide compatible success stories and optional approaches for collaboratively working toward a vision that focuses on motivation, learning, and achievement for all students.

A third and important point is that the culture of learning and change *must be built from within* the organization. The process must be one that supports continuous examination and improvement of the educational process at every level (Joyce & Calhoun, 1995). Critical inquiry into ways of helping students learn better must become a normal activity that involves the whole faculty and builds community. An important outcome of facilitating this kind of change from within, as reported by Joyce and Calhoun (1995), is that faculty begin to realize that teaching and learning involve a *never-ending process* of trying to reach all students in the best ways currently envisioned. The vision must be subject to change, the whole system must maintain flexibility and openness to new learning, transformation, and change. We assert that both learning and change are never-ending processes and, in fact, that learning is change and change is learning.

Collaboration is another important feature of learner-centered school cultures. It is sometimes addressed as a part of a culture of learning and change and sometimes independently. Fullan (1992–1993), for example, in discussing the need for teachers to be lifelong learners, highlights the importance of inquiry and *collaboration* along with technical skills and reflective practices. Collaboration, he says, includes sharing, trusting, and support; collaboration is central to daily joint work and facilitates growth. Working collaboratively, however, often necessitates overcoming problems. These include the problems of overload, isolation, groupthink (when individual intuition and experiential knowledge is suppressed and ill-conceived innovations flourish), untapped competence and neglected incompetence, narrow roles for teachers, administrative resistance to teachers' playing leadership roles, poor solutions, and failed reform—all of which have a negative impact on morale, motivation, energy, and enthusiasm for change.

Sharon Robinson (1995), the former Assistant Secretary of Education, argues for the importance of collaboration among researchers, universities, K–12 practitioners, parents, policymakers, and citizens. A four-and-a-half-year study of collaboration, supported by the National Science Foundation, is described by Bickel and Hattrup (1995). They found that for teacher-researcher collaborations to work, collaboration must be grounded in respect and equity among all participants. This respect and equity arises out of an evolving knowledge base and an appreciation for multiple perspectives. Participants must be willing to engage in hard work and effort over a long period of time to achieve effective and sustained collaboration. In this context, helping teachers to take increasing responsibility for leadership roles is critical.

In summary, the nature of a school's culture is critical to the likelihood of that school's becoming and remaining learner centered. We believe that cultures that support and nurture learner-centered education might be described as cultures of caring and as cultures committed to learning and change and to collaboration. We move next to an exploration of practices, structures, and policies that distinguish learner-centered schools.

School Practices, Structures, and Policies

All schools have practices, structures, and policies that reflect their philosophy, purpose, and goals. Schools that are learner centered, then, are distinguished by practices, structures, and policies that promote motivation, learning, and achievement for *all* students. In addition, these schools have practices, structures, and policies that support staff, parents, and others to accomplish school goals. As we have stated repeatedly, learner-centered education does not look one particular way. At the same time, certain practices, structures, and policies tend to be more facilitative than others of learner-centered education and to be more prevalent in learner-centered schools.

Structures and Practices That Support Students. A recent *USA Today* article (Henry, 1996) about the 1996 National Association of Secondary School Principals (NASSP) conference highlighted the principals' recommendation that high schools engage in practices and adopt structures that, we believe, make them more learner centered. It was strongly recommended that schools (1) be structured in units of not more than six hundred students so that teachers and students can get to know each other, (2) give each student an individual progress plan and an adult advocate who can act as a personal counselor, and (3) limit teachers to ninety students a term so that they can offer individual attention to student needs. That these recommendations are supported by administrators is borne out by the following statement from Marilyn Hohmann, senior associate for the Center for Leadership in School Reform (Henry,

1996, p. A9): "The [NASSP] document suddenly makes high school a different place. The student is the focus of every act and everything administrators and all of us do. No longer do we place emphasis on how time is used for the convenience of adults but rather for the learning of students."

Student grouping is one particularly important practice. At least three ways of grouping students may influence students' motivation, learning, and achievement. We consider two of the following three methods to be learner centered. What do you think?

Multiyear grouping places the same students and teachers together for extended periods of the students' schooling. For example, Burke (1996) reports results of long-term teacher-student relationships that show improvements in student performance and teacher job satisfaction. Both academic and emotional benefits of multiyear teaching strategies are also described by head teacher Barbara Hanson at Willett Elementary School in Attleboro, Massachusetts (Hanson, 1995). The school began to assign students to the same teacher for two years in the late 1980s, after starting with a pilot program with a few teachers. The pilot was so successful that the school system now requires all classroom teachers from grades 1 to 8 to spend two years with their classes. For example, those who teach first grade the first year teach the same students in second grade the next year; third-grade teachers move with their students to fourth grade, and so on. The school system is currently considering this arrangement at the high school level. Ms. Hanson researched the concept of multiyear assignments and found that the strategy has been used successfully in Germany where the same teams of six to eight teachers work with the same students from grades 5 to 10. In this country, multiyear grouping first appeared in 1974 in New York. Educator Deborah Meier of Central Park East considered the practice an essential component of her high school because it enhanced the ability of teachers and students to get to know each other well. The benefits of multiyear grouping to teachers include having extra time to spend teaching because the "get-to-know-you" time is minimal in the second year. Time spent developing social skills and cooperative group strategies also pays off in the second year, with students displaying better conflict resolution skills. Teachers are also able to give more focused attention to students needing social and language development. As Hanson (1995, p. 43) states: "Multiyear assignment is increasingly vital to the countless children whose lives are riddled with change—change of residence, change in family structure, change of economic status. Our kids come from broken homes, or go home to empty houses, or see parents only on weekends: They seem to really benefit from having a teacher as a role model, mentor, and friend." Parents also seem to appreciate this policy and the chance to become familiar with teachers' instructional styles and expectations for homework and classwork. In spite of these benefits, teachers must be sensitive to students new to the class and to difficulties in separating from the class at the end of the cycle. One of the learner-centered high schools we studied (Westbury in Houston, Texas) has addressed this issue by keeping students together with the same team of teachers for all four years of high school.

Multiage and multigrade groupings put together students of several ages or grade levels. Although many people intuitively like this strategy, remembering the times of the one-room schoolhouse, the research on its effectiveness is fairly limited. Countering what critics have said may be detrimental effects for some students, Veenman (1995) reports results of a comprehensive review of multigrade and multiage classes and finds that there is no evidence that students learn less or adjust less well in such classes. A benefit to teachers may be more time for direct instruction with those students who need it (given that most multigrade classes also make use of peer learning strategies). A benefit for students may be more time for projects and reflection (given that students are also given more time to work independently and assume responsibility for their own learning in effective multiage programs). Other advocates for multiage or multigrade groupings include Boyer (1996) and Gardner (1995), both of whom contend that to encourage respect for diversity as well as encourage creative and critical thinking, heterogeneous groupings show positive benefits.

Tracking is the practice of grouping students according to measures of their academic ability. This practice is increasingly out of favor, particularly with the current emphasis on inclusion. In a presentation of research on this topic, Brandt (1996) reported that the research is clear: ability grouping is detrimental to both student self-esteem and academic achievement. Researchers Oakes (1985) and Wheelock (1992) both argue that this practice must be reconsidered because it perpetuates inequalities and places limits on student potential and academic confidence. Alternative tracking strategies include Renzulli, Reis, Hebert, and Diaz's schoolwide enrichment mode (1995), which uses student interest as the sorting system for both gifted and special needs students. Research on this model confirms its benefits for students at all points on the ability continuum and also verifies the powerful role of motivation (interest, effort, perseverance) on achievement.

How do schools respond to special needs populations in a learner-centered manner? There are school-level practices that effectively meet the needs of *special populations* such as limited English proficiency, language minority, or English as a second language (ESL) students; students believed to be at risk for academic failure because of personal, family, or other social or cultural reasons; gifted students who have nontraditional ways of learning; and the like. Practices that are effective in this domain tend also to be learner centered. One such practice is the creation of *communities of support* or *families* (Raywid, 1995) that increase students' sense of belonging and ownership and their feelings of connection to the school. Such communities also support basic needs that may not be met outside of school. Communities that meet language minority student needs, according to Garcia (1995), also provide professional development in curricula, instructional strategies, and alternative assessments such that staff develop expertise and experience in multiple processes of communication that encourage students to take risks, construct meaning, and reinterpret knowledge in caring social contexts. Most important in the learner-centered model is to recognize and appreciate the rich intellectual, linguistic, and cultural attributes that all students bring to school.

Other structures at the school level that may be influenced by a learner-centered perspective are time schedules. Essential to *innovative time schedules* are what Canady and Rettig (1995) call the goals of (1) providing quality time, (2) creating a positive school climate, and (3) providing varying learning time. The four-block schedule is being used by more and more schools, but adjustments often have to be made to ensure that extended learning and enrichment times are available for those students who need it. O'Neil (1995) cautions that the research is sketchy on the effects of various forms of block schedules. It does appear, however, that both teachers and students like longer classes and that students do at least as well on measures of academic achievement. The 4x4 Plan described by Edwards (1995) is a four-period day of semester-length courses, with four blocks of 90 minutes each. This plan gives teachers a more manageable schedule than before, with fewer class preparations and fewer students per semester. Students also have simpler, more practical schedules, with twice the opportunities they once had to complete required courses in a 180-day schedule. Edwards (1995) reports that results in Orange County High School in California indicate that students are completing more courses, grades are going up, and more students are taking and passing advanced placement exams. Students have the opportunity to earn the privilege of controlling educational resources and acquiring the career and scholarship training they need. Whatever the scheduling model, however, what makes it learner centered is a focus on individual student needs and use of strategies that promote active, self-directed learning of personally meaningful and challenging academic standards.

Structures and Practices That Affect Staff and School. In addition to structures and practices that affect students, learner-centered administrators adopt structures and practices that support staff and school in becoming more learner centered. For example, administrators wanting to establish a learner-centered school culture, research shows, begin by establishing trust between themselves and teachers, students, and parents; then jointly develop a vision for what the school should look like; and finally discuss with teachers ways to build human capacity and maximize lifetime options for students (Barkley & Castle, 1993). Such administrators let teachers know that the process of teaching—how teachers teach—and a focus on the student are more important to learning than covering all the required curricula, although managing and tending to curricula is not to be abandoned. Keeping this broad purpose of school in mind can help teachers similarly widen their view of their job, reduce their fear of risk, increase creativity, and become more comfortable with learner-centered practices (Barkley & Castle, 1993).

Learner-centered administrators may also promote knowledge of research on intrinsic motivation, research that shows students naturally want to learn when basic needs are met (the needs to belong, be competent, and have personal control: for example, see, Deci & Ryan, 1991; McCombs, 1993). Peck, Law, & Mills (1989) suggest that administrators interested in creating what we call a learner-centered climate consider

- Organizational and administrative dimensions and policies affecting teachers' stress levels and their abilities to respond to the needs of troubled youth

- A range of legitimate school activities that reflect the interests of all groups of students and help students see the relevance of their education to their personal aspirations, strengths, and interests

- Factors affecting the overall motivational climate in the classroom and the ability of teachers to engage youth positively in learning

Similarly, administrators seeking a more learner-centered school, in searching out and trying out alternative structures and practices, often employ learner-centered accountability systems. According to Darling-Hammond and Snyder (1992), such a system might include

- Governance, decision making, and communication mechanisms that ensure that schools address important needs and issues
- School organization that fosters personalized relationships, pays attention to student needs and problems, and brings teaching and learning in line with learner-centered research
- Vehicles that encourage teacher interaction, collaborative inquiry, and ongoing learning to improve practice and allow for ongoing evaluation and improvement of teaching
- Student assessment that surfaces student strengths, talents, abilities, and performance capacities
- Evaluation of how well the school is functioning, using input from parents, students, staff, and external reviewers

Structures and Practices That Promote Parental and Community Involvement. Finally, learner-centered schools are those that recognize the importance of and actively seek parental and community involvement. According to a special report by the National Committee for Citizens in Education, the evidence is beyond dispute: parent involvement improves student achievement (Henderson, 1987). It improves positive attitude toward school and motivates children to succeed. These benefits are not confined to early childhood or the elementary level; there are strong effects from parent cooperation throughout high school (Wlodkowski & Jaynes, 1990). Henderson (1987, p. 19) says that "children whose parents are in touch with school score higher than those children of similar aptitude and background whose parents aren't involved. . . . Children who are failing in school improve dramatically when parents are called in to help." Further, having parents in schools results in having more information about their children and their children's particular needs. It provides information that allows teachers and administrators to *be* learner centered. As a bonus, when schools involve parents, "Parents get a greater appreciation of their important role in their children's education, a sense of adequacy and self-worth, strengthened social networks, and motivation to resume their own education. But that's not all. Not only do parents become more effective as parents, they become more effective as people. It is a matter of self-worth or confidence. Once they see they can do something about their child's education, they see they can do something about their housing, their community, and their jobs" (Liontos, 1991, p. 9).

Working with parents is particularly beneficial for students who are having problems in school because parents often provide key information about their children that helps teachers and schools more effectively deal with the problems. Yet these are the parents who are rarely considered by administrators and teachers as partners for solving learners' problems. Often these parents may be reluctant to participate in school activities because they have bad memories of their own schooling, are embarrassed about their child's behavior, or feel inadequate to take part in their child's education (Liontos, 1991). Because these parents frequently do not respond to invitations to traditional open houses or PTA meetings, teachers who are committed to educating all students may have to rely on other means of attracting these parents. For example, a teacher might attend a renters' meeting and help parents discover their political voice so they have a tool for changing aversive home and community conditions. Another way of including parents is to provide parenting workshops. Often such workshops can be coordinated with other community agencies that share a learner-centered perspective. In order to be consistent with the learner-centered principles, such workshops might address (McCombs, 1991):

- How a parental frame of reference involving parents' poor self-concept, insecurity about themselves and learning, and alienation influences their child's and their own moment-to-moment behavior, affect, and perceptions

- How parents can consistently maintain the positive, motivational interactions with their children that help children experience feelings of self-worth; how parents can better control their own feelings about situations or events and therefore help themselves and their children enjoy, grow, and learn successfully together

- How parents can alleviate the factors in the home environment that contribute to insecurity and reinforce a negative frame of reference as they also develop factors that contribute to a positive family climate and relationship

Other examples of ways to involve parents include encouraging them to provide service learning projects for their own children or their children's classmates, having them teach their own area of specialty, or asking them to take the lead in identifying school-community partners and mentors. In general, schools that create in-school programs that use parents' skills and make parents a vital part of the entire school community within a context that is collaborative and nonblaming are more successful (Comer, 1993). These programs have the additional benefit of bringing in support and partnerships for teachers from the community.

Given the importance of focusing on learners' holistic needs, which is an integral part of learner-centered education, many researchers and policymakers alike are calling for collaboration between schools, community groups, and social service agencies. Teachers can help promote linkages between schools and community agencies that might serve as the locus of nonacademic services. The *school of the future* is one example of a model service integration approach for highly economically disadvantaged populations that brings health, mental health, and social services into the school (Holtzman, 1992). Teachers can play a leadership role in researching models such as these, discussing the alternatives with their colleagues and administration, and bringing proposals for community support and involvement strategies to administrators, other staff, and parents.

Furthermore, the research clearly shows that a powerful tool for gaining community support and involvement is the students themselves. Teachers can involve students in the design of school and community programs that are relevant to their needs and interests and that can challenge them toward healthy self-development. Adults in partnership with youths help build connections between school and community and help establish attitudes of shared responsibility for personal and community well-being and health. Teachers, together with students, can reach out to communities to offer them assistance. Students have helped communities, for example, by conducting surveys for community organizations and volunteering in nursing homes, child-care agencies, and other local service agencies. Such services lead to better school-community relations and help communities see the many positive characteristics and qualities that youth possess.

Policies That Support All Learners.   The authors of the learner-centered psychological principles are quite explicit about the nature of policies that support learner-centered school systems. The principles suggest that policies should

- Recognize that learning can only be as enriching as the teacher's ability to foster it and the system's commitment to meeting the learner's needs. Teachers cannot automatically be assumed capable of facilitating learning and growth without ongoing administrative efforts to support teachers' self-development in intellectual, emotional, social, and behavioral areas. Thus, policy must address ways to ensure the reciprocal empowerment of both teachers and students such that teachers feel sufficiently supported and valued and can, in turn, empower their students.

- Allow for the construction of a learning environment that adapts to individual learner needs, avoiding overly rigid and reductionistic definitions of the curriculum, specification of objectives, and schedules for when and where learning occurs. Definitions and regulations of what, when, and for how long topics are to be studied and what resources are used should be drawn in a way that maximizes the flexibility and choice students and teachers have to organize learning to meet the needs of individual children.

- Reflect the need for learners to integrate and organize knowledge in personally meaningful ways. Curriculum and assessment processes should encourage learners to see the connections between what they are asked to learn and what they already know, how information being learned relates to other subjects and disciplines, and how the knowledge is used and connects with real-world situations—that is, situations that are not academically abstracted from natural phenomena and experiences. Policies should facilitate the organization of learning tasks around problem situations that integrate low- and high-literacy skills such as thinking about thinking and creative and critical thinking.

- Encourage the organization of sequences or hierarchies of learning tasks so that assessment of progress reflects the growth of the learner's skills and knowledge, not the matching of content rigidly tied to age or grade.

- Acknowledge the roles that personal beliefs about self, expectations about learning, and other cognitive constructions can play in learning and self-development. Furthermore, policies should acknowledge the importance of affective and cognitive development and give students the opportunity to increase their understanding of their psychological functioning (e.g., using psychological personnel to assist students in self-development).

- Encourage the creation of instructional settings that cross the full range of social mediation contexts needed for learning (e.g., working alone, working with others, and working with other groups as members of a team). Regulations and resources should be flexible and encourage this variety of settings; policies that promote only one perspective, such as individual isolation or competition among students, should be avoided.

- Acknowledge the diversity found in the United States among individual students' interests, cultural backgrounds, motivations, and abilities. The American school program needs to be diverse in character, structure, and intent to adequately meet the needs of the full range of these learners. Using single programs, standards, and learning goals for all learners ignores the fact and value of diversity.

- Facilitate the interaction of psychology with other disciplines such that concerns relative to the psychological health and functioning of learners are considered. Interactions among disciplines and their embodiment in funding and service provider agencies can mutually enhance the knowledge base and attention to the needs of the whole learner (emotional, intellectual, social, and physical).

- Enable schools to provide services for all of a child's needs and for all children, allowing schools to be the locus of services and connections to other service providers. Mechanisms for facilitating school-community linkages should be considered and promoted, as well as school-family and school-business linkages [Presidential Task Force on Psychology in Education, 1993, pp. 13–14].

In addition, policies should be sensitive to student needs and lives outside the school environment. This means that regulations and policies relative to such areas as suspension, expulsion, homework, and leaving campus need to consider students' family support needs or home and work responsibilities as well as school goals for learning and achievement.

These policy recommendations lead toward the creation of a vision and then a reality for schooling and school systems that value and support all learners and the learning process.

Summary

In this examination of the characteristics and features of learner-centered schools that are consistent with the learner-centered psychological principles, a number of common elements emerge. Many of these may be found in the checklist in Exhibit 4.1. Take a moment to look at how you might recognize a learner-centered school. We have organized these characteristics according to what you might notice about students; climate and culture; administration, support staff, and teachers; and physical characteristics of the school itself.

Like the learner-centered classroom, the learner-centered school does not look a particular way, because being learner centered represents as much a way of being or disposition as it does doing particular things. In fact, schools may actually be less learner centered when they apply a single supposedly learner-centered model or program to school redesign because doing so *reduces* flexibility and ownership by requiring everyone to conform to one model. The learner centered school is much more inclusive—it recognizes, values, and accommodates diversity among students and staff. Therefore, learner-centered schools may be detected by their cultures, practices, structures, and policies and the degree to which they are consistent with the knowledge base on learning and learners (that is, with the learner-centered psychological principles).

Basing school reform efforts on an understanding of the twelve principles leads to a concept of schooling different from the one that evolves from reform efforts focused *only* on the achievement of academic standards or a shift to performance-based assessment. The learner-centered model leads to a concept of schooling that has

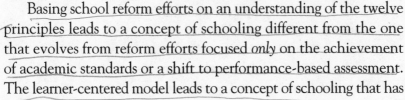

EXHIBIT 4.1   Characteristics of Learner-Centered Schools.

At this school, the **students** are
☐ Talking openly with teachers and administrators
☐ Happy to be at school
☐ Involved in school activities
☐ Proud of the school and respectful of its resources
☐ Involved in positively resolving their own conflicts
☐ Encouraged to get involved and take risks
☐ Involved in learning and school governance decisions
☐ Respectful toward school staff, administrators, and teachers
☐ Open and friendly

At this school, **climate and culture** characteristics are
☐ Administrators and teachers that actively solicit student input
☐ Students that are greeted by name and known by staff
☐ A school calendar that accommodates different student needs and cultures
☐ High daily attendance rates
☐ A visible theme of positive student growth and development
☐ Opportunities for long-term (multiyear) teacher relationships
☐ An expectation that all students will achieve high academic and personal standards
☐ An emphasis on intrinsic versus extrinsic incentives for learning

At this school, **administration, support staff, and teachers** are
☐ Emotionally responsive to all students
☐ Visible and accessible to students
☐ Respectful of students
☐ Sensitive and responsive to individual differences and needs
☐ Trusting of students
☐ Actively listening to students
☐ Engaging in mentoring relationships with students
☐ Sharing decision making with students
☐ Sensitive to students' mood levels

At this school, noticeable **physical characteristics** are
☐ Few locked doors
☐ A wide variety of learning spaces and activities

- [ ] Displays of student work
- [ ] Learning resources that are accessible to all students
- [ ] A variety of comfortable places for conversations
- [ ] Multiage groupings of students
- [ ] Active involvement and participation of parents
- [ ] Active involvement and participation of business and community members
- [ ] A school open at flexible hours to accommodate student and family schedules
- [ ] Cafeteria foods and school decor that reflect students' varied cultures
- [ ] Classes with low student-teacher ratios
- [ ] Flexible blocks of time to accommodate different learner needs and teacher planning time
- [ ] Availability of health, mental health, and social services

Source: Developed by Mid-continent Regional Educational Laboratory (McREL), 1994. Reprinted with permission of McREL.

at its center a commitment to the motivation, learning, and achievement of *all* students based on what is known about both learners and learning. This model fosters decisions about academic standards, curriculum, assessment, and instructional approaches that take into account learner needs, capacities, and frames of reference. There is, therefore, a focus on creating quality learning environments and personal relationships based on an understanding of learners and learning. There is a balance between individual learner considerations and what is known to be best for all learners. And there is a balance between concern for learner needs and concern for learning the knowledge and skills that define an educated and productive citizen.

It needs to be emphasized that *a learner-centered perspective is not just one more cookbook for better learning* to add to the never-ending parade of educational trends. A focus both on learners and learning and on the research base that supports each provides a foundation for school design decisions. It gives coherence to the myriad innovations so popular today—for example, site-based decision making, standards-based education, performance assessment, cooperative learning, and higher-order thinking. It gives educators a way to develop, organize, and plan significant educational innovations. When schools focus on both learners and learning, bringing students' frames of reference to the implementation of educational innovations, we believe—and research supports—that more students will be successful and satisfied in school and current innovations will be more effective in maximizing motivation, learning, and achievement for all students. We also believe that schools will begin to reinstall the love of learning in those growing numbers of students most alienated and turned off to school. Schools must be willing to value all learners, respect their differences, and challenge them. This includes addressing the needs of teachers as learners— teachers who have all too frequently been demoralized, frustrated, and burned out by the increasing demands placed on them by the reform agenda. The time for research-based learner-centered practice in this country's schools is now.

5

Making the Transition to Learner-Centered Classrooms and Schools

Look at your goals

Look at yourself

It means you have to look at yourself. For those people who cannot do that, change is really difficult. You've got to look at yourself honestly and then make changes in yourself. You've got to keep growing.
—Barbara Reed, Teacher, Westbury High School, Houston, Texas

Gradually we began trying some new approaches. One change led to another and another and another, like dominos. I started to see what people meant by systemic change. A new energy and excitement surged among us as hope grew and the cloudy vision of what we wanted became clearer and clearer.
—High School Principal

What is the journey of change that both research and practice have identified—the journey of personally transforming beliefs and practices toward a learner-centered model of schooling—that all of us ought to be embarking on, individually and in concert with whole educational systems? What is the nature of the change process and how does it unfold for those central to the process such as the teachers and other educators who aim to transform the system to better serve individual student learning needs?

This chapter focuses on examining this transition as it applies to changing roles for teachers, so that teachers can take control of their own personal change in the context of a complex educational system that extends outside their classroom to the school, the district, and beyond. The chapter begins with a brief overview of the nationally recognized need for a major reform and transformation of the educational system; how educators have responded to this need; the confusions that have existed over what exactly must be done; and the emerging consensus about the value of learner-centered models for reform. It then turns to a discussion of what a systemic perspective must address to successfully bring about far-reaching changes consistent with a learner-centered model. We address this systemic perspective to help teachers put their own personal change process in a larger context and better define lifelong learning and leadership opportunities for themselves.

More directly to the point of the journey of change, however, we consider what is required at the individual level to produce sustainable changes in thinking and practice, changes such that learners and the learning process become the central concerns of teachers. We provide examples of what teachers in three learner-centered high schools have shared about their stories of change, their personal learning and change processes, and describe how these examples mirror what research has shown to be critical aspects of the personal change process. Following the discussion of the ongoing journey of change and its implications for teachers, we conclude by examining how, by taking increased responsibility for their own learning and professional development, teachers may begin to recapture the excitement and enthusiasm of knowing they are making a difference in the learning and lives of all of their students.

The National Perspective on the Need for School Reform

As we illustrated at the beginning of this book, U.S. education is in an era in which reform is being demanded—traditional notions about teaching, learning, and the whole enterprise of schooling are being challenged. No longer are educators and psychologists aiming to improve the existing system. Instead there is widespread agreement that the existing system is not working and that basic assumptions underlying this system are fundamentally flawed (see, for example, Covington, 1992; Eisner, 1991; Hargreaves, 1995; Levin, 1991; O'Neil, 1995; Skrtic, 1991). Many educators, at least implicitly, acknowledge that comprehensive, learner-centered, and systemic redesign strategies are required. It is being recognized that these strategies must holistically address the unique needs of the learners, the families and social systems of which they are a part, and the educational and administrative systems that interface with the learners and their supporting social systems. Finally, strategies for improving student achievement are being seen in the larger context of the need to transform teaching and learning.

When we shift attention to what the national reform agenda identifies as the almost overwhelming needs facing American education, we see that they are consistent with the need to facilitate motivation, learning, and achievement for *all* students. Since the publication of *A Nation at Risk* (National Commission on Excellence in Education, 1983), national attention has focused on declining student achievement in critical subject areas (such as mathematics, science, reading, writing) and on the disparity in achievement between more advantaged and less advantaged students. More recently, first with the publication under President Bush and this nation's governors of the goals for America 2000 (U.S. Department of Education, 1991) and currently with the Goals 2000 agenda, this nation's awareness of the wide set of interrelated and systemic goals needed to increase achievement for all students has been on the rise. Parents and the general public are openly sharing their concerns about the quality of public schools, and parents of disadvantaged children, in particular, are becoming increasingly vocal about conditions they believe contribute to their children's failure in the traditional educational system. Issues of equity and parental involvement, standards that speak to an uneven playing field, and reform solutions that go beyond the school walls to families, communities, and businesses are all topics in the national discussion of factors that must be addressed to increase motivation, learning, and achievement for *all* students.

For example, a recent *Phi Delta Kappa* and Gallup poll of U.S. adults' attitudes toward public schools (Elam, Rose, & Gallup, 1994) names the five biggest problems facing schools as fighting, violence, and gangs; lack of discipline; lack of proper financial support; drug abuse; and standards and quality of education. Similarly, a national survey of the nation's educational leaders (Council of the Great City Schools, 1993), identified the issues of student performance assessment and alternative assessment; violence and gang-related activity; national standards and assessment; restructuring the management of schools; bilingual education; and early childhood education. Clearly, these polls and surveys show concerns that span many educational and social issues, thus calling for a *systemic* response, that is, one that addresses *all important components of the educational system.*

Educational Response

Related to the issues discussed in the last section is the concern of educators and researchers that prior reform efforts have been based on assumptions that are no longer tenable in their views of (1) what needs to change and (2) how to address the underlying factors affecting student motivation, learning, and achievement. For example, educators and researchers can no longer assume that changing one part of the system (say, the curriculum) happens in isolation; they now know that changing one part of the system will significantly affect and cause changes in other technical, personal, and organizational system components (Fullan, 1996). In the main, new designs for education are in response to an observed need for a change in educational outcomes—first in relation to an industrial society, then in relation to a competitive world, and then in relation to changing cultural values. Even in today's debates, all concerned face a dilemma: Different groups and different people have contradictory objectives. And even within groups there appear to be dual and conflicting goals for education (Cuban, 1986, 1990): socialize all children, yet nourish each child's individuality; teach history, but ensure that the child possesses practical skills that are marketable in the community; demand obedience to authority, but teach the child to think and question; teach the value of cooperation, but expect the child to be competitive.

Critics and advocates of public education do agree on one thing: the educational system must change to meet the needs of an increasingly diverse and seemingly less well educated or prepared group of young people so that they may do well in and meet the more complex needs of the twenty-first century in which they will live and work. If their needs are to be met, visionaries argue, the current system cannot merely be restructured; it must, they maintain, be transformed. What does this mean? In a literal sense, *transformation* is a shift in thinking, perception, or behavior. It results in a fundamentally different way of being. A transformation of the educational system means a rethinking of the basic purposes of schooling, the creation of a new vision, and the development of a new culture that will sustain these changes in purpose and vision. When a *living system* such as education, made up of human beings, supporting a human purpose, and dynamic and interactive in nature, is to be transformed, the transformation must consider the people the system serves and how best they can be served so as to accomplish the desired mission. In the case of education, this mission, we assert, must revolve around motivation, learning, and academic achievement for *all* learners.

For some, the revolution in thinking about the nature of things that occurred in the early part of this century with the revolution in the field of physics (Garmston & Wellman, 1995) is seen to have influenced the thinking about what is needed to remedy the current problems and shortcomings of education. Nothing short of a transformation of the outdated educational system will do. New fields of quantum mechanics, chaos theory, complexity theory, and fractal geometry and also the new biology have contributed to the reshaping of human thought. Such is the case for Garmston and Wellman (1995), who propose that schools must be adaptive as well as create adaptivity in order to be successful. They believe adaptivity is created by

- Basing decisions on the questions of who are we? and what is our purpose?—filtered through agreed-upon core values, such as a respect for human differences and respect and caring for others

- Shifting decision-making authority to the people most influenced by the decision

- Restructuring the day and year to increase the time teachers have to interact collegially with one another

- Setting outcomes and standards that signal a passion for excellence and attention to qualities that are based on real-world needs

- Supporting faculty members in collaboratively setting and working toward self-defined goals [p. 8].

Garmston and Wellman (1995) further argue that five human "energy fields" must be used to help schools and the people in them be continuously adaptive: efficacy (believing one can achieve and being willing to exert the effort necessary to achieve); flexibility (ability to appreciate multiple perspectives); craftsmanship (standards of excellence in thinking and actions); consciousness (awareness of thoughts, feelings, intentions, behaviors, and one's personal agency or control and also awareness of others' styles, values, and behaviors); and interdependence (seeing benefits of connections and collaboration as opportunities to learn). These energy fields or states of mind may be used to develop personal and organizational capacities in a shared leadership model that values and capitalizes on the diversity of those in the system.

In keeping with this vision, a current goal of educational reform is to create and sustain self-governing learning communities (Meier, 1995). Such communities require, at their heart, a *new school cul-*

ture—a culture dedicated to continuous learning and improvement. The purpose of such a culture is to better prepare students with the mental, moral, and social standards required for maximum productivity and personal development so they can meet the challenges of our complex and changing world. In a word, the culture must strive to develop the potential of *all* learners while respecting the diversity of their talents, interests, and capabilities. This new school culture is dedicated to helping all students understand and be able to use important knowledge and skills, and at the same time, it nurtures students' unique skills and abilities, a source of diversity and richness that contributes to the nation.

How does a culture dedicated to these goals, the culture discussed in Chapter Four, develop? Research on successful schools (that is, schools that are reaching the goal of high achievement for all students) shows that they have created a culture that values continuous improvement and learning as an ongoing goal for all— teachers, parents, administrators, and community members alike (see, for example, Anderson, 1993; Baum, Renzulli, & Hebert, 1994; Bennett & O'Brien, 1994; Boyd & Hord, 1994; Kruse, Seashore-Louis, & Bryk, 1994; Hargreaves, 1995; Meier, 1995). Such a culture develops through the sharing of a common purpose or goal, through dedication to continuous improvement and lifelong learning rather than to maintaining the status quo, and through a sense of shared responsibility for reaching the common goal among all system participants. There are shared norms and values at the core of the culture, along with a collective focus on learners and learning. The culture emerges through a process of reflective dialogue and collaboration (Floden, Goertz, & O'Day, 1995; Hasseler, 1995; Kruse, Seashore-Louis, & Bryk, 1994; McCombs, in press).

Where do teachers fit into this picture? What is important for them to understand about systemic change and the nature of educational systems if they are to help develop schools with cultures of the kind examined in Chapter Four, cultures committed to caring, learning and change, and collaboration? We believe that understanding the nature of systems and systemic change helps teachers better grasp both the complexities and the simplicities of solutions that define learner-centered model of schooling.

The Nature of Systemic Change

Complex systems that function to serve particular human needs can best be thought of as social systems, or living systems. Such systems are by their nature unpredictable; they can, however, be understood in terms of principles that define human needs, cognitive and motivational processes, and variabilities of behavior. Unlike mechanical, nonliving systems, living systems require a focus on concepts of interconnectedness, self-renewal, and interdependence because when one component of the system is "tinkered" with, all other components are affected, too. Implied in this view of living systems is a global, nonlinear, and dynamic view of learning and change (Banathy, 1992, 1995). In brief, living systems conform to the same basic psychological and sociological principles that define individuals and their interactions with others; thus, we are better able to understand complex living systems by understanding psychological and sociological principles.

To further our comprehension of living systems, it is helpful to appreciate how people within the system perceive the larger context, that is, the personal, technical, and organizational contexts that define the system. The learner-centered psychological principles are useful for understanding what systemic change means in a system such as the educational system that serves the primary function of supporting learning for individual learners. For example, it is helpful to note that what best supports learning also supports positive change; we know, then, that it is important to attend to individual needs, experiences, competencies, and special talents. Each of the twelve principles helps us see the design of the system in terms of human functioning and in terms of what must be present to support learning at all system levels—from classroom, to school, to district, to the community, and to society in general. This view fits with what other experts have to say about the nature and process of systemic change.

Fullan (1996), for example, argues that we need to view change as inherently "nonlinear" and fragmented and therefore not readily amenable to sophisticated linear plans. He suggests that the educational system begin the change process with a grounding in clear and coherent principles, strategies, and the like that are agreed to and believed by a majority of teachers. Successful strategies for building a foundation for change in a living system are networking, reculturing, and restructuring. Networks can provide multilevel staff development that is ongoing; a variety of ways to share ideas; an integration of priorities; and support for a commitment to inquiry, progress, and continuous improvement. *Reculturing* focuses on developing new values, beliefs, and norms. Importantly from the learner-centered perspective, Fullan stresses that systemic reform mainly involves changing conceptions, skills, and motivations in the minds and hearts of educators. The focus of such reform, then, must be on the people who change the system. This view brings a degree of simplicity to the complexity of change—it focuses attention on how to help change the thinking as well as the skills and motivations of critical players in the educational process, particularly the teachers. When thinking changes and when skills compatible with the new thinking are developed, motivation changes as well.

Similarly, Carr (1996) points out that unlike a systematic view which is linear, systemic thinking and change involve a global conception of problems that includes an understanding of interrelationships and interconnections. Systemic thinking is holistic rather than reductionistic and helps individuals change their perceptions of themselves, rather than putting the major focus on end goals. In systemic reform, as the focus turns to people, their thinking, and the interrelationships among them, the study of power relationships among people helps clarify and create a context for change and cultural understanding.

We turn now to a model based on the preceding ideas, a model of systemic change that can guide the rethinking required in the journey toward learner-centered practices at the school and classroom levels.

A Model of Systemic Change

We have used the metaphor of a journey to describe the change of a system—both take time, energy, and collective as well as individual will. The change of a system starts one person at a time and often involves a few committed teachers who recognize that the system is not working well for many of their students or for themselves. It is usually precipitated by a crisis at the personal, school, or community level, one that forces people to reexamine basic purposes, procedures, and policies being played out in the school and classroom that do not seem to be working together to achieve the goal of learning for all.

The model shown in Figure 5.1 is helpful for looking at the nature of social systems and the elements that must be addressed to design systems responsive to the needs of learners and to promote learning. These elements are defined by and aligned with *foundational beliefs and assumptions and a philosophy that describes and may guide system functioning*. That is, there are fundamental beliefs and assumptions about the primary processes of learning and motivation and how they operate differentially for individual learners in the system. From these core beliefs and assumptions, principles are defined. We have argued that these principles should be research based so that the philosophy that emerges from them can be informed by objective findings rather than subjective opinions. The need for a research base leads to the valuing of inquiry, collaboration, and ongoing assessment in support of system improvement. From principles and a philosophy, the purpose of the system is defined and educational processes, policies, practices, programs, and procedures are specified—all of which are thus aligned and consistent with the principles and philosophy.

Also important to systemic design is consideration of the differential needs of all learners at all system levels. Specifically, as shown in Figure 5.2, systemic design in education must be concerned with students, teachers, support staff, administrators, parents, and community members and with all levels of the system—classroom, school, district, and community. Design or redesign of the system

FIGURE 5.1 Elements of Social Systems.

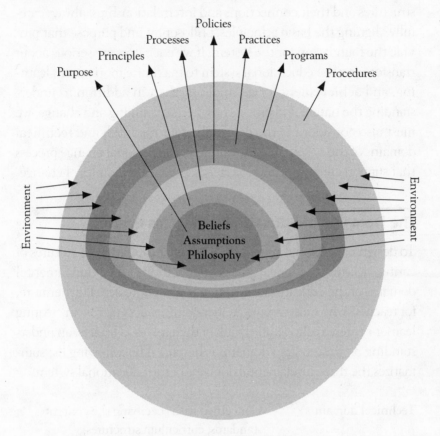

Constituencies: Students, Teachers, Parents,
Administrators, Business and Community Members

Source: Adapted from Burger, 1995.

thus needs to take into account simultaneously system functions and structures and their connections and interrelationships, always carefully aligning the basic principles, philosophy, and purpose that provide the foundation for the system. If we educators are serious about transforming the educational system to maximize motivation, learning, and achievement for *all* students, then in addition to understanding the nature and process of systemic thinking and change, we must also consider (1) the personal, organizational, and technical domains of the system; (2) the nature of the personal change process that supports redesign; and (3) research-based principles of change.

The Domains of Educational Systems Change

To design educational systems that foster the creation of cultures of caring, learning, change, and collaboration, three fundamental domains of the educational system must be addressed. Furthermore, for teachers who must assume an increasing leadership role in creating learner-centered schools and think of themselves as leaders, an understanding of these system domains is helpful. The following list summarizes the three fundamental domains of the educational system.

Technical domain	Concerned with specifying the content standards, curriculum structures, instructional approaches, and assessment strategies that best promote learning and achievement of all students
Personal domain	Concerned with supporting the personal, motivational, and interpersonal needs of those who serve and/or are served by the system (for example, teachers, administrators, students, parents)
Organizational domain	Concerned with providing the organizational and management structures and policies that support the personal and technical domains and, ultimately, motivation, learning, and achievement for all students.

FIGURE 5.2 System Levels.

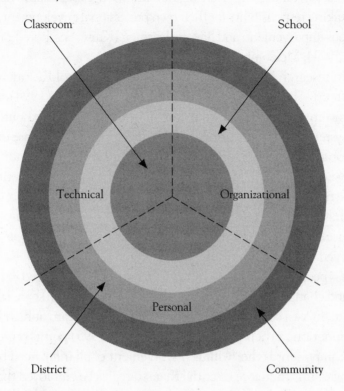

To bring about and sustain change of the educational system, then—to create a culture committed to ongoing learning and change as well as caring and collaboration—continual and simultaneous attention to all three domains is needed. Specifically, from the perspective of the *organizational* domain there must be time to meet and talk, physical proximity for team planning and collaboration, communication structures such as regular meetings or electronic mail systems, and shared decision-making strategies (Kruse, Seashore-Louis, & Bryk, 1994; Sagor, 1995). From the perspective of the *personal* domain, there needs to be a sense of community, high-quality personal relationships and constructive dialogue, an openness to improvement, trust and respect, supportive leadership, and processes for socializing new members into the culture (Kruse, Seashore-Louis, & Bryk, 1994; McCombs, 1995c). From the perspective of the *technical* domain, it is important to provide all members of the community with the knowledge and skills necessary to taking risks, learning new knowledge and skills as needed, and taking responsibility for their own professional development, continuous improvement, and lifelong learning (Kruse, Seashore-Louis, & Bryk, 1994; McCombs, 1991).

In research conducted by the Center for School Restructuring in fifteen schools, Kruse, Seashore-Louis, and Bryk (1994) found that attention to the personal domain—to the human resources in the system—was more critical to the development of a sense of professional community, or culture, than were structural conditions. They conclude that "this finding adds weight to the argument that the structural elements of restructuring have received too much emphasis in many reform proposals, while the need to improve the culture, climate and interpersonal relationships in schools have received too little attention" (p. 6).

As people develop new cultures that are caring, engaged in learning and change, and collaborative, that are centered on a shared vision that includes a commitment to having *all* students learn at high levels and function at their potential, Hargreaves (1995) points out that a key component is the "willful" involvement of all influenced by the changes. It is therefore essential that strategies be employed that are consistent with the transformed vision and respectful of the diversity of expertise that is available (even from the most critical and skeptical experts). This places a focus on the central importance of *building personal relationships* as an initial support system for sustaining change. These personal needs must be supported organizationally, and *collaborative cultures* that value both individual and shared learning must be established (Hargreaves, 1995). Change becomes learning, learning becomes intrinsically motivating and valued, and the negative predisposition to change as being aversive can be transformed into the view that "change is learning, and learning is fun" (p. 18).

Teachers and Principals as Leaders of Systemic Change

Boyd and Hord (1994) discuss the role of both teachers and school principals in bringing about systems change, specifically by creating schools as learning communities. Building on Senge's definition (1990), we see learning communities as organizations, or cultures, in which people are continually expanding their capacity to create what they desire, nurturing new and expansive patterns of thinking, and experiencing the freedom to be creative and continually learn how to learn together. Consistent with this definition, a learning organization has at its heart a shift to seeing people in the system as connected to each other and to the world. People begin to see that they create their reality and that they can change it. A particularly important shift is required in the leadership roles of teachers and school principals. They must see that learning and change are two sides of the same coin.

In Boyd and Hord's research (1994), the leadership functions most conducive to change are (1) reducing isolation; (2) increasing staff capacity; (3) providing a caring, productive environment; and (4) promoting increased quality. These functions are fulfilled by modeling; coaching; attending to detail; observing ceremonies, rituals, and traditions; and telling stories that identify heroes and heroines who support the school's mission. When these functions are fulfilled, norms change and a new culture develops. Furthermore, Reitzug and Burrello (1995) report that one of the most important things principals can do is facilitate teachers' reflective practice by asking challenging questions, providing constructive feedback from their own observations, challenging program regularities, and enhancing resource supports. Additionally, teachers need to be supported and encouraged to take increased responsibility for their own learning and professional development. For teachers to assume these leadership roles, a critical additional element is for teachers to see themselves as leaders.

Chen and Addi (1995) discuss the importance of empowering teachers to be more involved in decision making and school management. They argue that school administrators must engage not only in leadership activities but also in activities that set the stage for restructuring (for example, by establishing new organizational structures that encourage teachers to improve educational outcomes).

They must also influence the thoughts and actions of teachers through transformational activities and personal vision.

But how can teachers assume more of a leadership role in the change process? How can they become models of continuous, life-long learning? We believe that one key is for teachers to understand the nature of the personal change process.

The Personal Change Process

To facilitate and bring about the kind of changes we have been proposing, an understanding of the personal change process is important. Both teachers and students are required to "change their minds," to modify their current thinking about learning and schools.

As individuals change their thinking and practice, they progress through a dynamic process with several fundamental *stages*. These stages are not linear, and people do not go through them in one particular order, but each person will progress through a process that has distinct periods, or stages, of change. It is both illuminating and useful to learn ahead of time about the personal process in general and what must be attended to in specific stages. Knowledge is always power; here knowledge empowers those going through change or transformation. As a part of our work with teachers who were changing to a more learner-centered approach, we researched the literature on personal change, including the documentation of successful approaches in clinical and counseling settings. In this review (McCombs, 1994a), the following four stages were identified. They reflect the integration of several models, with a focus on will, skill, and social support strategies. Effective strategies at each stage of change will vary as a function of the context of change.

Stage 1: Increasing Awareness and Inspiration to Change

This stage of the personal change process shows the person who needs to change that *change is personally relevant and possible*; this stage *inspires hope*.

The initial phase of the change process requires a willingness to change. Whether the change is in one's personal life (for example, losing weight) or in one's professional life (for example, learning to see all children as naturally motivated to learn), people must believe that the change they are considering is possible, regard it as meaningful, and have a sense of hopefulness about a life that includes the change. Without the will or inspiration to change, the person may go through the motions, but sustainable change is not likely. A truism about real change is that it cannot be mandated; it must be chosen willingly and must result in a transformation of thinking, feeling, and behaving. These general findings may be applied as teachers are supported in becoming more learner centered. The first step for teachers is to become more aware of (1) what is happening in the area of school reform; (2) the impact of current practices on individual students; (3) what learner-centered characteristics and strategies are; and (4) what these characteristics and strategies are intended to accomplish. Teachers must also become personally convinced of the importance of a learner-centered perspective when deciding what innovations to implement and how to implement them. In short, teachers must become inspired to change their beliefs or practices. They become inspired when they have an understanding of the personal benefits and relevance of change; see the possibility it holds for enhanced motivation, learning, and achievement for all learners; and have evidence that change will actually produce positive results with real teachers and actual students.

Stage 2: Observing Models and Building Understanding

Stage 2 of the personal change process involves *looking at models and discussing the what and how*; this stage *builds understanding*.

Once a willingness and desire for change are present, it is helpful for teachers to see models of how learner-centered practices are implemented in diverse settings and with diverse populations. At this stage, what is important is that teachers see the *what* and *how* of various strategies, have opportunities to discuss what makes various practices learner centered or not, and begin the dialogue that will lead them to a deeper understanding of how such practices might work for them.

Stage 3: Adopting Strategies and Developing Ownership

Stage 3 of the process concerns *tailoring strategies, coaching, trying out, and revising;* this stage *develops ownership.*

After opportunities to observe models—whether in person or via videotape—teachers are ready to try out some of the modeled practices for themselves. This stage works best when teachers are encouraged to take risks and to experiment with selected practices, adapting the practices to their own styles and personalities. It is important for them to keep in mind that there is no one best way to be learner centered—it is a function of both disposition and specific behaviors and practices. At this stage, teachers need to be supported by other teachers and their administration in taking risks and beginning their own change process.

Stage 4: Adopting and Maintaining New Attitudes and Practices

In stage 4, the person working on personal change adopts strategies for *ongoing self-assessment, networking, and support;* this stage *maintains and sustains new attitudes and practices.*

As teachers become comfortable with changes in practice as well as with ongoing assessment and evaluation of the effectiveness of these changes (evidenced by increased student motivation, learning, and achievement), they will begin to develop a positive attitude toward ongoing learning and change. For a learner-centered approach to be sustained, this attitude must be maintained. Ongoing self-assessment, networking, and support are as important as the specific practices that are adopted. In fact, if practices do not undergo assessment, refinement, and continued change over time, teachers are not being learner centered; they have forgotten that learner centered is a perspective and disposition that focuses attention on learners and learning so as to promote motivation, learning, and achievement for all students. Students change from class to class and from year to year; the knowledge base on learning and learners also continually changes. Teachers must be adaptive and maintain the conviction that learning must be supported by continuous change and improvement of practices. Teachers may need support in maintaining this stance because it involves ongoing evaluation and modification of practices and thus requires them to take an active role in creating their own professional development plans and support systems. Support systems might include professional networks at the building level or at the national level via electronic or organizational networks.

Principles of Change

We have derived a number of *principles of change* from the literature on change. These principles help explain conditions that best support change, or transformation, at the systemic level. Because these principles help connect the psychology of learning and the psychology of change and because they are apparent in the stories of change from learner-centered high school teachers that we relate later, we think it useful for educators to be aware of them. These principles of change are overarching principles that facilitate change independently of, but in interaction with, contextual and environmental factors. Furthermore, although many of these principles have been associated with school administrators and principals, it is our position that they apply to teacher leaders as well.

1. Change begins with believing change is possible, with the inspiring of hope.

2. Leadership qualities that contribute to the establishment of empowering contexts for change include sharing power, facilitating discussions and active communication, being inclusive, and having effective conflict resolution and negotiation skills.

3. Change occurs one person at a time and is, in essence, a change in thinking such that people see themselves as learners and have a willingness to share the ownership of knowing.

4. Change is a lifelong process, similar to learning, that is continuous and ongoing.

5. For change to be sustained, new attitudes, perspectives, and ways of thinking about change must be internalized; trying to sustain particular programs, practices, or policies without corresponding changes in attitude may impede change.

6. A respectful change process is invitational, not mandated; it includes time for reflection and practice.

7. The establishment of learning communities can support change and enhance motivation for change.

8. A focus on learners and learning can create a common vision and common directions for change.

9. Change strategies must attend to participants' levels of will, skill, and social support.

10. Change is facilitated by empowering contexts in which individuals feel ownership, respect, personal support, and trust.

11. Change involves believing that all learners have the ability to make choices about their own learning, and seeing students and parents as customers of the system.

12. Effective change requires commitment to making necessary resources, including needed knowledge and skill training, available to all.

13. Change is viewed differently by different cultures and groups.

14. The purposes and plans for change must be understood and accepted by all stakeholders.

We would like to ask you to try an experiment now. Review the list of principles of change, substituting the word "learning" for the word "change." What did you discover? We suggest that, for the most part, the words are interchangeable; that is, change is learning and learning is change. The following section examines how these principles and the ideas about systemic and personal change that we have discussed relate to the actual experiences of teachers who are on the journey of change toward learner-centered classrooms and schools.

Teachers' Journeys of Change in Three High Schools

As we ourselves began to explore the implications of the learner-centered psychological principles for the purpose of redesigning schools and classrooms and guiding the change process, we looked for schools that were in the process of changing their practices based on the current knowledge of learners and learning. We then, for several reasons, decided to focus on three high schools going through the process. First, it is in high schools that problems of low achievement, dropping out, alienation, and perceived irrelevance of schooling are most prevalent. Second, high school teachers have been educated and trained in institutions and staff development programs that typically focus on skills for teaching content rather than on skills for teaching diverse learners and promoting learning for all students. Much of the knowledge base represented by the twelve learner-centered psychological principles has been absent from their preparation. Third, it is in high schools that there is an opportunity to make a real difference for students before they enter adulthood by (1) reenergizing both students and teachers as learners and (2) discovering learner-centered ways to turn around the current negative trends in students' levels of motivation, learning, and achievement. In order to ensure the usefulness and transferability of any conclusions we might draw from our study, we elected to look at a rural, a suburban, and an urban high school.

The Context of Change

To help you understand the stories of change from the teachers in the three high schools we selected to study, we offer a brief description of each.

The rural school is Nederland High School in Nederland, Colorado, a small mountain community outside of Boulder. The community is a mix of low- and middle-income families. Many of these families settled in Nederland during the late 1960s and early 1970s, and the town remains something of a sixties community. The school population of approximately 400 students is characterized by diverse family backgrounds and an increasing number of Hispanic students. In 1990, school staff began to recognize, in their words, that "things were in turmoil." Teacher morale was low, as was student achievement. Teachers felt isolated, and students complained that the curriculum was irrelevant to their needs. The change started with a small group of teachers who believed that things could be better if the focus of schooling was turned to the students and their needs. A new principal provided support for building a school community dedicated to learners and learning; he encouraged teachers to explore the research and to innovate with new curricula and instructional methods. He also began to involve students and their parents in designing a new system. With the focus on learners and learning, students began to see Nederland High as their school, and the community beyond the school also began to own the school. Student input became a key way in which new programs started.

The suburban school is Mundelein High School in Mundelein, Illinois. This primarily blue-collar community on the northwest side of Chicago sits between very affluent and very low-income communities. Like the Nederland community, the Mundelein community had been becoming increasingly diverse, with growing numbers of Hispanic families. The high school population of nearly 1,200 students began to experience growing segregation and racial tensions; at the same time, student achievement, attendance, and behavioral problems were becoming serious issues. A small group of language arts teachers discovered a draft copy of the learner-centered psychological principles in 1991, at a time when they had decided to research the issue of tracking. (They had observed that tracking was not meeting the needs of students and was contributing to increased student segregation and tension.) They had begun a process of researching how curriculum and instruction could be changed to meet the changing needs of students, with the principles providing the research base for guiding the process. These language arts teachers began to come together as a department to experiment and to redesign the curriculum with a learner-centered focus. Their primary emphasis was to approach education from the students' perspectives by creating a learning community in which students might feel more connected to each other and to their teachers. With administrative and community support, the change has moved out from the language arts department to the math, science, and social studies departments.

The third school we looked at is Westbury High School, a large urban school in the heart of Houston, Texas. For Westbury, the change process began in the early 1980s when the problems of poverty, drugs, chaos, fragmentation, and alienation found in many urban schools began to reach crisis proportions. Faculty members realized that students were changing (the nearly 2,500 students represented sixty different cultures), student motivation to learn was decreasing, and teachers were having trouble reaching the overwhelmingly diverse population of students. The teachers discovered, too, that they were not meeting the needs of the students who historically attended Westbury. After several changes in leadership and an increased district focus on problems of student achievement (and the labeling of Westbury as "Wastebury" by students and the surrounding community), a new principal arrived in 1988. She became a catalyst for the creation of a common mission of "service to all students." Although the faculty members were different from one another in many respects, they did have one thing in common: they cared about their students. With supportive leadership, they began to find out what learners needed and to value the students' diversity for the richness it brought to the learning experience. By appreciating their students, understanding student backgrounds and experiences, acknowledging the knowledge students did have, and believing in what students could achieve, teachers at Westbury began their journey to becoming a learner-centered school.

Common Experiences and New Learnings

We recently had the opportunity to bring teachers who played a key leadership role in each of the three high schools together, along with their principals, to tell their stories of change in creating learner-centered schools. They had the opportunity to hear each other's stories, dialogue about common learning experiences, and share new learnings. The following sections summarize what they had to say.

Common Experiences. One commonality reported by the teachers is that they were supported in coming to a common focus on learners and the learning process. The change evolved from a concern with what was happening to students and a perceived need to better serve an increasingly diverse population of students. Teachers were able to get support from administrators, school boards, and communities to innovate, take risks, and engage in research that could guide their understanding of changes needed in their practices and in themselves.

At the beginning of the process, teachers who played a leadership role were those who felt hopeful, thought that they could make a difference, and believed that change was possible. They felt empowered by the administration with the freedom to do what was needed and to see any failures as opportunities for learning and change. These teachers began to see themselves as learners and, as a result, recognized that they needed to talk to students and get them involved in shaping the curriculum and in showing teachers what they perceived to be "real learning." For example, students at

Nederland chose projects they wanted to work on, problems they wanted to explore, and ways to demonstrate their knowledge and skills. There was a recognition of the need to create a caring environment in which everyone could be successful, in which student perspective would be honored, and in which students would feel a part of the school. There was a collective recognition that when teachers put students first, relationships become the critical vehicle for increasing the experience of comfort, safety, and trust required for learning.

Teachers recognized the importance of opening up the dialogue in the school to include students, and saw the importance of understanding each other and their students in achieving meaningful change. At Mundelein, for example, teachers spend the first nine weeks of school "building a learning community"and helping students get to know each other and their teachers. Students are also included in curriculum and assessment decisions. This valuing of student voice and including that voice as part of the change and design processes required a change of mind-set and heart on the part of many. Teachers further realized that building trust is a foundation for change and that their own personal changes, while more difficult, would make the difference. Teachers also began to see that content could be a vehicle for change, that change needs to start with alterations in what students learn and with teachers' honoring how students learn, and that how students learn must be considered before making decisions about scheduling and grouping. Teachers also began to recognize that change is ongoing learning. It is not static; it is not a matter of arriving somewhere and staying there but of always moving. Teachers recognized that change must be inclusive and that it involves permission to make mistakes. A new excitement grew out of being involved in ongoing change, and this excitement took students to new levels of motivation, learning, and achievement.

As to their leadership roles, teachers said that they needed the freedom to make changes and take responsibility for student outcomes. For example, teachers at Westbury took the initiative in forming study and inquiry groups and going to the school administration with proposals for learner-centered changes in curriculum and structures for grouping students in teams. Being able to make meaningful decisions, becoming learners, and getting district and parental support were all seen as important to teachers' evolving roles as leaders and to the success of their learner-centered approaches. Teachers discovered that the students were the best "salespersons" for change, especially when they were able to demonstrate new competencies to parents and community members as part of exit interviews and performance demonstrations. Teachers found that involving other teachers in the process needed to be invitational and not forced. As they became more successful with students, they counted on the natural curiosity of other teachers to be the main motivator for moving the change beyond themselves to others in their buildings. Teachers also saw that *they* needed to take increased responsibility for (1) creating a learning community with opportunities for staff dialogue, (2) creating a new culture of support and risk taking, (3) keeping the change ongoing, (4) keeping student involvement and voice at the center of changes, (5) creating opportunities for teachers to be models and learners, (6) giving time willingly to what is being done as long as the task is seen as meaningful (and no longer seeing time as a barrier), and (7) taking an active role in keeping people on the "same page" with changes. Teachers recognized the importance of their own learning and personal development, of forming inquiry groups, and of building relationships and understanding among themselves as keys to their own creativity and commitment to lifelong learning.

New Learnings. As these high school teachers listened to each other and reflected on their common experiences, they also had an opportunity to think about new learnings. Among the most profound was their recognition that the change had to start within each of them, and that change happened one person at a time. It then had to move out and deepen to create a learning community and a new culture of caring, learning, change, and collaboration.

Trust was key to understanding and the building of relationships. Teachers had first to see themselves as learners in order to appreciate their students' perspectives. They had to learn to trust that students had valuable input and that students could make responsible choices about their own learning. Most importantly, the teachers recognized that, as one of them put it, "the common enemy is us" when it comes to deepening the change and turning hearts and minds around to embrace the value of the students' perspective in informing the teaching and learning process. In regard to true and lasting change, the teachers expressed again that they had learned that "the common enemy is us"—that the place where change starts is "with me" rather than with working on someone else and that they needed to come together as a faculty and truly value and respect each other as learners before they could model learning for students and take the change to a deeper level.

Listen to the shared, summarized voices of some of these teachers as they described their journey of change:

Resistance is mostly about "voice" and the process used to make decisions.

It is important to be willing to share mistakes "with our own" and not give into pressure to be perfect.

We need to work with parents and students in rewriting the curriculum and not let insecurity get in the way.

We need to negotiate changes with students.

We need to see curriculum documents as "never done" and always changing—as living documents.

We need to see "learning as learning" regardless of level of schooling, and see assessment as informing instruction.

We need to negotiate with students about the types of demonstrations that will show their individual learning and understanding and about what quality criteria should be used for assessing final products and for grading, and we need to allow students to be empowered through shared ownership of knowing.

We need to understand the nature of learning and knowing if we are to allow ourselves to turn more control and responsibility over to students and not feel threatened.

We must let students "tell us whether it is working"; seeing the increased student comfort level opens up "a whole new world."

Unwavering Focus on Learners and Learning for All

Now listen to observations from individual teachers from each of the schools.

Mundelein High School Teachers

JOHN: But it's not going to stop because you're going to go back and look at it, and you're going to say, "Well, now we can do this and now we can improve on this." And then you find out that it still changes and you still need to work on it and you still need to do things with it. . . .

My role . . . I guess I didn't for one thing realize that . . . levels of participation . . . led to commitment on people's parts. If they're part of that process, they were so much more committed. . . .

DENNIS: . . . You have the original cadre of people that have been very involved in the process, and I think the real challenge is to . . . increase that group to become bigger and bigger so that the change is schoolwide and it's solid and it can evolve.

JOHN: . . . When you're gonna change anything . . . you have to celebrate those small successes. . . . I guess what encouraged me was . . . change seems to be very divisive, but once you've gone through the change and people see it was the right thing to do, then it becomes even more unifying.

CAROL: Well, we began to look at ourselves as learners instead of as teachers.

JANELL: . . . And now I think what helps me continue to be excited about teaching and about being an administrator is that we're not going to get there . . . or we'll get there, but getting there will only take us to another level of where we need to get later on down the road. And that's exciting.

Nederland High School Teachers

PAT: Students became part of the process instead of the recipients of it.

JOHN:. . . You can't hide. And so when we talk about change, every teacher has to address it.

ED:. . . As we continue to talk about the change process, one of the things that occurs to me is that the change is evolutionary and it's continual. Just like the change in society is continual. You know, we encourage students to be lifelong learners and . . . risk takers, and I think we have to do that as adults in the building.

. . . It takes a lot of work. It takes high energy. It takes a high level of commitment, but the product you get is certainly worth it.

Westbury High School Teachers

BARBARA: We really care about kids. That is the commonality.

SHIRLEY: . . . It really is a change of heart, in how I look at kids and how I react.

BARBARA: . . . And that means you have to look at yourself.

YUKARI: . . . It's constantly evolving, and constantly learning about new things . . .

SHIRLEY: . . . And, your work is making a difference. And, it is worth the struggle and it is worth the effort that you make.

High School Teachers' Roundtable

BARBARA: Putting the emphasis on the student is really very important. It's not something that is just mouthed. It is truly at the core of what we are doing.

DENNIS: . . . It's a whole different system and we're no longer the experts; we're learning as well, and we're incorporating these concepts into our teaching.

JANELL: . . . It's respecting the individual needs of the learner, what that learner needs. It's celebrating their growth; it's doing all the things we know about learning.

High School Administrators' Roundtable

SHIRLEY: It is all very possible, and it's in the future. It's very hopeful. . . . I think our message could be that this isn't impossible. Yeah, it's complex, but it can be done.

We have drawn some conclusions from these people's voices. First, to support a personal change process of continuous learning, teachers need to help create a professional development model that meets their own needs for reduced isolation, for time and resources for inquiry and learning, and for access to research and experts on learning or the change process. Second, to competently assume leadership roles, teachers themselves must be empowered to take increased responsibility for and higher levels of control over their own learning and professional development processes. Teacher education and professional development programs must teach basic principles of motivation, learning, and psychological functioning and engage participants in learning activities that are in keeping with these principles. Therefore, we describe next what current research suggests to be promising professional development directions for preparing teachers for learning and leadership roles.

Implications for Professional Development and Leadership

In addressing emerging professional development models that attempt to incorporate research on learners and learning, Stocks and Schofield (1995) point out that such models must be flexible and incorporate teacher feedback on how best to implement this knowledge base. Because many teachers were exposed to a didactic teaching model in their own education, staff development programs must help them see why a change in their own similarly didactic practices is necessary, feel a sense of ownership of such a change, and create a network of support for change with other teachers.

Supporting teachers in a personal change process requires changes in how professional development is viewed (see, for example, Anderson, Blumfeld, Pintrich, Clark, Marx, & Peterson, 1995; Little, 1993; McCombs & McNeely, in press). Little (1993, p. 133), for example, proposes that "the most promising forms of professional development engage teachers in the pursuit of genuine questions, problems, and curiosities, over time, in ways that leave a mark on perspectives, policy, and practice. They communicate a view of teachers not only as classroom experts, but also as productive members of a broader professional community and as persons embarked on a career that may span 30 years or more."

Little also spells out six principles for professional development:

(1) Professional development offers meaningful intellectual, social, and emotional engagement with ideas, with materials, and with colleagues both in and out of teaching; (2) Professional development takes explicit account of the contexts of teaching and the experience of teachers; (3) Professional development offers support for informed dissent; (4) Professional development places classroom practice in the larger contexts of school practice and the educational careers of children; (5) Professional development prepares teachers (as

well as students and their parents) to employ the techniques and perspectives of inquiry; and (6) The governance of professional development ensures bureaucratic restraint and a balance between the interests of individuals and the interests of institutions [pp. 138–139].

Little also argues that (particularly to meet the needs of urban children) these changes in teacher education must be systemic and far-reaching. She asserts that bringing about such change will involve "political will," because, she believes, we have sufficient knowledge to move forward and apply this knowledge in the service of urban education.

Fullan (1995) points out that professional development has not had a theoretical base and coherent focus. He proposes a framework that addresses three components: moral purpose, the culture of the school, and the linking of preservice and in-service teacher education. With respect to moral purpose, professional development is "learning how to make a difference through learning how to bring about ongoing improvements" (p. 255). To accomplish the purpose of continuous learning requires personal vision building, inquiry, mastery, and collaboration. In building a culture that supports professional development, Fullan believes it is necessary for teachers to have a personal commitment to learn individually and together, to have a questioning attitude, and to be willing to take risks. When a professional community develops, it must be dedicated to discourse and be structurally and culturally embedded in the regular work experiences of teachers, with collaboration and experimentation that develops trust and an attitude of continuous learning and improvement. The skills of collaboration and continuous learning are considered essential and must, he asserts, be fostered at the beginning of teacher preparation programs—with collaboration and partnerships with schools and districts built into a synergistic relationship between pre- and in-service components. He suggests the idea of a *professional development school* (PDS), as a model to produce learning educators and learning organizations through school-university partnerships. Fullan concludes that for PDSs to be successful, university programs themselves must change to become collaborative learning environments.

Swanson (1995) found successful university preservice programs to be those that "emphasized . . . school/university partnerships to enhance the connection between theory and practice, training and socialization in a culture of inquiry, collaborative practice, reflection, and careful placement of student teachers in schools that model 'best practices'"(p. 37). Similarly, successful in-service programs were those that had new teacher leadership opportunities and extensive ongoing learning opportunities through such vehicles as discussion groups, professional networks, institutes, and university-sponsored extended educational offerings. When these collaborative experiences and teacher opportunities for inquiry and learning were carried over to teachers' restructuring efforts in their schools, changes that were successful were those that provided time for teachers to plan and work together, engage in shared decision making, participate in professional networks, coordinate consistent standards and expectations for student learning, and develop cooperative and collaborative cultures within their schools.

As Weinstein (in press) has maintained about the value of extending the learner-centered psychological principles to teacher education and professional development, the principles provide a foundation for guiding this learning process and point to the importance of seeing both learning and motivation to learn as inherently natural processes for all learners, when supported by cultures of collaboration and caring. Weinstein states that "critical to promotion of a positive expectancy climate was the creation of consistent, stimulating, and supportive conditions for school staff to question their expectations for students, not only in addressing beliefs about ability but also in examining teaching practices and policies. Perceived obstacles were translated into opportunities, as teachers collaboratively reframed their work with students, other teachers, and the administration."

In a different vein, a number of educators have argued that an overemphasis in staff development on teaching *content* can interfere with the primary role of teaching *students*. For example, Darling-Hammond (1996) explains that schools now are expected to both educate and ensure learning, meaning that "covering the curriculum" must also be combined with helping each learner attain challenging learning goals. To meet these expectations, teachers must "*understand learners and their learning as deeply as they comprehend their subjects*, and schools (*must*) structure themselves to support deeper forms of student and teacher learning than they currently permit" (p. 5, emphasis added). Along these lines, Darling-Hammond notes several promising strategies for transforming teacher preparation. One such strategy is helping prospective teachers develop reflective, problem-solving orientations to teaching by engaging them in research and inquiry about learning and each student's experiences. Another strategy helps teachers to assume a greater leadership role in the management of their own learning and inquiry and to take greater responsibility and assume a more significant role in making decisions that affect the learning of all at the classroom and school levels. Darling-Hammond also discusses the need for teachers to be prepared for what schools must *become*, not just for how they *are*, observing that "teacher educational reforms are beginning to recognize that prospective teachers, like their students, learn by doing. As teacher educators, beginning teachers, and experienced teachers work together on real problems of practice in learner-centered settings, they can begin to develop a collective knowledge base and a common set of understandings about practice" (p. 6).

In response to the current reality that teachers must educate an increasingly diverse student population, Delattre (1995) argues that teachers must be prepared to understand learning and individual differences and, in particular, to understand cultural diversity. From a study of teacher preparation experiences that support teachers in working with students of diverse backgrounds, Reimer and Lapp (1995) found that there were four elements that student teachers could use to increase their ability to shift their perspectives toward cultural awareness and intercultural sensitivity: (1) using an inclusion approach that promotes social and structural equality and using a cultural pluralism that respects cultural differences throughout the curriculum, both in coursework and field experiences; (2) actively engaging student teachers in culturally diverse classroom settings while they are studying multiculturalism in their college courses; (3) encouraging a broad variety of perspectives by both faculty and student teachers; and (4) supporting student teachers in reflecting on their experiences and own cultural backgrounds and in making connections with these experiences. A variety of approaches was needed to shift student teachers' ideas, as was openness and cultural sensitivity on the part of the classroom teacher with whom student teachers had their field experiences.

To encourage teachers to become more culturally sensitive, Ladson-Billings (1995) recommends preservice or in-service opportunities for teachers to observe models, to reexamine and rethink their practices, and to develop the ethic of caring and personal accountability. One very important dimension in encouraging cultural sensitivity is teachers' conceptions of themselves and others, including beliefs (1) that all students are capable of academic success, (2) that pedagogy is an art that is always in the process of becoming, (3) that as teachers they are members of a learning community, and (4) that learning is a lifelong commitment. It is also important that preservice and in-service programs promote the maintenance of positive teacher-student relationships, the ongoing connectedness with students, the development of a community of learners, and the encouragement of collaborative and responsible learning. In addition, professional development programs should foster the view of knowledge as dynamic and personally constructed, promote a passion for knowledge and learning, and encourage an appreciation of multiple forms of assessment.

In terms of practical implications for all learners, three general principles that must be addressed by staff development emerge. First, learners are motivated by situations and activities that (1) challenge them to be personally and actively involved in their own learning and (2) allow them personal choice and control matched to their abilities and learning task requirements. Second, learners' motivation is enhanced if they perceive that learning tasks (1) directly or indirectly relate to personal needs, interests, and goals and (2) are of appropriate difficulty levels so that they can accomplish them successfully. Finally, learners' natural motivation to learn is elicited in safe, trusting, and supportive environments characterized by (1) quality relationships with caring persons who see the learners' unique potential; (2) instructional supports tailored to learners' unique learning needs; and (3) opportunities for learners to take risks without fear of failure.

These three principles also apply to the design of teacher education programs and to the way teachers design learning environments for their own students. In addition, these basic principles underscore the importance of the following teacher roles, which also must be dealt with by professional development:

- Diagnosing and understanding students' unique needs, interests, and goals

- Helping students define personal goals and see how they relate to school learning goals

- Relating learning content and activities to students' personal needs, interests, and goals, and helping students define these relative to learning goals

- Structuring learning goals and activities such that each student can accomplish his or her own goals and experience success

- Challenging students to invest effort and energy in taking personal responsibility and being actively involved in learning activities

- Providing students with opportunities to exercise personal control and choice over carefully selected task variables such as type of learning activity, level of mastery, amount of effort, or type of reward

- Creating a safe, trusting, and supportive climate by demonstrating real interest, caring, and concern for each student

- Attending to classroom goal structures and goal orientations so that noncompetitive structures and learning goals are emphasized over competitive structures and performance goals

- Highlighting the value of student accomplishment, the value of students' unique skills and abilities, and the value of the learning process and learning task

- Rewarding students' accomplishments and encouraging them to reward themselves and develop pride in their accomplishments

These practices are themselves in keeping with basic principles of learning, motivation, and psychological functioning and are best learned when experienced as part of teacher preparation and professional development. In addition, new understandings of changes in teacher and student roles in the learning process emerge.

This examination of the implications of changing to a learner-centered approach to schooling in staff development (pre- and in-service) has led to a recognition that educational systems are more successful when they are designed from a research-based set of principles *that focus on both learners and learning and on basic principles of psychological functioning* that are translated into a core philosophy and culture. For example, staff from all three of our featured learner-centered high schools report increasing student achievement and attendance. We have also realized that change is more likely to occur when educators and others are assisted in self-assessing and reflecting on their basic beliefs and assumptions, and in engaging in critical inquiry on issues identified in the research on learners and learning. We believe these are essential aspects of the change process.

Barriers still exist to fostering the changes needed in pre- and in-service programs. For example, veteran classroom teachers and student teachers do not always understand why it is important to pay attention to students' perspectives. Because administrators and university faculty do not necessarily focus on this aspect of teaching and learning, administrators do not provide in-service training that addresses the issue and trains teachers how to be sensitive to and include students' perspectives. Neither do universities provide this information and training in preservice experiences. We believe it critical that teachers become aware and respectful of students' views as well as the backgrounds that influence those views (for example, culture, gender, race, family experiences, and the like), and that teachers understand these views' impact on motivation, learning, and achievement, as we have emphasized throughout this book. Another barrier is the notion that "this is the latest bandwagon" and "this, too, shall pass." Teachers often resist in-service staff development opportunities because so many prior innovations have gone by the proverbial wayside. It is useful to point out that most innovations, regardless of their eventual favor or disfavor as theories, nevertheless contribute to teachers' repertoires of strategies and practice when the theory or specific strategies have been seen and experienced as making a difference with students.

Self-assessment and reflection tools are needed to increase staff awareness of the need to consider alternative perspectives as a strategy to stimulate change. Many current staff development models emphasize the importance of teachers taking increased responsibility for their own professional development, and these models advocate self-assessment and reflection strategies as well as learning through inquiry. Tools do not currently exist, however, that assist teachers in engaging in a continuous, ongoing, respectful, nonthreatening, supportive, and self-directed process of assessing and changing their practices so as to increase their instructional effectiveness with individual students. Furthermore, tools do not exist for aligning this type of self-assessment with a consideration of students' (or other constituencies') perspectives. Such a tool might facilitate change itself and also shift how we think about change—that is, change as learning and learning as change. Such a shift would necessitate ongoing self-assessment and revision of practices. Our work with the Learner-Centered Battery (described in Chapter Six) is focused on developing and validating these tools.

In conclusion, professional development that enhances motivation, learning, and achievement *must* be based on an understanding of the psychology of learning and change as well as an appreciation of personal needs and individual perceptions that enhance or inhibit motivation, learning, and change. The particular variables related to teachers include (1) creating a positive learning context, (2) supporting personal changes in teachers' own thinking, and (3) enhancing students' motivation, learning, and academic achievement. The following characteristics related to these variables are identified in the literature as among the most critical. Teachers must acknowledge the importance of students'

Feelings of interpersonal caring, acceptance, and support

Sense of personal voice, control, and autonomy

Perceptions of meaningfulness and relevancy of learning activities

Feelings of personal competence and capacity to succeed

Being understood and respected as individuals

Addressing these variables is necessary not only for teachers but for all constituents at all levels of the system—students, teachers, building and central office administrators, and community members.

Current research indicates that teacher changes in thinking and practice have the highest payoff in terms of student motivation, learning, and achievement. The importance of such changes in thinking is reflected in emerging models of staff development and teacher education. In addition to the implications of changes in thinking for teachers' roles, the models highlight implications for the design of curricula and instructional practices, administrative supports, and interfaces for schools and the larger community. People are at the heart of any living system; attention to learners and learning in educational redesign puts the focus where there is the maximum probability of enhancing positive outcomes. We believe that teacher education and staff development programs that focus on the research on learners and learning, as well as on the research on personal and systemic change, have all those concerned with education looking in the right direction.

Summary

This chapter has explored the journey of change teachers take as they apply the learner-centered psychological principles to their personal learning and change process within the complex arena of educational systems change. We started by overviewing the nationally recognized need for a major transformation of the educational system and the need for a learner-centered model to guide this reform. We next explored why a systemic perspective is necessary and how teachers need to understand this perspective in order to better place their own personal change process in a larger context that can help them identify learning and leadership opportunities. We focused in on the personal change process and what this means for teachers and shared what other teachers who have been and continue to be involved in this process say about their personal experiences. Finally, we looked at what all of this implies for teachers' ongoing learning, leadership, and professional development and at what changes are needed and are beginning to be made in pre- and in-service teacher preparation programs.

In our personal journey to define the personal change process that occurs in those classrooms and schools that exemplify the learner-centered model, we have made friends with administrators, teachers, and students in three high schools: Mundelein High School in Illinois, Westbury High School in Houston, and Nederland High School in Colorado. We brought key leaders in each of these schools together to share their stories of change.

We end this chapter with the "voice" of these learner-centered schools, as staff summarized the journey of change and how they have become lifelong learners and leaders of change. Here are some of their most profound ideas and insights.

"Mistakes are great moments" to develop a love of learning.

Communication, trust, and relationships are key—not ideas and programs.

Moving toward learner-centered practices begins with each person and ultimately the whole school wanting what is best for *all* students and wanting *all* students to succeed.

Teachers need to see themselves as learners and to model lifelong learning skills before they can be truly learner centered.

Change cannot be forced—it must be learner centered and begin with those who are most comfortable and interested.

True change is "change of heart"—"keeping kids in front of us."

6

An Action Plan for Ongoing Learning and Change

Only in a learning community can adults and children together explore and practice the mutuality and reciprocity essential to sustaining human life and democratic society.
   —Joan Lipsitz, "Prologue: Why We Should Care About Caring," 1995

Culture is more than ways of doing; it also involves beliefs or interpretations. . . . Teachers need time and "permission" to talk and listen to their students and colleagues and to attend to their needs.
   —George W. Noblit, Dwight L. Rogers, and Brian M. McCadden, "In the Meantime: The Possibilities of Caring," 1995

Throughout this book, as we have looked at the need for learner-centered classrooms and schools, defined what learner centered means, discussed how it might look in practice in classrooms and schools, and talked about the journey of change toward becoming more learner centered, we have stressed the critical role of teachers' basic beliefs and assumptions about learners, learning, and teaching. One pivotal assumption in the learner-centered model is that it is important to acknowledge and honor students' perspectives about what *they* need to make learning more personally relevant, meaningful, and challenging, what *they* need to feel competent and supported in being successful in the learning process, and what *they* need in terms of alternative methods and special help when current methods are not working for them. By looking at and respecting students' perceptions of their teachers' educational practices, seeing how these perceptions differ from their teachers' perceptions of those practices, and identifying and dealing with the discrepancies between the two views, teachers can take the first step in their own personal change process. Through reflection, teachers can begin to identify areas in which change may have the most impact on individual student motivation, learning, and achievement.

Because the information revealed by the discrepancies between teachers' and students' beliefs and perceptions of practice is so critical to (1) motivation, learning, and achievement and (2) teachers' ability to identify areas of change likely to have high payoffs, we are devoting this final chapter to ways you can initiate a personal change process based on self-assessment and reflection. We will ask you to repeat the exercise that assesses your beliefs, reflecting on any differences between your responses now and the responses you gave in Chapter Two, and we will ask you to begin to articulate an action plan that can lead to or enhance your own learning, change, and increased leadership in becoming more learner centered.

Assessment of Personal Change: Tools for Taking Charge of Your Personal and Professional Growth and Development

In Chapter Five, we described how new models of professional development for teachers focus on empowerment, taking responsibility for one's own growth and professionalism, becoming leaders, developing higher-order thinking and problem-solving skills, and using personal reflection skills. A key to teachers' success with any of these new models is the availability of support for teachers as they develop the knowledge and skills necessary to understanding, accepting, and implementing the models. One source of such support is self-assessment tools that help teachers become more aware of their beliefs and practices and of the impact these beliefs and practices have on students. Self-assessment information may then be used by teachers—in a nonthreatening and nonjudgmental context—to identify the changes in practice that may better serve the learning needs of all students. By engaging in such reflection and self-assessment, teachers may take responsibility from the very beginning of the process for the creation of their own professional development plan.

The Learner-Centered Battery

How do you see yourself? How do you view your students? How do you perceive other teachers? How can you increase your impact on the motivation, learning, and achievement of all of your students? The Learner-Centered Battery (McCombs & Stiller, 1995) is a set of short self-assessment tools, or surveys, that may help educators answer these questions at the classroom and school levels.*

The battery consists of five surveys in all. The first two are for individual classroom teachers. The Teacher Beliefs Survey and the Teacher Practices Survey, respectively, help teachers assess (1) what they believe about learners, learning, and teaching; and (2) what they believe to be their instructional practices in the classroom. (You were introduced to the Teacher Beliefs Survey in Chapter Two and to the Teacher Practices Survey in Chapter Three.)

The third survey is for students. It tells teachers what each of their students experiences in their classroom. This tool helps teachers become aware of differences between what they think they are doing to assist learning and how what they are doing is perceived and experienced by each student. Discrepancies between student and teacher perceptions of classroom practice can then be plotted for four major domains: creating positive interpersonal relationships and classroom climate; honoring student voice, providing academic

---

*This section includes information from McCombs, Bishop, Jesse, and Peralez, *Test Manual for the Learner Centered Battery*, which will be published by the Mid-continent Regional Educational Laboratory (McREL) in 1997. The complete Learner-Centered Battery described here may be obtained from Barbara L. McCombs at McREL.

challenge, and encouraging perspective taking; encouraging higher order thinking and self-regulated learning; and adapting to individual differences among students.

The fourth survey is for peer teachers. It provides information about teachers' perceptions of each other's classroom practices, giving peer teachers a tool for reflecting on differences between their own and another's perceptions of their practice. More importantly, however, it gives teachers a source of information for discussions and *collaboration* on the differences between their own and their students' perceptions. In these discussions, it is essential that teachers learn to focus on seeing their practices from their students' perspectives if they are to improve student motivation, learning, and achievement. Becoming aware of how their students perceive and experience teacher practices in particular domains provides an impetus for change when teachers understand that it is students' perspectives that determine student motivation, learning, and achievement. By focusing on discrepancies between their own and their students' perceptions of practice, they gain important information about particular practices that can better meet the needs of each student.

The fifth survey is for school administrators and their faculties. It allows individuals to assess their own beliefs and perceptions of practices at the school level in the domains of instruction, motivation and expectations, curriculum, assessment, instructional management, staff development, and leadership and policy. The feedback allows administrators and faculty members to examine discrepancies between, on the one hand, their own beliefs about ideal practices and their assessment of actual school practices and, on the other hand, overall administrator and faculty beliefs and practices. This survey thus becomes a leadership tool for identifying which faculty members have differing perceptions and in what areas they differ in terms of both beliefs and practices. Discussion groups may be formed to discuss differences and to begin or strengthen the process of becoming a culture of caring, learning, change, and collaboration.

Why Is the Battery Important?

Administrators and teachers usually engage in practices that they think will be best for their students. Sometimes they are unaware of how these practices are perceived and experienced by others, particularly their students. It is valuable for teachers to have tools for becoming more aware of how their practices are perceived by those most important to them—their students and their peers. By using tools that increase their awareness and knowledge of the personal impact of their classroom practices on each of their students' learning experiences—and ultimately, students' motivation, learning, and achievement—teachers have information for making *self-initiated changes* that can improve the learning of *all* of their students. Similarly, it is valuable for administrators to have tools for becoming more aware of how school practices and policies are perceived by their staff. The battery thus becomes a mechanism for personal reflection and encourages a willingness to look at and change thinking and practices as necessary and appropriate.

What Is the Personal Payoff of Using Self-Assessment and Reflection Tools?

One of the greatest payoffs of using self-assessment tools is that teachers are able to take personal responsibility for their own growth and professional development. They are able to determine how they might best influence each of their students. This determination helps teachers focus their effort where it counts—on what matters to their students. They then are able to make the best use of their own resources—their time, energy, and talents. In addition, knowing the personal impact teachers have on their students and being able to have a positive impact on more students can potentially revitalize teachers' sense of personal control, accomplishment, and professionalism. These benefits, plus the empowerment that results from diagnosing and meeting their own needs, help reduce feelings of frustration and professional burnout. Teachers can recapture the joy and excitement that initially brought them into the field.

For administrators, the self-assessment tools help them identify those teachers who have different views of what should be and what is in practice at the school level. Administrators are thus able to see areas of difference that need to be addressed if they are to build a learning community committed to developing a culture of caring, learning, change, and collaboration. Like teachers, administrators receive information that allows them to tailor their leadership practices so as to foster personal trust, quality relationships, and commitment to lifelong learning—elements that are so important to the development of learner-centered classrooms and schools. Acting on this information can therefore have the personal payoff for administrators of renewing their excitement as they create schools that are more in touch with the general vision of a learner-centered school and their personal vision of making a difference with more students. Administrators can also capture the excitement that comes from watching others grow and change.

Reassessing Your Own Beliefs

In Chapter One, we asked you to take a look at your beliefs about learning, learners, and teaching by completing a self-assessment survey. As a way for you to examine any changes in your thinking that may have occurred as a result of considering issues raised so far in this book, this chapter provides you with an opportunity to reassess these beliefs to see whether they are substantially the same as they were in Chapter One, substantially different, or somewhere in between. We will then suggest how you can use this information to inform a personal action plan for change. Please take a few minutes to engage in the self-assessment exercise (Teacher Beliefs Survey) in Exhibit 6.1. Again, the more truthful you can be and the more you can resist the temptation to give what you believe to be "acceptable" or "right answers," the more useful you will find the results of this exercise.

EXHIBIT 6.1 Teacher Beliefs Survey.

Please read each of the following statements. Then decide the extent to which you agree or disagree. Circle the number to the right of the question that best matches your choice. Go with your first judgment and do not spend much time mulling over any one statement. PLEASE ANSWER EVERY QUESTION.

	Strongly Disagree	Somewhat Disagree	Somewhat Agree	Strongly Agree
1. Students have more respect for teachers they see and can relate to as real people, not just as teachers.	1	2	3	4
2. There are some students whose personal lives are so dysfunctional that they simply do not have the capability to learn.	1	2	3	4
3. I can't allow myself to make mistakes with my students.	1	2	3	4
4. Students achieve more in classes in which teachers encourage them to express their personal beliefs and feelings.	1	2	3	4
5. Too many students expect to be coddled in school.	1	2	3	4
6. If students are not doing well, they need to go back to the basics and do more drill and skill development.	1	2	3	4
7. In order to maximize learning, I need to help students feel comfortable in discussing their feelings and beliefs.	1	2	3	4
8. It's impossible to work with students who refuse to learn.	1	2	3	4
9. No matter how bad a teacher feels, he or she has a responsibility not to let students know about those feelings.	1	2	3	4

	Strongly Disagree	Somewhat Disagree	Somewhat Agree	Strongly Agree
10. Addressing students' social, emotional, and physical needs is just as important to learning as meeting their intellectual needs.	1	2	3	4
11. Even with feedback, some students just can't figure out their mistakes.	1	2	3	4
12. My most important job as a teacher is to help students meet well-established standards of what it takes to succeed.	1	2	3	4
13. Taking the time to create caring relationships with my students is the most important element for student achievement.	1	2	3	4
14. I can't help feeling upset and inadequate when dealing with difficult students.	1	2	3	4
15. If I don't prompt and provide direction for student questions, students won't get the right answer.	1	2	3	4
16. Helping students understand how their beliefs about themselves influence learning is as important as working on their academic skills.	1	2	3	4
17. It's just too late to help some students.	1	2	3	4
18. Knowing my subject matter really well is the most important contribution I can make to student learning.	1	2	3	4
19. I can help students who are uninterested in learning get in touch with their natural motivation to learn.	1	2	3	4

EXHIBIT 6.1 (*continued*)

	Strongly Disagree	Somewhat Disagree	Somewhat Agree	Strongly Agree
20. No matter what I do or how hard I try, there are some students who are unreachable.	1	2	3	4
21. Knowledge of the subject area is the most important part of being an effective teacher.	1	2	3	4
22. Students will be more motivated to learn if teachers get to know them at a personal level.	1	2	3	4
23. Innate ability is fairly fixed and some children just can't learn as well as others.	1	2	3	4
24. One of the most important things I can teach students is how to follow rules and to do what is expected of them in the classroom.	1	2	3	4
25. When teachers are relaxed and comfortable with themselves, they have access to a natural wisdom for dealing with even the most difficult classroom situations.	1	2	3	4
26. Teachers shouldn't be expected to work with students who consistently cause problems in class.	1	2	3	4
27. Good teachers always know more than their students.	1	2	3	4
28. Being willing to share who I am as a person with my students facilitates learning more than being an authority figure.	1	2	3	4

	Strongly Disagree	Somewhat Disagree	Somewhat Agree	Strongly Agree
29. I know best what students need to know and what's important; students should take my word that something will be relevant to them.	1	2	3	4
30. My acceptance of myself as a person is more central to my classroom effectiveness than the comprehensiveness of my teaching skills.	1	2	3	4
31. For effective learning to occur, I need to be in control of the direction of learning.	1	2	3	4
32. Accepting students where they are—no matter what their behavior and academic performance—makes them more receptive to learning.	1	2	3	4
33. I am responsible for what students learn and how they learn.	1	2	3	4
34. Seeing things from the students' point of view is the key to their good performance in school.	1	2	3	4
35. I believe that just listening to students in a caring way helps them solve their own problems.	1	2	3	4

Source: Developed by Mid-continent Regional Educational Laboratory (McREL), 1994. Reprinted with permission of McREL.

Comparison and Reflection on Results
(Chapter One and Chapter Six Differences)

To score your responses, refer again to the information in Appendix A. Compare your present results to those from Chapter One for each of the three factors described in the scoring instructions, looking to see whether your scores went up, down, or stayed the same. Take a few minutes to consider and reflect upon the items you rated differently this time from the first time. What is your reaction to the change? Why do you think your responses changed? What difference, if any, does or will this change make for you and your students? What thoughts or insights do you have about yourself, your students, teaching and learning, your role, and so on as a result of your reflection on your reassessment?

It is important to keep in mind that most teachers do not fall totally within one profile or the other but share some attributes of each. In general, however, we have found that teachers who tend more toward the non-learner-centered profile are likely to believe they should direct what students learn and how students learn it, that they should assert their authority, that it is best to concentrate on building students' intellectual capacity, and that they should focus on getting through the required curriculum.

Those who tend more toward the learner-centered profile focus on the student and the student's frame of reference. Such inclusion of the student generally means there is better communication and cooperation with the student. These teachers are more likely to believe they should take into account what students want to learn, include students in the setting of learning goals, and support students as they bring about their own learning, sometimes individually and sometimes in cooperative groups. These teachers are more inclined to believe they should draw on students' unique experiences, talents, capacities, and strengths to bring about desired learning outcomes—that is, they focus on learning outcomes desired by both teacher and student. Learner-centered teachers also have a propensity to believe that they should cultivate not just intellectual but also social and emotional growth within and among students.

As we have pointed out a number of times now, underlying teachers' actions and practices are their beliefs about learners, learning, and teaching. In fact, in our research with the Learner-Centered Battery (McCombs, Ridley, & Stiller, 1995; McCombs & Stiller, 1995), we found that when teachers' beliefs about learners were non–learner centered (that is, when teachers did not believe that all students can be helped to learn), then students tended to perceive classroom practices in negative ways. And when student perceptions were negative, both student motivation and classroom achievement were low. Thus, although it is also important for teachers to assess differences between their own and their students' perceptions of classroom practice, becoming more aware of non-learner-centered beliefs is crucial if teachers are to have a positive impact on each student's motivation and achievement. Once teachers identify the beliefs they hold that are non–learner centered, they can examine them in terms of their consistency with the research base on learners and learning as represented in the learner-centered psychological principles. You may now wish to go back to the comparison you made between your responses to the first and second Teacher Beliefs Survey and to reconsider this information in the context of creating a personal action plan for change. We suggest that you pay particular attention to how you responded to items for factor 3, non-learner-centered beliefs about learners.

No Change in Assessment Results. It is possible that your scores on the three belief factors did not change much from your first to second self-assessment. Take note of those items to which you did respond differently. Note the direction of these changes and whether they are now more consistent with the research we have presented in this book. Ask yourself if there are some areas you might want to reexamine and, perhaps, specifically plan to address.

More Learner Centered in the Second Assessment. It is likely that your scores on the second survey are higher (or more learner centered) than on the first survey. We believe this is a positive sign. It indicates that you have altered your thinking in some ways—ways that are likely to show up in more learner-centered practices in your classrooms or schools. Again, you may wish to note specific items that have changed and reflect on how these changes might manifest themselves in changed practices in your classroom or school.

Less Learner Centered in the Second Assessment.   Occasionally teachers' beliefs actually become less learner centered between the first and second assessment. If this is so for you, it may be that you disagree with your previous answers or that you have altered your thinking in some way. For whatever reason, we hope you might be willing to reevaluate your beliefs in the context of the research we have presented—especially if your goal is to enhance the motivation, learning, and achievement of all your students. Note those beliefs that you think may be contrary to the learner-centered psychological principles by looking at the items that define learner-centered beliefs in factor 1 (as shown in Appendix A); these beliefs indicate areas you may be willing to further explore on your own, discuss with colleagues, or plan to change.

Creating a Vision and Plan for Change

To get started with a plan for change, it is first helpful to create a vision that can become the magnet that draws you toward a new future.

Your Vision for Change

Many teachers we have worked with use the information from the Teacher Beliefs Survey in the Learner-Centered Battery, as we are suggesting to you, to identify areas they would like to change or strengthen, and then to create a personal plan for change. Most of the teachers have begun by creating a vision of the teacher they would like to be, the difference they would like to be making with all their students, the way their classrooms would look if they were successful in enhancing motivation, learning, and achievement for all of their students, and the like. We recommend that you create your own personal vision, one that fits with, furthers, and exemplifies the changes you would like to make. This vision should be described as clearly as possible, as if it is happening now, and should include statements about what you are doing, what your students are doing, and what results are being produced. For example, one teacher we know described her vision in the following way:

> I see myself as a teacher kids feel comfortable talking with— both in the classroom and around the school. I feel respected and I also respect my students. I challenge students to do their best and they tell me that I make a real difference in their lives. Other teachers in my building are starting to come to see my classroom and talk to me about the strategies I'm using to involve students in their own learning. My students do so well on the end-of-course test that a local newspaper interviews me and I receive a special award. My students surprise me with a party!

As you can see, a vision is not just a single statement. It is most effective when it is a powerful story that can inspire and reenergize a commitment to change.

One last word about *your* vision. Be sure to create a vision that reflects something you are committed to. That is, when considering changes in beliefs and practices, select those that are really important to you, those that you are willing to work for. Likewise, create a vision based on those changes that "turn you on," that will get you up in the morning, that you will be willing to "fight" for. Once you have created such a vision, it can continually inspire and energize you as you pursue your commitment to change.

Your Personal Plan for Change

Once you have formulated a clear and compelling vision, one you are truly committed to, you are ready to develop a personal plan. To create your personal action plan, start with notes you have made about any changes in your beliefs. This action plan may take any number of forms. Exhibit 6.2 illustrates a planning guide that many teachers and administrators have found useful.

If you wish to use this format, start by stating a specific area you would like to change or enhance in either your beliefs or practices. Note that area in the first column. For the area you select, outline what steps you would take or the process you would go through to make the change and list them in the second column. The third column is used to outline steps you might want to take to monitor how well you are doing as a result of the change in terms of increased student motivation, learning, and achievement. As a way to enhance your effectiveness in making the change, specify in the fourth column strategies you might use to model how to make the change or to mentor other teachers. Finally, the fifth column is used to outline actions you might take to maintain, sustain, or further the changes you are making so that you will do what is necessary to continuously improve student outcomes.

Exhibit 6.3 is an example of how this action planning guide might look for a particular area of change: in this case, creating student teams within a large high school to increase students' feelings of belonging. In this example, the area "create student teams" is named in column 1. In column 2, the teacher has listed three action steps she will take to further formulate her personal change process. For monitoring the effectiveness of this change in practice (column 3), the teacher is going to use the Learner-Centered Battery, and she has noted steps to follow in using the battery. Another part of her plan involves how she will use modeling and mentoring strategies to create more effective teams; these steps are specified in column 4. Finally, the action steps chosen to sustain the plan are specified in the column 5. Reviewing this sample can familiarize you with the important pieces of an effective action plan.

Identifying and Dealing with Barriers and Resistance

It is all well and good to talk about creating learner-centered classrooms and schools, assessing and changing one's beliefs and practices,

Exhibit 6.2 Action Planning Guide.

Area of Change Toward Learner-Centered Practice	Personal Change Process: Action Steps	Monitoring Strategies: Action Steps	Modeling and Mentoring Strategies: Action Steps	Sustaining the Change Process: Action Steps

EXHIBIT 6.3 Example of Completed Action Planning Guide.

Area of Change Toward Learner-Centered Practice	Personal Change Process: Action Steps	Monitoring Strategies: Action Steps	Modeling and Mentoring Strategies: Action Steps	Sustaining the Change Process: Action Steps	
Create student teams where students stay with the same group of teachers and students for multiple years	1. Discuss with administration, students, and faculty 2. Create pros and cons from each group's perspective 3. Find models of schools with successful team approach	1. Use entire Learner-Centered Battery as pretest before starting 2. Schedule periodic re-assessment with battery 3. Implement team model in a pilot team of teacher and students 4. Analyze results and decide how well team approach is working	1. Create schoolwide teacher teams aligned with student teams 2. Discuss various mentoring strategies 3. Choose mentoring approach to help other teachers with teaming based on preferred approach of each team	1. Arrange schedule for teacher inquiry groups to discuss how to make teaming better 2. Decide on structure to support teachers and to provide ongoing learning and research on best practices 3. Design process for ongoing evaluation of teaming	

committing oneself to learning and change, and even generating an action plan. In the real world of education, however, as teachers engage in this journey they often find that it is "easier said than done." Inevitably, they meet reticence within themselves and encounter both resistance from others and barriers in the system—all of which thwart attempts to move forward. It is important therefore for teachers and administrators to anticipate such reticence, resistance, and barriers by identifying what is likely to surface and thinking in advance about how they might effectively deal with these potential obstacles or situations. That way, at least, teachers may not be taken by surprise and may, in being prepared, (1) be more effective in heading off the potential negative effects of any resistance and barriers and (2) actually be more successful in bringing about desired changes at both the personal and systems levels.

A helpful process for handling situations in which a problem or issue arises and there is a difference between your goals and those of others is called a *force field analysis* (Lewin, 1951). This process is based on the idea that social or psychological problems or issues exist because opposing forces are keeping them "in place." The force field analysis is helpful in identifying forces that are working for and against your goals, thus putting resistances and obstacles in a context in which they may be more clearly articulated and, ultimately, addressed. You start by writing your goal (for example, "to become a more learner-centered school"). You then write down all the important "forces" that could help you achieve this goal. That is, you list all of the things—situations, beliefs, people, policies, practices, and so on—that might work in favor of your achieving this goal. Next you think about what could get in the way of your reaching this goal and write these obstacles down also. Try to be as specific as possible. For example, instead of "poor communication" write "teachers don't have opportunities to discuss their beliefs and examine differences in their practices." Consider categories of forces in yourself, in others, in special groups, and the like. Exhibit 6.4 illustrates a completed force-field analysis.

Once you have identified "for" and "against" forces, you must break the balance, so to speak. That is, you must change strengths of

Exhibit 6.4 Example of Completed Force Field Analysis.

Goal: Become a More Learner-Centered School	
Forces for My Goal	Forces Against My Goal
Several teachers who are well respected and seen as leaders are learner centered and are in favor of the school becoming more learner centered.	Several teachers see this goal as too affective; they're only interested in their content.
We have money for staff development.	There is a general reaction to change and innovation: "This, too, shall pass." People therefore tend not to take new ideas seriously.
Our test scores went down, so people acknowledge the importance of doing something.	Our community is very pro "back to basics." It wants increased test scores and more focus on reading, writing, and math.
Staff are committed to improving student achievement.	There is no agreement on a vision or way to increase student achievement.

forces, change directions of forces, eliminate against forces, or add for forces so that the balance of forces favors your goal. Examples of actions that might be taken to break the balance described in Exhibit 6.4 are shown in Exhibit 6.5 in boldface. Breaking the balance is particularly important when there are more againsts than fors or when specific critical forces for the goal do not exist. In the previous example of a force field analysis (Exhibit 6.4), for example, "principal is in favor of the change" is an important but missing force.

Brainstorming is a process that may be useful in generating ideas for dealing with the forces. Remember that in brainstorming there

Exhibit 6.5 Example of Breaking the Balance in a Force Field Analysis.

Goal: Become a More Learner-Centered School

Forces for My Goal	*Forces Against My Goal*
Several teachers who are well respected and seen as leaders are learner centered and are in favor of the school becoming more learner centered. **Ask them to do little action research projects and share their results and excitement with others.**	Several teachers see this goal as too affective; they're only interested in their content. **Bring examples of research and case studies that show that student achievement in content areas rises with learner-centered practitioners and practices; have teachers consider their own experience.**
We have money for staff development.	There is a general reaction to change and innovation: "This, too, shall pass." People therefore tend not to take new ideas seriously. **Dialogue about innovations from the past that have "passed away." Have teachers identify elements that they still use or do because they make a difference with students.**
Our test scores went down, so people acknowledge the importance of doing something.	Our community is very pro "back to basics." It wants increased test scores and more focus on reading, writing, and math. **Provide information that demonstrates the positive difference that learner-centered practices and practitioners have**

Exhibit 6.5 (*continued*).

	made in student achievement of basic knowledge and skills.
Staff are committed to improving student achievement.	There is no agreement on a vision or way to increase student achievement. **Given that the principal is not "on board," find a teacher-leader who's respected by the principal. Try to gain support of principal through this person and his or her interactions and sharing.**

are no bad ideas. This means no one evaluates any of the suggestions until the brainstorming process is over. The force field analysis is a powerful vehicle for *anticipating* problems and solutions, thus empowering you to be proactive. It is equally useful for dealing with problems that arise during the change process.

Another useful process for anticipating and dealing with change and potential resistance is the concerns based adoption model (Research and Development Center for Teacher Education, 1979). It suggests that change progresses in stages, each of which is characterized by a different set of concerns. Briefly, the stages may be described as follows:

1. People want information about the change and want to know what it will do for them.

2. People then shift to more personal concerns such as what risks they might have to take, what the change might mean to them in terms of workload, and so on.

3. People next want to know how the change works, what exactly they have to do (this is a "mechanical use" level).

4. People then shift their attention to performance, wanting to know if the change is producing the desired outcome. It is during this stage that commitment to the change is developed.

5. Finally, once the change is integrated, people look for ways to improve the innovation.

Being aware of, monitoring, and responding appropriately to these levels of concern is important and can head off obstacles. (CBAM also has usefulness as a means to determine the level of *use* of an innovation; it also provides valuable evaluation information as educators begin to implement particular changes.)

There are many other vehicles and processes for dealing with potential barriers to change. We highlighted two that could be easily discussed here. The important point is, we believe, to be aware of and anticipate potential problems before they occur and before you are "up to your eyebrows in alligators," or obstacles. Your *commitment* to learning and change, coupled with an intelligent evaluation of the situation at hand, makes effective change more likely.

Finally, as you deal with internal and external pressures to change or run into barriers or resistance with the potential to hinder your plans for change toward more learner-centered beliefs and practices, the words of Margaret Metzger (1996), a veteran teacher of twenty-five years, may be helpful. She provided the following advice to student teachers as they move from competence to excellence, but it is also appropriate for experienced teachers striving to become more learner centered:

Be gentle and fair with yourselves, help students take responsibility for their own learning, give students the message that education is important, help students be dedicated to their own growth and willing to take academic risks, convey a passion for a discipline or idea, be truthful about what is important to learn, emphasize how to learn rather than what to learn, empower students by including them in the process of teaching and learning, explain the purpose of every assignment, model that you are a member of a community of learners, connect classroom learning to the outside world, challenge students to think carefully about their assumptions, help students ask the big questions and give them the big ideas, help students envision their own futures, control your workload by helping students do more of the work and having them take more control and responsibility, give students multiple opportunities to master skills, keep pushing students to not be passive and to be thoughtful and responsible, take care of yourself by keeping your mind enriched by learning and cultural events and by maintaining a life.

Good advice, isn't it? We invite you to keep it in mind on your journey toward ongoing learning and change toward learner-centered teaching.

Getting the Support You Need

It is hard to change by yourself, and it is hard to keep a vision alive without support from others. As we learned from our learner-centered teachers, it is critical to form networks and inquiry groups within your school. When the focus is on the learner and the learning process, teachers themselves have to stay vitalized as learners. One way to keep passion and vision alive is through ongoing dialogue, research, and the search for ever-better solutions that may enhance the motivation, learning, and achievement of all students. We encourage you to share this book with your colleagues and invite them to consider their own beliefs and practices and to join you in your journey toward creating more learner-centered classrooms and schools.

Getting Support from Your Administration.   Administrators can offer support for teachers' own learning as well as for their intellectual, emotional, social, and behavioral development. The factors that encourage the growth, development, and self-regard of a school's staff are the same as those necessary for fostering these attributes in students in a classroom (McCombs, 1991; McCombs & Whisler, 1989; Sarason, 1990). However, teachers may find themselves in settings in which administrators' beliefs are insufficiently learner centered: for example, rather than involving teachers in decision making administrators may think it is up to them to structure the school so that teachers know how they should operate within it. Under these circumstances, teachers need to remember that the best strategy to encourage change in others is one that is invitational and nonthreatening. That is, even if it is one teacher all alone who gets started with learner-centered practices in a school, he can win others over by the model he provides and the successes he has with students in terms of higher motivation, learning, and achievement.

It is important to remember that administrators are empowered to share their control over instructional decisions with teachers only to the degree to which *they* are supported by district- and state-level administration in implementing policies that focus on students rather than solely on performance goals tied to accountability (see for example, Ames, 1992; Maehr, 1992; Dweck & Legget, 1988; Meece, 1991). Unfortunately, policymakers, particularly at the state level, often send conflicting messages. For example, policies sometimes require schools administrators to develop personalized learning environments and encourage team teaching and cooperative learning while also demanding tests that focus on rote memorization and promote directive teaching (Darling-Hammond & McLaughlin, 1995). If teachers understand the larger contexts in which decisions are being made, they may be able to better deal with frustrations that arise when things do not change as quickly as or in the directions they would like.

Getting Parent and Community Support and Advocacy.   Beyond the support teachers can get from administrators, however, it is also essential that teachers understand the importance of gaining support from parents and the community for learner-centered practices at the classroom and schools levels. For teachers to get this support and advocacy, they must first of all recognize that being learner centered means having a commitment to working closely with parents and community members, welcoming them into the school, and inviting their participation in meaningful ways. Teachers themselves can take the lead in identifying in-service training opportunities that will help them better understand the important roles that parents and community members play in the effective education of students. They can learn how to obtain parental and community involvement and advocacy for learner-centered education.

Engendering advocacy for any innovation requires education. That is, people are unlikely to support anything new or different unless they understand what difference such a change might make or why it is needed. Thus, providing information about the benefits of learner-centered classrooms and schools to parents and community members is the first step toward gaining their support. Information may be disseminated in written form, through meetings, or via observations of learner-centered practices in action—live or as captured by video or film. Such information might include research data about the impact of learner-centered practices on student motivation, learning, and achievement as well as descriptions of what learner-centered classrooms and schools look like. We have listed in the Appendix B several video programs that we developed for use in the education of parents and community members. The video program . . . *And Learning For All* can be particularly helpful for parents and community members, letting them see what learner-centered practices look like and how these practices enhance student motivation, learning, and achievement.

Once information is disseminated, it is important to invite and encourage discussions, questions, and input from parents and community members. It is necessary both to access their thoughts and ideas *and* to develop buy-in and support. This is also a practice consistent with the learner-centered psychological principles and the constructive nature of learning. Only if parents and community members are a *vital* and *real* part of the process of defining the change will they become supporters and advocates of learner-centered practices at the classroom and school levels. Not enough can be said about the criticality of this support and advocacy. It is not uncommon for new ideas and innovations to be dismantled by a public that neither understood nor bought into a proposed (or even already instituted) change. But beyond this practical reason for gaining support and advocacy, parents and the public *ought to be* an important part of a school community—particularly one that considers itself to be learner centered. And they often bring a different and valuable perspective as well as fresh ideas to the table.

Finally, we want to note the important and unique role parents and community members can play in responding to dissent from other parents and the community. People who vocalize concern and opposition to change are often more open to information and explanations from one of their own than from school staff, who may be regarded as the "them" in a "we versus them" view. Furthermore, in their book about how differences in worldviews, philosophies, and values can underlie conflict between the public and educators over educational change, Gaddy, Hall, and Marzano (1996, p. 213) state: "The roots of any successful response to criticisms of educational materials and programs can be found in the school's ongoing efforts toward developing a strong sense of community among parents, teachers, administrators, community members, and students. A vital community with an established network of working relationships has laid groundwork to successfully deal with controversies should they arise." Perhaps the best advice of all that Gaddy, Hall, and Marzano offer is that teachers and administrators spend time getting to know parents and community members in one-to-one sessions that build trust and mutual respect. Once participant partnerships are established, the job of community building becomes a reality. It is from this larger community of educators, parents, and the public that viable change comes about.

Keeping the Vision Alive

One defining attribute of learner-centered practice as we have explored it throughout this book is its concern with individual learner needs and its valuing of the rich diversity of learners' backgrounds, talents, experiences, and perspectives. We have seen that when learner-centered practices are implemented, students know it and are able to describe their experiences quite eloquently. Here are a few of the comments we have heard from students we have talked with during our exploration of what learner centered means from the students' perspectives. Consider these comments as "clips" or "scenes" from visions that inspired learner-centered classrooms and schools.

> The teacher listens, understands. In Miss Johnson's English class, it's just like a big family. We have disagreements and we argue over it and she basically says we're both right. And she gives her point of view, we argue a little bit more, which gives more points of view of how to look at it, and she sits there as a chairman and just makes sure there's no fist fights or anything like that. Because she says everyone's right and there's no wrong answer. It's all our point of view, how we see it.

> This is the first class I've ever had where they asked us questions, like, you know: "Guys, how do you feel about doing this? How does this work in what you're doing? Does this help you out? Will this help you remember for the essay test?" We had a lot of interaction between teacher and student because they wanted our feedback so they could make the upcoming block schedule easier and better for their students. I like that. I like expressing my opinion. It's not the same as being told "just sit down and do the work." We had a lot of interaction between student and parent . . . and teacher.

> This class, it's challenging. It's challenging, but it's not one of the ones where you say, "Oh God, I'm not going to pass." The

teachers help you out to where they make sure you don't fail. 'Cause that's what Mr. McDonald first said when we first got here. "Nobody is going to fail this class. Nobody." He goes, "The only way you'll fail is if you just come in here and sit and not do anything." And none of us do that. We sit in here you know like everyday, you know, like quit talking—we want to get to work. And we just come in here and we just start working. It just seems like the teacher is there to help us out. And in my case when I have another class, I look at that class like this one. So I'll start doing the projects like I do in this class. Start researching, making models, making this, making that. And it just makes them classes even better.

Listening to these students' voices is a reminder that educational needs be personalized and learner differences taken seriously. As Gardner (1995) argues, a uniform educational approach will serve only a minority of students, unlike a school set up to address a wide range of individual differences in learners. He states: "I would be happy to send my children to a school with the following characteristics: differences among youngsters are taken seriously, knowledge about differences is shared with children and parents, children gradually assume responsibility for their own learning, and materials that are worth knowing are presented in ways that afford each child the maximum opportunity to master those materials and to show others (and themselves) what they have learned and understood" (p. 208).

If educators are to design an educational system and classroom practices that meet the academic and personal needs of each learner, we have argued that it is beneficial for them to understand the research base on learners and learning. The learner-centered psychological principles may be seen as a framework for describing this research base, the base that becomes a foundation for designing a personalized educational system. We think you will find, as you begin your process of becoming more learner centered, that you will have increasing support among your colleagues and in the world outside school—support that will help you keep the vision alive. As evidence that such support for learning-centered education is increasing, consider, for example, a recent report from the National Association of Secondary School Principals (1996) about two years of reviewing research and conferring with educators. The report recommends that instruction and other services be tailored to students' individual needs. It points to the impersonal nature of high schools in particular, which the report asserts leaves too many students alienated from the learning process, and it concludes that "future schools must be much more student-centered and, above all, more personalized in programs, support services and intellectual rigor" (p. 54). We would go further and recommend that schools be *learner centered* and personalized for *all* learners, including teachers and administrators.

The learner-centered psychological principles have powerful implications for creating new visions of instruction, curriculum, assessment, teacher education, parent and community involvement, and educational policy. The following story shows how two high schools that we studied kept their visions alive.

A large urban high school in a low-income culturally diverse community decided that to best meet the needs of all students in their school, the school needed to create smaller units of students that would stay together with teams of teachers over the four years of high school. Teachers and administrators believed this strategy would allow students who had little or no "family" of their own but had high needs for belonging to connect with both their teachers and peers. This connection would, they thought, create a positive environment for learning, reduce feelings of alienation, and help keep students in school. Across town in the same urban school district, the neighborhood consisted primarily of families with high income in a racially homogeneous community where families tended to be intact and actively supportive of learning. However, students in this school were often bored in class and did not always learn to their capacity. Here, a learner centered approach focused on helping students see school as relevant to their personal interests and goals. The staff at this school believed that they had to begin with a focus on redefining the curriculum so that it included topics relevant to students, integrated multiple disciplines, and was challenging for all students.

Both these schools reflect a learner-centered perspective. Their visions differed in where they started because they were based on the different needs and issues of the students and communities involved. In both cases, however, the visions were kept alive by responsiveness to particular needs of students and the communities around the school.

At this point, you have probably created a conceptual understanding of what it takes to transform practice in the direction of a learner-centered model. To further show how such a goal might become a reality and to spark, inspire, and help keep alive your own vision, we present an interview with Janell Cleland from Mundelein High School in Illinois. Cleland was one of the initiators of the transformation of the school's English department and an inspirer of teachers in other departments to become more learner centered themselves. As a teacher with fifteen years experience, Cleland exemplifies many educators who have gradually evolved their practice into a commitment to a learner-centered model. Her reflections about the challenges, realities, and rewards she has encountered as she and her colleagues shifted to a learner-centered perspective offer enlightenment about this educational journey.

Q: *When did you become interested in a learner-centered model of teaching?*
A: Well, I was fortunate enough to work with a teacher before I came to Mundelein who was very concerned that we not teach anything in the classroom that students couldn't use outside of it. Then I came to Mundelein and met a colleague who had been really looking into how to better reach students in her classroom. Three years ago, the administration pulled the two of us together and asked us to target juniors and seniors who were below grade level in reading, writing, or

both—but not so far below that they received any type of support. These were students who generally kind of fall between the cracks. The administration told us we could have free rein. They just let us experiment with what we thought would improve the students' reading and writing. It turns out that what we were doing was consistent with the learner-centered psychological principles that we found later and worked with more formally. And it worked! Then two years ago, we got a new superintendent, and she further supported our work. She began to say that if the curriculum and instruction are working so well with the juniors and seniors in this classroom, why doesn't the entire English department look like this? And so began an entire reform movement in the English department to become, what we later discovered, was more learner centered.

In this vein, we now begin the school year using the first nine weeks getting to know each other and building a learning community. We want the students to get to know the students across from them and the people at their tables so they can get insights into and from each other. It's not easy for them to come together and appreciate each other. We spend a lot of time just creating an atmosphere in our classroom where the kids feel safe to share, where their ideas are not scoffed at, and where they can learn to take responsibility for their own learning.

The other big difference is that we changed the way we viewed ourselves. I began to see myself as a co-learner and realize that I don't have all the answers. I have an answer, but so do all my students. And if we work together, then we become co-learners and more of a community, rather than teacher-performer, student-listener.

Q: *What did you and your colleagues do to begin?*

A: Our superintendent allowed us a year of research so we could learn what we needed to do to meet the needs of all freshmen. Usually high school teachers have a fifty-minute period a day where they have a study hall period or whatever. Our superintendent said we should use that fifty minutes a day to research and log in our journals some of the things that we were discovering about learning. It was during this time that I first saw a rough draft of *Learner-Centered Psychological Principles*. Those principles and the research we did to further support each principle provided us with the knowledge base we used as we began the task of redesigning our curriculum and instruction. So we used the learner-centered psychological principles to guide our thinking about what we taught and how we taught it to individual learners.

Our department then met as professionals throughout the year to discuss how we might implement what we were finding out about motivation and learning in our classrooms. A core of eight teachers really felt strongly that we were moving in the right direction and were very excited about the changes that might take place. Now we meet once a week as a team.

Q: *Would you say that all of you are united in this process?*

A: No, not yet. It's a slow process. I think we are still amazed at how far we've come in the year and one-half that the new curriculum and instruction have been underway. I think every teacher has grown immensely but that we still have probably a few that are a little reluctant about the changes that we're making and are more comfortable with the methods that they were using.

Q: *How do you know being learner centered is better for your students?*

A: One of our goals was to really improve students' attitudes toward reading and writing. So one of the things that we instituted initially was an attitude survey that we administered to our students three times a year. What we are beginning to see is that our students do love to read and reading a novel every day is just a part of life for them. Last year, we charted the number of novels that our students read and they skyrocketed.

Q: *Do you have any numbers on that?*

A: At first, students, on average, said they read one to three novels per grading period. When they left us they were circling the highest response which was eight or more novels—so that was a number that was very encouraging for us.

agreements

Another one of the strongest components of our program was the reflective writing component. This is where students step back and look at their learning. They also talk about what's working for them and where they can apply the strategies that they are learning. I don't believe I have ever had such a strong feeling that students were able to read and write across all their content areas. They were able to give very specific examples of where their reading and writing had improved in history and in biology.

Application had never been part of my teaching. Now application is a very important component to what we are doing. I don't think in my earlier years of teaching that my students really owned their learning. I don't think they knew what was working for them and why it was working and how they could reproduce that. Occasionally students would hand in a good paper, but not consistently because they didn't know what they were doing that made it good. Now I really believe that our freshmen have a very strong understanding and can put that in place.

Q: *Well, I've heard you say many things about how it works for the students and why you believe that it's a helpful approach. What about for you?*

A: I'm probably more stimulated that I have ever been in my entire career. It's very hard for us in the English department to even go down to eat lunch with another group of people because we are so excited about what we are doing. It seems we have so many exciting ideas to share that whenever we have a free minute, we want to spend that time together, figuring out what to do with these new ideas. I don't ever remember being that enthusiastic when I was using traditional curriculum and instruction. I remember lunches where we did a lot of complaining but that doesn't happen in our office anymore. So for me, I think that's been the most invigorating part—so that in my professional life I think I'm really modeling what I'm hoping the students are taking away from my classroom.

Q: *How has your teaching changed since you were more conventional or traditional?*

A: Probably the boldest difference is that before, I put the responsibility for learning solely on my shoulders. I prepared everything very carefully. I tested, graded papers, recorded them, returned the test, and then started all over again. I was so busy being very prepared that students kind of got lost in the whole process. I loved my students as people but my classroom demeanor would not have reflected that. So I think it's the responsibility that I took for learning and seeing myself as a learner, too—that's what has changed.

Q: *What's the biggest change that you personally had to overcome in order to be more learner centered?*

A: The biggest change, probably the scariest change, is that I have to accept my students and take them from where they come to me. I'm somewhat embarrassed to admit it now, but I frequently came back from the summer with everything done for the first semester and I hadn't met one single student yet. Now I know I have to meet my students first, and I have to take them from where they are to that next step. I gave up some control and that was initially a little scary.

Q: *How could administrators help teachers to be more learner centered?*

A: That's a hard question for me to answer. I think what teachers are most fearful of is that move from the front of the classroom, because they think that when administrators walk into the room, they expect to see you in front of the class disseminating information. I think initially what administrators can do is to be very supportive of new strategies, to be very supportive of those small steps that teachers make as they move from the front of the class to becoming kind of one of the co-learners in the class.

Q: *What about parents?*

A: I think as a school district you have to be very conscientious about parent input and informing parents about some of the decisions you're making because what they are going to see their children doing doesn't look like traditional homework. So we did some informational meetings for parents. We set up some sample classrooms where eighth-grade parents could see literature discussions in action, where they could see authoring circles in action. We had a room of freshmen talking, letting parents ask freshmen what this was all about. We also had a room where last year's freshmen parents could answer the questions of the incoming freshmen parents.

Q: *If a more conventional teacher wanted to become more learner centered, what's the first thing you would recommend to that person?*

A: First of all, my advice is to be excited about those first small steps that you take to change your classroom—taking those little steps and seeing how they all accumulate. One of the other things I suggest first is giving students more choice. Instead of saying, "Tomorrow we are going to read this novel," why not say, "Here are two novels. Which one would you prefer to read?"—rather than directing everything. Just begin to look at the ways in which students can have voice. But at the same time, keep some of the things that work well for you until you are comfortable taking that next step. I really feel the frustration comes when you try to do too much too fast. Then you're just certain that this isn't the way to go.

Q: *Among the people who read this interview, some are not going to be learner centered. Some are going to be very learner centered. And some will be someplace in between. So let's take those that are in between. Do you have any advice to them? Our hunch is that they are in a lonely position?*

A: I think that many times the people in the middle are people who have been operating from a gut feeling. They know what they are doing is right, they know that they have the concerns of their students at heart. However, they haven't made the tie between what they know feels right and what we understand about learning. That's the next step for these people, for them to tie their application—their "what feels right"—to research. For me, that was the biggest revelation and the most exciting part of my move to learner-centered instruction—because there was validation. That spurs me to go even further and to take some more risks because now I know I have that research behind my application.

Again, we have offered Cleland's experiences as a potential spark to ignite or rekindle your own vision. Her thoughtful answers to our questions may also have given you some helpful suggestions for getting the support you need from administrators and parents.

Final Review

This closing review summarizes our findings, views, and suggestions.

• In Chapter One, we addressed the question what is learner centered? and contrasted learner centered with child or student centered. We stated that learner centered has to do with the context for learning that is created primarily by the teacher and where that teacher is "coming from" in the teaching and learning process. We explained that the concept of learner centered comes out of an understanding of the research base on the psychology of learning and individual differences in learners. We also defined learner centered in terms of our understanding of the twelve learner-centered psychological principles across five major domains (metacognitive and cognitive, affective, personal and social, developmental, and individual differences). We noted that these principles further lead to five premises. These premises speak to (1) learners' uniqueness; (2) what learners' unique differences include (their emotional states of mind, learning rates, learning styles, stages of development, abilities, talents, feelings of efficacy, and other academic and nonacademic attributes and needs); (3) learners' constructive ways of making meaning and connecting new information to prior knowledge and experiences; (4) the positive climate needed to support learning and motivation for all learners, in and out of school, young and old; and (5) the naturalness of the learning process. The definition of learner centered was also related to the beliefs, characteristics, dispositions, and practices of teachers that (1) include learners in important teaching and learning decisions, (2) take learner's unique perspectives seriously as part of the learning process, (3) respect and accommodate individual differences, and (4) treat learners as cocreators of knowledge and learning. We stressed that what defines learner centered is not one kind of teacher or one set of practices. Rather, to be learner centered is to have a perspective that focuses equally on individual learners and their needs and on the process of learning itself. Knowledge about both learners and learning, then, forms the basis for decision making, so that motivation, learning, and achievement are enhanced for *all* learners.

- In Chapter Two, we explored the question why learner centered? in the context of what many consider to be the alarming problems facing schools and the larger society. These problems, we asserted, have necessitated that schools focus on both the learner and the process of learning. We argued that it is especially important to serve the needs of the learner as a whole person, which translates to a concern with each learner's nonacademic as well as academic needs. We spoke to the frustrations of both teachers and students when what is needed for the teaching and learning process is not present (that is, opportunities for choice and control, personally relevant and interesting curricula, opportunities to exhibit personal strengths and talents and to excel, encouragement and support from teachers and peers, standards that are rigorous and personally challenging) and the results are feelings of alienation, boredom, anger, and hopelessness. We looked at research that shows successful schools to be those that focus on both learners and learning, and we argued that the benefits of such a focus extend to all learners in the system, including students, teachers, administrators, and parents. Finally, we suggested that for the educational system to meet the needs of all learners, the type of change required is a transformation in thinking. This transformation in thinking, we asserted, must be informed by research that focuses on learning and individual differences in learners and that provides a foundation for creating learner-centered classrooms and schools.

- In Chapter Three, we looked at classroom practices consistent with the learner-centered psychological principles. Again, we pointed out that these practices are not limited to one particular set but are based on commonalities in the beliefs, qualities and characteristics of teachers and include many overlapping practices that tend to be learner centered. These practices acknowledge and attend to learner uniqueness across metacognitive and cognitive, affective, developmental, and personal and social domains and to other individual differences. Learner-centered teachers, we said, understand that learning is a constructive process and must be meaningful and relevant. It must promote active learning so that learners are aided in creating knowledge and understanding by making connections to what they already know or have experienced. Learner-centered teachers, we professed, also understand that they must create positive classroom climates for learning and that these become personal learning communities of support, appreciation, acknowledgment, and respect for all learners. Finally, we suggested that to facilitate motivation, learning, and achievement teachers must come from an assumption that all students want to learn and that students do not need to be "fixed." We argued that the most important parts of the learner-centered classroom are the teacher's qualities of heart and mind that respect and value each learner. This is in addition, of course, to the teacher's competence and expertise in understanding and guiding the learning process in partnership with students.

- In Chapter Four, we explored practices, structures, and policies that define the learner-centered school. Again, we found that such schools are not defined by a single model but are considered learner centered if they promote (1) cultures of caring, learning, change, and collaboration and (2) inclusive, respectful, and flexible practices that value and capitalize on diversity among students and staff. We stressed that learner-centered schools are learner centered for everyone involved at the school—students, staff, and parents alike—and that support is available to carry out learner-centered structures, practices, and policies at the building level. We also mentioned in passing that learner-centered schools have physical characteristics that convey a welcoming atmosphere that values students and learning. Throughout, we emphasized the theme that a critical ingredient in learner-centered schools is that the attitudes and beliefs of teachers and staff are consistent with the knowledge base on learners and learning, the base represented in the learner-centered psychological principles, for example.

• In Chapter Five, we explored what the journey of change, the journey toward learner-centered classrooms and schools, might look like from a research and practice perspective. We talked about what teachers can do to become models of lifelong learners and to assume increasingly proactive and responsible leadership roles in their own professional development process. We described the larger context for personal change, a context that involves the whole system. We suggested how systemic change applies to living systems such as education and that living systems must be concerned with personal as well as technical and organizational aspects of change. We described a personal change process that involves seeing relationships between the psychology of learning and the psychology of change. We stated that change must be built from within—from within each person as a transformation of heart and mind and from within each classroom, school, and district. From teachers in three learner-centered schools, we heard that trust must be a foundation for change, that change takes time, and that teachers must come to the place where they see themselves as learners. We suggested that when teachers are able to see themselves as learners, they are better able to understand their students' perspectives. They also become better able to assume responsibility for their own professional development, which involves a commitment to ongoing learning and change.

• And so we arrived at Chapter Six, where we considered some tools that may assist anyone engaged in constructing and following an action plan for ongoing learning and change toward more learner-centered practice. We stressed the importance of becoming more aware of beliefs—particularly about learners—that may not be consistent with the knowledge base and with what growing numbers of educators know can best enhance motivation, learning, and achievement for all learners. We suggested that you create a personal action plan to focus on those areas in which you believe you can become more learner centered. Finally, we talked about some strategies that you may find helpful in dealing with barriers and resistance to change that you may encounter at a personal or systems level. We encouraged you to form inquiry groups and networks among your colleagues to keep the vision alive.

As we close this final chapter, we invite you to dare to dream. If you could wave a magic wand and with that wave find yourself in the classroom or school of your dreams, what would you find? Who would be there? What would they be doing? How would they be doing it? How would they look and feel? Describe or depict your dream classroom or school in as much detail as possible. Find an appropriate medium for your expression. It might be an essay, a poem, a picture, a model, or even a song!

Once you have dared to dream, we suggest that you take the following statement to heart. It expresses the thoughts of Sir Edmund Hillary, who successfully climbed Mt. Everest.

Until one is committed there is hesitancy, the chance to draw back, always ineffectiveness. Concerning all acts of initiative (and creation), there is one elementary truth, the ignorance of which kills countless ideas and splendid plans: that the moment one definitely commits oneself, then Providence moves too.

All sorts of things occur to help one that would never otherwise have occurred.

A whole stream of events issues from the decision, raising in one's favour all manner of unforeseen incidents and meets and material assistance, which no man could have dreamt would have come his way.

I have learned a deep respect for one of Goethe's couplets:
Whatever you can do, or dream you can, begin it.
Boldness has genius, power, and magic in it.

Appendix A: Teacher Beliefs Survey: Self-Scoring Instructions and Explanation

The Teacher Beliefs Survey contains thirty-five items that form three major factors or categories of beliefs (listed below). These factors were defined on the basis of the research base contained in the learner-centered psychological principles (Presidential Task Force on Psychology in Education, 1993). They were verified in a large-scale validation of the survey with more than 660 middle and high school teachers from diverse rural, suburban, and rural school districts and geographic regions all over the United States.

The Three Factors and the Items Contained in Each

Factor 1: learner-centered beliefs about learners, learning, and teaching (survey items 1, 4, 7, 10, 13, 16, 19, 22, 25, 28, 30, 32, 34, 35)

Factor 2: non-learner-centered beliefs about learners (survey items 2, 5, 8, 11, 14, 17, 20, 23, 26)

Factor 3: non-learner-centered beliefs about learning and teaching (survey items 3, 6, 9, 12, 15, 18, 21, 24, 27, 29, 31, 33)

Scoring Instructions

When you completed the survey, you gave each item a value ranging from 1 to 4. Now, working by factor, add together the values for all the items in each factor. For factor 1, there are fourteen items. The total score possible on factor 1 ranges from a low of 14 (14 × 1) to a high of 56 (14 × 4). For factor 2, there are nine items. The total score possible on factor 2 ranges from a low of 9 (9 × 1) to high of 36 (9 × 4). For factor 3, there are twelve items. The total score possible on factor 3 ranges from a low of 12 (12 × 1) to a high of 48 (12 × 4).

Calculating Your Score

Once you have totaled your score for the items in each factor, divide that total by the number of items in the factor to get your mean score. For example, if your total score on factor 1 is 30, your mean score is 30 divided by 14, or 2.14. Factor means for the validation sample are shown below. This sample contained results for 796 teachers, primarily in high schools but some in middle schools, from around the country. They represent urban, suburban, and rural schools with a diversity of student populations.

Validation Sample Means for Each Factor

Factor 1: 3.22

Factor 2: 2.28

Factor 3: 2.31

Interpreting Your Score

Once you have calculated your mean for each factor, you can compare your mean scores with those of the validation sample to see how similar your beliefs are to this sample. The standard deviations for each factor are .40, .56, and .49, respectively. You can see whether your means differ significantly from those of the validation sample by seeing whether your means are more than a standard deviation higher or lower for each factor.

In general, teachers with learner-centered beliefs are those with means above 3.4 on factor 1 and below 2.0 on factors 2 and 3. Teachers with non-learner-centered beliefs are those with means below 2.8 on factor 1 and above 2.4 on factors 2 and 3.

Appendix B:
Learner-Centered Resources

This appendix describes five learner-centered resources: *Learner-Centered Psychological Principles* (document), *For Our Students, For Ourselves* (videotapes), *Reinventing Schools* (videotapes), . . . *And Learning for All* (videotapes), and *The Learner-Centered Battery* (assessment tools). To obtain more information about any of these materials, contact the Mid-continent Regional Educational Laboratory (McREL), 2550 S. Parker Road, Suite 500, Aurora, CO 80014; (303) 337–0990; fax (303) 743–3005.

Learner-Centered Psychological Principles (Document)

Learner-Centered Psychological Principles: Guidelines for School Redesign and Reform was produced in conjunction with the American Psychological Association's Presidential Task Force on Psychology in Education. This document outlines twelve psychological principles that can provide the foundation for improving the quality of teaching and learning in U.S. schools. These principles, many of which are already implemented in exemplary classrooms, represent an organized knowledge base that supports a learner-centered perspective or model. This model leads to a concept of schooling that has at its center a concern with each student and that student's maximum achievement and development.

When used as a basis for school reform, the principles guide decisions about learning standards, curriculum, assessment, and instructional approaches by helping decision makers consider learner needs, capacities, and frames of reference. The model focuses on respecting individual student perspectives, unique talents, and special learning needs and interests. Individual learner considerations are balanced with what is known to be best for all learners and with concerns for learning the standards and content that define an educated and productive citizen.

For Our Students, For Ourselves (Videotapes)

For Our Students, For Ourselves consists of two four-part videos that demonstrate the essence of the learner-centered psychological principles and their implications for educational practice at the high school level. Viewers visit three high schools and observe students, teachers, and administrators using the principles to guide their educational reform efforts. Learner-centered practice is shown as an approach that makes learning personalized and relevant in a climate of personal consideration, mutual respect, and student responsibility. The three featured high schools include a small rural school, a school in a suburban setting, and an inner-city school with nearly 2,500 students.

Tape one, *Learner-Centered Principles in Practice*, gives a concise overview of the twelve principles followed by demonstrations in the classrooms of the three example schools. In tape two, *Stories of Change*, the key participants in the restructuring of the three schools convene two years following the taping of the first video to discuss the process of change that occurred. Teachers and administrators describe the creation of their vision for change, the transformation in their thinking that resulted in mission statements, the consequences of change including mistakes that resulted in reflection and growth, and finally, the evolution to a new school culture dedicated to lifelong learning and improvement.

A printed aid (*Facilitator Manual*) that accompanies the video-tapes describes separate workshops that are to be held in conjunction with each video. In the first workshop, the facilitator trainer guides the participants through a set of key questions leading to the creation of their own learner-centered model. In the second workshop, the facilitator trainer takes the participants through four stages of change, helping individuals examine personal, technical, organizational, and collaborative strategies that lead to the implementation of a learner-centered approach to education. To facilitate group discussions, the manual also includes viewer guides for the four parts of each video.

Reinventing Schools (Videotapes)

The two videotapes that make up *Reinventing Schools* describe a K–8 school in Williston, Vermont, that has implemented ideas and concepts from the learner-centered psychological principles. Tape one, *Student Voices in a Learner-Centered School*, shows teachers and children interacting in a school where teachers take primary responsibility for all students, and support personnel act as case mangers on multiaged teaching teams. Students, parents, and teachers describe their reactions to the constructivist and inquiry approach to learning, in which students take personal responsibility for their learning plans, including resources and applications, and teachers use quality indicators for assessment of student work. Tape two, *Gathering the Dreamers: The Transformation Process to a Learner-Centered School*, reviews the process that Williston Central followed in its transformation from a traditional approach to one based on learner-centered concepts. The tape describes how the creation and implementation of the vision of a unified school required personal, organizational, and technical changes. Teachers, parents, and administrators discuss the challenges they faced in their school and community in creating professional interdisciplinary teams developed through faculty, parent, and community participation.

... And Learning for All (Videotapes)

Americans have become increasingly aware of the need to strengthen this country's educational system. . . . *And Learning for All* identifies successful educational programs and provides a way of gaining community support for their adoption and maintenance over an extended period of time. . . . *And Learning for All* videotapes are part of a flexible comprehensive package of video and print materials organized around the National Goals for Education. The materials are intended to inspire new visions of education and to provide the tools to organize the community action necessary to realize those visions. The package includes six goal-related video programs highlighting exemplary practices, one overview tape, a community action packet and facilitators' guide for encouraging citizen involvement and gaining community support at the local level, and a resource directory describing research results and successful educational practices related to the national educational goals.

The Learner-Centered Battery (Assessment Tools)

The purpose of *The Learner-Centered Battery* is to support a personal process of change in which teachers and administrators use self-assessment tools to reflect on (1) discrepancies between their own and student or faculty perceptions of practices and (2) areas of needed change and the strategies to achieve them. For teachers, *The Learner-Centered Battery* is part of a professional development model that focuses on empowerment, teachers' responsibility for their own growth and professionalism, teachers as leaders, and teachers' development of higher-order thinking and personal reflection skills. The battery includes five types of surveys. The first two are for individual classroom teachers. The Teacher Beliefs Survey and the Teacher Practices Survey, respectively, help teachers assess (1) what they believe about learners, learning, and teaching; and (2) what they believe to be their instructional practices in the classroom. (You were introduced to the Teacher Beliefs Survey in Chapter Two and to the Teacher Practices Survey in Chapter Three.)

The third survey is for students. It tells teachers what each of their students experiences in their classroom. This tool helps teachers become aware of differences between what they think they are doing to assist learning and how what they are doing is perceived and experienced by each student. Discrepancies between student and teacher perceptions of classroom practice can then be plotted for four major domains: creating positive interpersonal relationships and classroom climate; honoring student voice, providing academic challenge, and encouraging perspective taking; encouraging higher order thinking and self-regulated learning; and adapting to individual differences among students.

The fourth survey is for peer teachers. It provides information about teachers' perceptions of each other's classroom practices, giving peer teachers a tool for reflecting on differences between their own and another's perceptions of their practice. More importantly, however, it gives teachers a source of information for discussions and *collaboration* on the differences between their own and their students' perceptions. In these discussions, it is essential that both teachers learn to focus on seeing their practices from their students' perspectives if they are to improve student motivation, learning, and achievement. Becoming aware of how their students perceive and experience teacher practices in particular domains provides an impetus for change when teachers understand that it is students' perspectives that determine student motivation, learning, and achievement. By focusing on discrepancies between their own and their students' perceptions of practice, they gain important information about particular practices that can better meet the needs of each student.

The fifth survey is for school administrators and their faculties. It allows individuals to assess their own beliefs and perceptions of practices at the school level in the domains of instruction, motivation and expectations, curriculum, assessment, instructional management, staff development, and leadership and policy. The feedback allows administrators and faculty members to examine discrepancies between, on the one hand, their own beliefs about ideal practices and their assessment of actual school practices and, on the other hand, overall administrator and faculty beliefs and practices. This survey thus becomes a leadership tool for identifying which faculty members have differing perceptions and in what areas they differ in terms of both beliefs and practices. Discussion groups may be formed to discuss differences and to begin or strengthen the process of becoming a culture of caring, learning, change, and collaboration.

References

Alexander, P. A. & Murphy, P. K. (in press). The research base for APA's *learner-centered psychological principles*. In B. L. McCombs & N. Lambert (Eds.), *Issues in school reform: A sampler of psychological perspectives on learner-centered schools*. Washington, DC: APA Books.

Ames, C. (1992). Achievement goals and the classroom climate. In D. H. Schunk & J. L. Meece (Eds.), *Student perceptions in the classroom* (pp. 327–348). Hillsdale, NJ: Erlbaum.

Ancess, J., & Darling-Hammond, L. (1995). Collaborative learning and assessment at International High School. In L. Darling-Hammond, J. Ancess, & B. Falk (Eds.), *Authentic assessment in action* (pp. 115–167). New York: Teachers College Press.

Anderson, B. L. (1993). The stages of systemic change. *Educational Leadership, 51*(1), 14–17.

Anderson, L. M., Blumfeld, P., Pintrich, P. R., Clark, C. M., Marx, R. W., & Peterson, P. (1995). Educational psychology for teachers: Reforming our courses, rethinking our roles. *Educational Psychologist, 30*(3), 143–157.

Anson, R., & Fox, J. (1995). Studies of education reform: An overview. *Phi Delta Kappan, 77*(1), 16–18.

Banathy, B. H. (1995). Developing a systems view of education. *Educational Technology, 35*(3), 53–57.

Banathy, B. H. (1997). Designing educational systems: creating our future in a changing world. *Educational Technology, 32*(11), 41–46.

Barkley, R., Jr., & Castle, S. (1993, April). *Principles and actions: A framework for systemic change*. Paper presented at the annual meeting of the American Educational Research Association, Atlanta.

Bartolome, L. I. (1994). Beyond the methods fetish: Toward a humanizing pedagogy. *Harvard Educational Review, 64*(2), 173–194.

Baum, S. M., Renzulli, J. S., & Hebert, T. P. (1994). Reversing underachievement: Stories of success. *Educational Leadership, 52*(3), 48–52.

Bennett, J. K., & O'Brien, M. J. (1994, July). The building blocks of the learning organization. *Training*, pp. 41–47.

Berliner, B., & Benard, B. (1995, September). How schools can foster resiliency in children. *Western Center News*, pp. 1, 6.

Bernieri, F. J. (1991). Interpersonal sensitivity in teaching interactions. *Personality and Social Psychology Bulletin, 17*(1), 98–103.

Bickel, W. E., & Hattrup, R. A. (1995). Teachers and researchers in collaboration: Reflections on the process. *American Educational Research Journal, 32*(1), 35–62.

Bosworth, K. (1995). Caring for others and being cared for: Students talk caring in school. *Phi Delta Kappan, 76*(9), 686–693.

Boyd, V., & Hord, S. M. (1994, April). *Principals and the new paradigm: Schools as learning communities*. Paper presented at the annual meeting of the American Educational Research Association, New Orleans.

Boyer, E. (1996). *The basic school*. Ewing, NJ: California Princeton Fulfillment Services.

Brandt, R. (1996, February). *Why tracking is never a good alternative*. Annual meeting of the Colorado Chapter of Phi Delta Kappa, Denver.

Brooks, J. G., & Brooks, M. G. (1993). *In search of understanding: The case for constructivist classrooms.* Alexandria, VA: Association for Supervision and Curriculum Development.

Brown, A. L. (1994). The advancement of learning. *Educational Researcher, 23*(8), 4–12.

Brown, A. L., & Campione, J. C. (in press). Designing a community of young learners: Theoretical and practical lessons. In B. L. McCombs & N. Lambert (Eds.), *Issues in school reform: Perspectives on learner centered practices*. Washington, DC: APA Books.

Burger, D. (1995, April). Designing a sustainable standards-based assessment system. *What's Noteworthy on Learners, Learning, and Schooling*. Aurora, CO: Mid-continent Regional Educational Laboratory.

Burke, D. L. (1996). Multi-year teacher/student relationships are a long-overdue arrangement. *Phi Delta Kappan, 77*(5), 360–361.

Canady, R. L., & Rettig, M. D. (1995). The power of innovative scheduling. *Educational Leadership, 53*(3), 4–10.

Carr, A. A. (1996). Distinguishing systemic from systematic. *Techtrends, 41*(1), 16–20.

Chaskin, R. J., & Rauner, D. M. (1995). Youth and caring: An introduction. *Phi Delta Kappan, 76*(9), 667–674.

Chen, M., & Addi, A. (1995, April). *Educational leaders' influencing behaviors and school restructuring.* Paper presented at the session "Creating Success: Studies of School Change" at the annual meeting of the American Educational Research Association, San Francisco.

Clark, D. C., & Clark, S. N. (1996). Building collaborative environments for successful middle-level school restructuring. *NASSP (National Association of Secondary School Principals) Bulletin, 80*(578), 1–16.

Comer, J. (1993, March). *Creating learning communities: The Comer process.* Experimental session. Annual Conference of the Association for Supervision and Curriculum Development. Washington, DC.

Council of the Great City Schools. (1993). *Diversifying our great city school teachers: Twenty-year trends.* Washington, DC: Author.

Covington, M. V. (1992). *Making the grade: A self-worth perspective on motivation and school reform.* Cambridge, MA: Cambridge University Press.

Cuban, L. (1986). *Teachers and machines: Classroom use of technology since 1920.* New York: Teachers College Press.

Cuban, L. (1990). Reforming again, again, and again. *Educational Researcher, 19*(1), 3–13.

Damico, S. B., & Roth, J. (1994, April). *Differences between the learning environments of high and low graduation schools: Listening to general track students.* Paper presented at the annual meeting of the American Educational Research Association, New Orleans.

Darling-Hammond, L. (1993). Reframing the school reform agenda: Developing capacity for school transformation. *Phi Delta Kappan, 74*(11), 753–761.

Darling-Hammond, L. (1994). Who will speak for the children? How "Teach for America" hurts urban schools and students. *Phi Delta Kappan, 76*(1), 21–34.

✗ Darling-Hammond, L. (1996). The quiet revolution: Rethinking teacher development. *Educational Leadership, 53*(6), 4–10.

Darling-Hammond, L., & McLaughlin, M. W. (1995). Policies that support professional development in an era of reform. *Phi Delta Kappan, 40*(7), 597–604.

Darling-Hammond, L., & Snyder, J. (1992). *Reframing accountability: Creating learner-centered schools.* New York: ERIC Clearinghouse on Urban Education/National Center for Restructuring Education, Schools, and Teaching.

Deci, E. L., & Ryan, R. M. (1991). A motivational approach to self: Integration in personality. In R. Dienstbier (Ed.), *Nebraska symposium on motivation: Vol. 38. Perspectives on motivation* (pp. 237–288). Lincoln: University of Nebraska Press.

Deci, E. L., Vallerand, R. J., Pelletier, L. G., & Ryan, R. M. (1991). Motivation and education: The self-determination perspective. *Educational Psychologist, 26*(3–4), 325–346.

Delattre, E. J. (1995, April 5). The Holmes impairment. *Education Week,* pp. 60–61.

✳ DeVries, R., & Kohlberg, L. (1987). *Constructivist early education: Overview and comparison with other programs.* Washington, DC: National Association for the Education of Young Children.

Dweck, C. S., (1991). Self-theories and goals: Their role in motivation, personality, and development. In R. Dienstbier (Ed.), *Nebraska symposium on motivation: Vol. 38. Perspectives on motivation* (pp. 199–235). Lincoln: University of Nebraska Press.

Dweck, C. S., & Legget, E. L. (1988). A social-cognitive approach to motivation and personality. *Psychological Review, 95,* 256–273.

Edwards, C. M., Jr. (1995). The 4x4 plan. *Educational Leadership, 53*(3), 16–19.

Eisner, E. W. (1991). What really counts in schools. *Educational Leadership, 48*(3), 10–17.

Eisner, E. (1994). Opinions clash on curriculum standards. *ASCD Update, 36*(1), 6–7.

Elam, S. M., Rose, L. C., & Gallup, A. M. (1994). The 26th annual Phi Delta Kappa/Gallup Poll of the public's attitudes toward the public schools. *Phi Delta Kappan, 76*(1), 41–56.

Feldman, D. H. (1988). Creativity, dreams, insights, and transformations.

In R. J. Sternberg (Ed.), *The nature of creativity* (pp. 277–297). Cambridge, MA: Cambridge University Press.

Fiske, E. B., & Clinchy, E. (1992). Habits of the mind: Essential classrooms in action at Fairdale High School in Louisville, Kentucky. *Equity and Choice, 8*(3), 6–13.

Floden, R. E., Goertz, M. E., & O'Day, J. (1995). Capacity building in systemic reform. *Phi Delta Kappan, 77*(1), 19–21.

Fullan, M. (1992–1993). *Managing change.* Toronto: University of Toronto.

Fullan, M. G. (1993). Why teachers must become change agents. *Educational Leadership, 51*(7), 12–17.

Fullan, M. G. (1995). The limits and the potential of professional development. In T. R. Guskey & M. Huberman (Eds.), *Professional development in education: New paradigms and practices* (pp. 253–267). New York: Teachers College Press.

Fullan, M. G. (1996). Turning systemic thinking on its head. *Phi Delta Kappan, 77*(6), 420–423.

Gaddy, B. B., Hall, T. W., & Marzano, R. J. (1996). *School wars: Resolving our conflicts over religion and values.* San Francisco: Jossey-Bass.

Garcia, E. E. (1995). The impact of linguistic and cultural diversity on America's schools: A need for new policy. In M. C. Wang & M. C. Reynolds (Eds.), *Making a difference for students at risk: Trends and alternatives* (pp. 156–180). Thousand Oaks, CA: Corwin Press.

Gardner, H. (1992). *The unschooled mind.* New York: Basic Books.

Gardner, H. (1993). *Multiple intelligences: The theory in practice.* New York: Basic Books.

Gardner, H. (1995). Reflections on multiple intelligences: Myths and messages. *Phi Delta Kappan, 77*(3), 200–209.

Gardner, H., & Boix-Mansilla, V. (1994). Teaching for understanding within and across the disciplines. *Educational Leadership, 51*, 14–18.

Garmston, R., & Wellman, B. (1995). Adaptive schools in a quantum universe. *Educational Leadership, 52*(7), 6–12.

Glasser, W. (1984). *Control theory: A new explanation of how we control our lives.* New York: HarperCollins.

Glasser, W. (1990). *The quality school: Managing students without coercion.* New York: HarperCollins, Perennial Library.

Glasser, W. (1994). Foreword. In B. Greene (Ed.), *New paradigms for creating quality schools* (p. iv). Chapel Hill, NC: New View Publications.

Goldenberg, C. (1991, June). *Two views of learning and their implications for literacy education*. Paper presented at the Language Minority Literacy Roundtable, University of California, Santa Barbara.

Gordon, D. (1992). *Beating the odds*. New York: HarperCollins.

Grayson, D. A., & Martin, M. D. (1977). *Gender/ethnic expectations and student achievement*. Earlham, IA: GrayMill.

Haas, T. (1990, Fall). Goal 2: School completion. *Noteworthy* (pp. 14–21). Aurora, CO: Mid-continent Regional Educational Laboratory.

Hanson, B. J. (1995). Getting to know you—Multiyear teaching. *Educational Leadership, 53*(3), 42–43.

Hargreaves, A. (1995). Renewal in the age of paradox. *Educational Leadership, 52*(7), 14–19.

Hasseler, S. S. (1995, April). *Missing links: The complexities of supporting teacher learning in school contexts*. Paper presented at the annual meeting of the American Educational Research Association, San Francisco.

Helmke, A., & Shrader, F. W. (1991, April). *Cognitive, affective, and motivational goals of classroom instruction: Are they incompatible?* Paper presented at the annual meeting of the American Educational Research Association, Chicago.

Henderson, A. (1987). *The evidence continues to grow: Parent involvement improves student achievement. An annotated bibliography*. Special Report. Columbia, MD: National Committee for Citizens in Education.

Henry, M. A. (1994, February). *Differentiating the expert and experienced teacher: Quantitative differences in instructional decision making*. Paper presented at the annual meeting of the American Association of Colleges for Teacher Education, Chicago.

Henry, T. (1996, February 22). Principals urge broad changes in high schools. *USA Today*, p. A9.

Holtzman, W. H. (Ed.). (1992). *School of the future*. Austin, TX: American Psychological Association and Hogg Foundation for Mental Health.

Joyce, B., & Calhoun, E. (1995). School renewal: An inquiry, not a formula. *Educational Leadership, 52*(7), 51–55.

Karsenti, T. P., & Thibert, G. (1995, April). *What type of motivation is truly related to school achievement? A look at 1,428 high school students*. Paper presented at the annual meeting of the American Educational Research Association, San Francisco.

Katsiyannis, A., Conderman, G., & Franks, D. (1996). Students with disabilities: Inclusionary programming and the school principal. *NASSP (National Association of Secondary School Principals) Bulletin, 80*(578), 81–86.

Keller, B. M. (1995). Accelerated schools: Hands-on learning in a unified community. *Educational Leadership, 52*(5), 10–13.

Kermon, S., Kimball, T., & Martin, M. (1980). *Teacher expectations and student achievement (TESA): Coordinator manual.* Bloomington, IN: Phi Delta Kappa.

Kindel, S. (1995, May). Building bridges: An interview with Lois Loofbourrow. *Hemispheres,* pp. 19–24.

Kruse, S., Seashore-Louis, K., & Bryk, A. (1994). *Building professional community in schools.* Madison: University of Wisconsin, Center for School Restructuring.

Ladson-Billings, G. (1995). Toward a theory of culturally relevant pedagogy. *American Educational Research Journal, 32*(3), 465–491.

Levin, H. M. (1991, April). *Building school capacity for effective teacher empowerment: Applications to elementary schools with at-risk students.* Paper presented at the annual meeting of the American Educational Research Association, Chicago.

Levine, A., & Nidiffer, J. (1996). *Beating the odds: How the poor get to college.* San Francisco: Jossey-Bass.

Lewin, K. (1951). *Field theory in social science.* New York: HarperCollins.

Lewis, C. C., Schaps, E., & Watson, M. (1995). Beyond the pendulum: Creating challenging and caring schools. *Phi Delta Kappan, 77*(11), 547–554.

Lieberman, A. (1995). *The work of restructuring schools: Building from the ground up.* New York: Teachers College Press.

Lincoln, Y. S. (1995). In search of students' voices. *Theory into Practice, 34*(2), 89–94.

Liontos, L. B. (1991, January). Involving the families of at-risk youth in the educational process. *Trends and Issues.* Eugene, OR: ERIC Clearinghouse on Educational Management.

Lipsitz, J. (1995). Prologue: Why we should care about caring. *Phi Delta Kappan, 76*(9), 665–666.

Little, J. W. (1993). Teachers' professional development in a climate of educational reform. *Educational Evaluation and Policy Analysis, 15*(2), 129–151.

Maehr, M. L. (1992, April).*Transforming school culture to enhance motivation*. Paper presented at the annual meeting of the American Educational Research Association, San Francisco.

Marshall, H. H. (1992). *Redefining student learning: Roots of educational change*. Norwood, NJ: Ablex.

Marzano, R. J. (1992a). *A different kind of classroom: Teaching with dimensions of learning*. Alexandria, VA: Association for Supervision and Curriculum Development.

Marzano, R. J. (1992b). The many faces of cooperation across the dimensions of learning. In N. Davidson & T. Worsham (Eds.), *Enhancing thinking through cooperative learning* (pp. 7–28). New York: Teachers College Press.

Marzano, R. J., Pickering, D. J., Arredondo, D. E., Blackburn, G. J., Brandt, R. S., & Moffett, C. A. (1992). *Dimensions of learning*. Alexandria, VA: Association for Supervision and Curriculum Development and the Mid-continent Regional Educational Laboratory.

McCarthy, B. (1980). *The 4MAT System: Teaching to learning styles with right/left mode techniques*. Barrington, IL: Excel.

McCarthy, B., & Leflar, S. (1983). *4MAT in action*. Barrington, IL: Excel.

McCarthy, B., Samples, B., & Hammond, B. (1985). *4MAT and science: Toward wholeness in science education*. Barrington, IL: Excel.

McCombs, B. L. (1991). Motivation and lifelong learning. *Educational Psychologist, 26*(2), 117–127.

McCombs, B. L. (1993). Learner-centered psychological principles for enhancing education: Applications in school settings. In L. A. Penner, G. M. Batsche, H. M. Knoff, & D. L. Nelson (Eds.), *The challenges in mathematics and science education: Psychology's response* (pp. 287–313).Washington, DC: American Psychological Association.

McCombs, B. L. (1994a, March). *Development and validation of the Learner-Centered Psychological Principles*. Aurora, CO: Mid-continent Regional Educational Laboratory.

McCombs, B. L. (1994b). *The personal change process: Applications to teachers' professional development*. Working paper. Aurora, CO: Mid-continent Regional Educational Laboratory.

McCombs, B. L. (1994c). Strategies for assessing and enhancing motivation: Keys to promoting self-regulated learning and performance. In

H. F. O'Neil, Jr., & M. Drillings (Eds.), *Motivation: Research and theory* (pp. 49–70). Hillsdale, NJ: Erlbaum.

McCombs, B. L. (1995a). Alternative perspectives for motivation. In L. Baker, P. Afflerbach, and D. Reinking (Eds.), *Developing engaged readers in school and home communities.* Hillsdale, NJ: Erlbaum.

McCombs, B. L. (1995b). Commentary to Renzulli and Hebert's "The plight of high-ability students in urban schools." In M.C. Wang & M. C. Reynolds (Eds.), *Making a difference for students at risk: Trends and alternatives* (pp. 90–91).Thousand Oaks, CA: Corwin Press.

McCombs, B. L. (1995c, May). *Facilitating change at the personal level.* Invited presentation at the "Facilitating Systemic Change" Conference, University of Nebraska-Lincoln.

McCombs, B. L. (in press). Integrating metacognition, affect, and motivation in improving teacher education. In B. L. McCombs & N. Lambert (Eds.), *Issues in school reform: A sample of psychological perspectives on learner-centered schools.* Washington, DC: APA Books.

McCombs, B. L., Burrello, L. C., & Dudzinski, T. (1996). *Telling the stories of change: Perspectives from three learner-centered high schools.* Aurora, CO: Mid-continent Regional Educational Laboratory.

McCombs, B. L., & Lambert, N. (Eds.) (in press). *Issues in school reform: A sampler of psychological perspectives on learner-centered schools.* Washington, DC: APA Books.

McCombs, B. L., & McNeely, S. (Eds.) (in press). *Psychology in the classroom: A mini-series on applied educational psychology.* Washington, DC: APA Books.

McCombs, B. L., & Pope, J. E. (1994). Motivating hard to reach students. In B. L. McCombs, & S. McNeely (Eds.), *Psychology in the classroom: A mini-series on applied educational* psychology. Washington, DC: APA Books.

McCombs, B. L., Ridley, D. S., & Stiller, J. (1995, April). *Self-assessment and reflection tools for teachers: Validation of the Learner-Centered Battery.* Paper presented at the annual meeting of the American Educational Research Association, San Francisco.

McCombs, B. L., & Stiller, J. R. (1995, October). *Development and validation of the Learner-Centered Battery: Self-assessment tools for teachers and administrators.* Aurora, CO: Mid-continent Regional Educational Laboratory.

McCombs, B. L., Swartz, D., Wlodkowski, R., Whisler, J. S., & Stiller, J. (1994). *The learner-centered school and classroom*. Aurora, CO: Mid-continent Regional Educational Laboratory.

McCombs, B. L., & Whisler, J. S. (1989). The role of affective variables in autonomous learning. *Educational Psychologist, 24*(3), 277–306.

McKeachie, W. J. (1990). Learning, thinking, and Thorndike. *Educational Psychologist, 25*(2), 127–142.

McKeachie, W. J. (1992). Research on college teaching: The historical background. *Journal of Educational Psychology, 82*(2), 189.

McKeachie, W. J. (1995, August). *What makes a good teacher great!* Invited address at the annual meeting of the American Psychological Association, New York.

Meece, J. L. (1991). The classroom context and students' motivational goals. In M. Maehr and P. Pintrich (Eds.), *Advances in motivation and achievement* (Vol. 7, pp. 261–286). Greenwich, CT: JAI Press.

Meier, D. (1995). How our schools could be. *Phi Delta Kappan, 40*(4), 369–373.

Merenbloom, E. Y. (1996). Team teaching: Addressing the learning needs of middle-level students. *NASSP (National Association of Secondary School Principals) Bulletin, 80*(578), 45–53.

Metzger, M. (1996). Maintaining a life. *Phi Delta Kappan, 77*(5), 346–351.

Miles, M. B., & Louis, K. S. (1990). Mustering the will and skill for change. *Educational Leadership, 48*(9), 57–61.

Murray, H. G., & Renaud, R. D. (1995). Disciplinary differences in classroom teaching behaviors. *New Directions for Teaching and Learning, 64*(Winter), 31–39.

Murray, W. B. (1951). *The Scottish Himalayan expedition*. London: Dent.

National Association of Secondary School Principals (1996). Breaking ranks: Changing an American institution. *NASSP Bulletin, 80*(578), 54–67.

National Commission on Excellence in Education (1983, April). *A nation at risk: The imperative for educational reform*. Washington, DC: U.S. Department of Education.

Natriello, G., Pallas, A. M., McDill, E. L., McPartland, J. M., & Royster, D. (1988). *An examination of the assumptions and evidence for alternative dropout prevention programs in high school* (Center for Social Organization of Schools, Report No. 365). Baltimore, MD: Johns Hopkins University.

Noblit, G., Rogers, D., & McCadden, B. (1995). In the meantime: The possibilities of caring. Phi *Delta Kappan,* 76(9).

Noddings, N. (1995). Teaching themes of care. *Phi Delta Kappan,* 76(9), 675–679.

Nolen, S. B. (1994, April). *Learning from students.* Paper presented at the annual meeting of the American Educational Research Association, New Orleans.

Oakes, J. (1985). *Keeping track: How schools structure inequality.* New Haven, CT: Yale University Press.

Oakes, J. (1992). Can tracking research inform practice? Technical, normative, and political consideration. *Educational Researcher,* 21(2), 12–21.

Ogle, D. (1986). K-W-L: A teaching model that develops active reading in expository text. *The Reading Teacher,* 39(11), 564–576.

Oldfather, P. (1991, April). *When the bird and the book disagree, always believe the bird: Children's perspectives of their impulse to learn.* Paper presented at the annual meeting of the American Educational Research Association, Chicago.

Oldfather, P. (1993, Summer). *Students' perspectives on motivating experiences in literary learning.* Athens: University of Georgia, National Reading Research Center.

Oldfather, P. (1994, Winter). *When students do not feel motivated for literary learning: How a responsive classroom culture helps.* Reading Research Report No. 8. Athens: University of Georgia, National Reading Research Center.

O'Neil, J. (1995). On lasting school reform: A conversation with Ted Sizer. *Educational Leadership,* 52(5), 4–9.

Ornstein, A. C. (1993). How to recognize good teaching. *American School Board Journal,* 80(1), 24–27.

Peck, N., Law, A., & Mills, R. C. (1989). *Dropout prevention: What we have learned.* Ann Arbor: ERIC Counseling and Personnel Services Clearinghouse, University of Michigan.

Piaget, J. (1954). *The construction of reality in the child.* New York: Basic Books.

Pintrich, P. R., Brown, D. R., & Weinstein, C. E. (1994). *Student motivation, cognition, and learning: Essays in honor of Wilbert J. McKeachie*. Hillsdale, NJ: Erlbaum.

Poplin, M., & Weeres, J. (1992). Listening at the learner's level. *The Executive Educator, 15*(4), 14–19.

Presidential Task Force on Psychology in Education, American Psychological Association (1993, January). *Learner-centered psychological principles: Guidelines for school redesign and reform*. Washington, DC: American Psychological Association/Mid-continent Regional Educational Laboratory.

Ramirez-Smith, C. (1995). Stopping the cycle of failure: The Comer model. *Educational Leadership, 52*(5), 14–19.

Raywid, M. A. (1992). Why do these kids love school? *Phi Delta Kappan, 73*(9), 631–633.

Raywid, M. A. (1995). Alternatives and marginal students. In M. C. Wang & M. C. Reynolds (Eds.), *Making a difference for students at risk: Trends and alternatives* (pp. 119–146).Thousand Oaks, CA: Corwin Press.

Reimer, K. M., & Lapp, A. S. (1995, April). *Preparing prospective teachers for multicultural classrooms*. Paper presented at the annual meeting of the American Educational Research Association, San Francisco.

Reitzug, U. C., & Burrello, L. C. (1995). How principals can build self-renewing schools. *Educational Leadership, 52*(7), 48–50.

Renzulli, J. S., Reis, S. M., Hebert, T. P., & Diaz, E. I. (1995). The plight of high-ability students in urban schools. In M. C. Wang & M. C. Reynolds (Eds.), *Making a difference for students at risk: Trends and alternatives* (pp. 61–98). Thousand Oaks, CA: Corwin Press.

Research and Development Center for Teacher Education. (1979). *Concerns Based Adoption Model (CBAM): Procedures for adopting educational innovations*. Austin: University of Texas.

Resnick, L. B. (1987). Learning in school and out. *Educational Researcher, 16*(9), 13–20.

Ridley, D. S., McCombs, B. L., & Taylor, K. (1994). Walking the talk: Fostering of self-regulated learning in the classroom. *Middle School Journal, 26*(2), 52–57.

Robinson, S. P. (1995). Forging a new agenda for educational research. *Phi Delta Kappan, 77*(1), 15–16.

Roesener, L. (1995). Changing the culture at Beacon Hill. *Educational Leadership, 52*(7), 28–32.

Rossi, R. J., & Stringfield, S. C. (1995). What we must do for students placed at risk. *Phi Delta Kappan, 77*(1), 73–76.

Ryan, T. M. (1995). Psychological needs and the facilitation of integrative processes. *Journal of Personality, 63*(3), 397–427.

Sagor, R. (1995). Overcoming the one-solution syndrome. *Educational Leadership, 52*(7), 24–27.

Sarason, S. B. (1990). *The predictable failure of educational reform: Can we change course before it's too late?* San Francisco: Jossey-Bass.

Sarason, S. B. (1995a). *Parental involvement and the political principle: Why the existing governance structure of schools should be abolished.* San Francisco: Jossey-Bass.

Sarason, S. B. (1995b). Some reactions to what we have learned. *Phi Delta Kappan, 77*(1), 84–85.

Scherer, M. (1994). On schools where students want to be: A conversation with Deborah Meier. *Educational Leadership, 52*(1), 4–8.

Senge, P. (1990). *The fifth discipline.* New York: Doubleday.

Sizer, T. (1992). *Horace's school.* Boston: Houghton Mifflin.

Skrtic, T. M. (1991). The special education paradox: Equity as the way to excellence. *Harvard Educational Review, 61*(2), 148–206.

Smith, B. M. (1995). The editor's page: That's no techno-fix. *Phi Delta Kappan, 76*(9), 659.

Sternberg, R. J., & Horvath, J. A. (1995). A prototype view of expert teaching. *Educational Researcher, 24*(6), 9–17.

Stocks, J., & Schofield, J. (1995, April). *Educational reform and professional development.* Paper presented at the annual meeting of the American Educational Research Association, San Francisco.

Strong, R., Silver, H. F., & Robinson, A. (1995). What do students want (and what really motivates them)? *Educational Leadership, 53*(1), 8–12.

Swanson, J. (1995). Systemic reform in the professionalism of educators. *Phi Delta Kappan, 77*(1), 36–39.

Sylwester, R. (1994). How emotions affect learning. *Educational Leadership, 52*(2), 60–65.

Thorkildsen, T. A., Nolen, S. B., & Fournier, J. (1994). What is fair? Children's critiques of practices that influence motivation. *Journal of Educational Psychology, 86*(4), 475–486.

U.S. Department of Education (1991, October). *Striving for excellence: The national education goals*. Washington, DC: U.S. Department of Education.

Vatterott, C. (1995). Student-focused instruction: Balancing limits with freedom. *Middle School Journal, 27*(11), 28–38.

Veenman, S. (1995). Cognitive and noncognitive effects of multigrade and multi-age classes: A best-evidence synthesis. *Review of Educational Research, 65*(4), 319–381.

Voelkl, K. E. (1994). School warmth, student participation, and achievement. *Journal of Experimental Education, 63*(2), 127–138.

Wang, M. C. (1992). *Adaptive education strategies: Building on diversity*. Baltimore: Paul H. Brookes.

Weinert, F. E., & Helmke, A. (1995). Learning from wise Mother Nature or Big Brother instructor: The wrong choice as seen from an educational perspective. *Educational Psychologist, 30*(3), 135–142.

Weinstein, R. S. (in press). Promoting positive expectations in schooling. In N. Lambert & B. L. McCombs (Eds.), *Issues in school reform: A sampler of psychological perspectives on learner-centered schools*. New York: APA Books.

Wells, A. S., & Serna, I. (1995, April). *The politics of culture: Understanding local political resistance to detracking in racially mixed schools*. Paper presented at the annual meeting of the American Educational Research Association, San Francisco.

Wheelock, A. (1992). *Crossing the tracks: How "untracking" can save America's schools*. New York: New Press.

Wiggins, G. (1992, January). Systematic quality: Curricula and assessment for ensuring excellent performance. General session paper presented at the Second Annual International Conference on Restructuring Curriculum-Assessment-Teaching for the Twenty-First Century, Phoenix, AZ.

Williamson, R. D. (1996). Modifying structure: A resource for improved student achievement at the middle level. *NASSP (National Association of Secondary School Principals) Bulletin, 80*(578), 17–23.

Wlodkowski, R. J., & Ginsberg, M. B. (1995). *Diversity and motivation: Culturally responsive teaching*. San Francisco: Jossey-Bass.

Wlodkowski, R. J., & Jaynes, J. H. (1990). *Eager to learn: Helping children become motivated and love learning*. San Francisco: Jossey-Bass.

Wynne, E. A., & Walberg, H. J. (1995). The virtues of intimacy in education. *Educational Leadership, 53*(3), 53–54.

Zimmerman, B. J. (1994). Dimensions of academic self-regulation: A conceptual framework for education. D. H. Schunk & B. J. Zimmerman (Eds.), *Self-regulation of learning and performance: Issues and educational applications* (pp. 3–21). Hillsdale, NJ: Erlbaum.

Index

1 Peter 2:16-18
Isaiah 41:10-15

1 Peter 4:1,2

1-800-727-WORD

www.Jmministries.org

Parents Family Home Evening
Teacher Development Class

Personal Learning Development Class

This could be the basis of single adult
+ adults without children Family Home
Evening.

Also Include Spiritual Boosters
+ Family Boosters

Individual Study with Helps.

VIDEO TEACHING BANK
or maybe something on the
WEB or digital camera
newsletter

GLORY SHARING
Digital News Sheets

NOTEBOOK
SUNDAY SCHOOL REFLECTIONS

FAMILY HOME STUDY   IS THE KEY
PERSONAL

The Art of Virtue

Chris Evans
7379 Gore Range Bld 2-305
Littleton, Co 80127